LANDMARKS IN THE
HISTORY OF EDUCATION

LANDMARKS
IN THE HISTORY OF
EDUCATION

*English Education as part of
the European Tradition*

T. L. JARMAN
M.A., B.Litt. (Oxon), A.M. (Harvard)
Reader in the History of Education,
University of Bristol

Foreword by
ROGER WILSON
Professor of Education,
University of Bristol

JOHN MURRAY
Fifty Albemarle Street London

TO MY PARENTS

© *T. L. Jarman* 1963

First published (Cresset Press) 1951
Second edition (John Murray) 1963
Reprinted 1966
Made and printed by offset in Great Britain by
William Clowes and Sons, Limited, London and Beccles

FOREWORD

by Professor Roger Wilson

EDUCATIONAL change is in the air and in my view this is important, for the pattern of the secondary education of able boys and girls is far more static than it ought to be in contemporary Britain. But one element in considering what educational change is desirable is an intelligent grasp of the important historical factors which lie behind present practice. Some understanding of what has been important in the past, and why, gives depth to critical and constructive ideas about schooling to-day and to-morrow.

The influence of the past on contemporary education is often neglected because the books about it are almost unreadable. One of the great merits of this book is that it is splendidly readable. Its second great merit is that it relates the tradition of education in this country to powerful influences on the European mainland, and it consequently stimulates thought about the contemporary relationships between Great Britain and her continental neighbours. For the sake of any overseas readers, of whom I hope there may be many, it is perhaps important to say that when Mr. Jarman deals with the educational changes that have taken place since 1947, his views and comments are not necessarily shared either by all his university colleagues or by all those who teach in schools or who are engaged in educational administration. Mr. Jarman has a stronger belief in the virtues of tradition in education than many of us, but this does not detract from the general importance and attractiveness of this book, which I commend particularly to those who are interested in educational change but who are sceptical of the value of an historical approach.

BRISTOL

January 1963

v

PREFACE

THE Englishman often displays a certain healthy scepticism towards education. He is more impressed by what a man can do than by what he knows; he is more impressed by results than by any amount of theory, and prefers stolid character to intellectual agility. Yet in every age there has been the need for specialized training in one field or another, whether in that of the soldier, the priest, the scholar, the man of affairs, or the scientist and the technician, and much of the interest of the history of education lies in discovering how each age dealt with its own particular educational problems. In the present volume the evolution of education in England is traced as part of the historical development of European education, from its origins in ancient Greece to the modern practice of education for all. I have tried to delineate clearly the landmarks in this long history, and to illustrate it by reference at each stage to the education actually experienced by some outstanding and characteristic figure.

A book of this kind must be largely dependent upon the specialized work of others, and my debt in this respect is acknowledged in the footnotes and bibliography. Among friends and colleagues who have helped, at Bristol and elsewhere at home and abroad, I owe a special debt of gratitude to Dr. T. K. Derry, who has read the book in proof and made a number of comments and suggestions. But for any expressions of opinion the author is, of course, himself responsible. I feel that I should thank also the librarians and library staffs who have assisted my studies at Bristol, in the British Museum, the libraries of the Ministry of Education, University College, London, and Harvard University, in the Bodleian, in the Bibliothèque Nationale and the Bibliothèque Sainte-Geneviève, Paris, and the Bibliothèque Royale, Brussels.

T.L.J.

vii

CONTENTS

Part One: ORIGINS

Part Two: MEDIEVAL EDUCATION

Part Three: MODERN EDUCATION

CONTENTS

PART ONE

Origins

CHAPTER I

IN GREECE

WHEN Tom Brown was sent to Rugby School his father had a fairly clear idea of what he expected of education. 'Shall I tell him', pondered Squire Brown, 'to mind his work and say he's sent to school to make himself a good scholar? Well, but he isn't sent to school for that—at any rate, not for that mainly. I don't care a straw for Greek particles, or the digamma; no more does his mother. What is he sent to school for? If he'll only turn out a brave, helpful, truth-telling Englishman, and a Christian, that's all I want.' Though the reference to the Greek language was a slighting one the fact is remarkable that an English country squire looked back, two thousand years later, to Greek as a standard of scholarship. In spite, also, of the implied contradiction between schooling and character, the Englishman's opinion of the object of education would not have been unfamiliar to the Greeks. Scholarship and character, for them, went together. A proper patriotism and the worship of the gods were virtues esteemed in the ancient world. 'We must', said Plato, 'assimilate ourselves to God, seeking to become like him, wise and just and holy'. To mould the character of the young, he said, 'teachers are enjoined to look to the child's manners even more than to his reading and music', and the only education which truly deserves the name is 'that education in virtue from youth upwards, which makes a man eagerly pursue the ideal perfection of citizenship'.

The character of Greek civilization was such that it has never lost its attraction for those who have come under its influence. It is one of the main sources from which the cultural life of to-day has sprung. It is for this reason that so much of Greek thought is still clear and significant to us in a different age, often clearer and more direct than what has been written in recent times. The Greeks were lucid thinkers, and as, in many spheres of human thought, we have merely added to or elaborated upon their work, to turn back to it is to rediscover its pristine purity and simplicity. In art and architecture, in literature and philosophy, in the highest expression of human sentiment, of personal development and of social idealism, the Greeks have scarcely been surpassed; it is hard to conceive that in these spheres they can be surpassed. They set the standards and drew the patterns which, when fully known, have evoked imitation and admiration in every age and land.

The education of the Greeks was but a part of their civilization, though an important part. The problem of how to train the young in the fullest sense was ever present to the politician as he planned the way of life of the Greek city. To think of Greek civilization, however, as one complete and finished stage in the human story, to picture it as something capable at a given date of final definition, is misleading—and the same is true of Greek education. We speak of Greece and of Rome, or of Greek or Roman civilization, as though these were entities, each with its recognizable and definable characteristics and qualities. But these entities are no more than generalizations or approximations. 'The glory that was Greece' . . . but where and when? In Athens, was it, or on the field of Troy, in Sparta, or in the cities of Asia Minor? For the Athenians at the height of their political and cultural development Homer was already a classic figure of the past; yet the story he told was of an age even more remote. The gigantic walls of Mycenaean Samothrace were already an antiquity of which—like the Cretan civilization—the Greeks whom we know best knew but little. Yet to the glory something was contributed by all. Between the end of the early invasions of Greece by the Dorians and the time of Plato seven centuries went by; with the conquests of Alexander of Macedon the Near and Middle East were hellenized; by extending her power over the lands of the eastern Mediterranean Rome entered into the heritage of Greece. But Rome, herself no newcomer to the political scene, was undergoing fundamental political change: the centuries-old republic became an empire, an empire which endured for four hundred years. In those centuries of political rise and decline and of the development of human arts and ways of life whose influence was to persist for another fifteen hundred years and more, there were not one, but many, Greeces and Romes. And the changes which marked the course of their history marked also their education.

The earliest glimpses of Greek life which literature gives show a people among whom the virtues of war and husbandry were supreme. In *Works and Days* Hesiod describes the seasonal labours of agriculture and urges the need for self-denial, persistence, and unremitting effort: 'Work the work which the gods ordained for men.' Stick to the simple and essential things required—'get a house, and a woman, and an ox for the plough'. Such maxims indicate the rural character of life where education consisted in learning by doing, practising the arts of agriculture under the guidance of father or master or elder brother. At the same time Homer's epic tells the story of peoples whose life was influenced through and through by war. In the *Iliad*, Hector, before going out to battle, bids farewell to Andromache who is followed by her serving woman carrying Hector's infant son. The baby whimpers and draws back, frightened by its father's mail and the helmet with its 'nodding dreadful crest'. The parents smile, and Hector asks of Zeus a blessing:

> . . . Grant him the spoils
> Of war, grant him to slay his enemy,
> And make his mother glad because of him.

The education of the Greek warrior is briefly indicated by the *Iliad*. Achilles, as the old horseman Phoenix reminds him, left home when he was 'unskilled as yet in remorseless war or in the councils where men also gain renown'. It was for this reason, said Phoenix, that 'your father sent me to instruct you in all these things, to be both a speaker of words and a doer of deeds'. The skill of the orator was valued as a practical art in the affairs

5

of man; and, in an age of force, prowess in arms was beyond all price. For the services of Achilles King Agamemnon offered tripods and talents of gold, twelve strong horses, seven women of Lesbos 'skilled in goodly handiwork', the fair daughter of Briseus, and promises of spoils and glory more by far than all these, if Troy should fall. Yet this matchless warrior was found by Agamemnon's envoys 'delighting his soul with a clear-toned lyre, fair and richly wrought, whereon was a bridge of silver; this had he taken from the spoil when he had laid waste the city of Aëtion. Therewith was he delighting his soul, and he sang of the glorious deeds of warriors.'

Into these passages of the *Iliad* are packed brief though brilliant pictures of a barbaric age—but it is a refined and brilliant barbarism which, in later ages of sophistication, has shone undimmed. The clash of conflict on the bloody field ennobled only by human courage and devotion unto death, the play of passion and ambition in the council of the chiefs offset by the caution and experience of the sage, the dawn of literature and history, of music and the arts—all this is to be found in the epic poetry of Greece. The strife of warriors is, indeed, a common theme in the epic poetry of the Greeks and of other races. The rivalry of the warriors Arjun and Karna is a principal theme of the Hindu *Mahabharata* as is that of Achilles and Hector of the *Iliad*. War and the council of chiefs are ever-recurring notes in the description of the conflict of nations on the upper Ganges about thirteen centuries before Christ when the Pandu warriors

> Came in various battle-chariots drawn by steeds of every hue,
> Various were the chieftains' standards which the warring
>   nations knew.

The *Ramayana*, the other great epic of ancient India, speaks of the council when the king bids his chiefs:

> Therefore freely speak your counsel and your monarch's task
>   shall be
> But to shape in deed and action what your wisest thoughts
>   decree.

War was the main occupation of the ruling classes of mankind, and the education of young men of good birth was a training for the field of battle.

War did not cease to be a preoccupation of the Greek statesman who had to consider the security and defence of his city. But by the fifth and fourth centuries B.C.—the greatest days of ancient Greece—Athens had developed an urban and maritime civilization in which all the arts of peace could flourish and where the human spirit flowered more finely perhaps than it has done elsewhere or since. In Sparta, however, war remained of primary importance and government continued to be based upon force. Isolated by the northern mountains and confined by them and the sea to the southern peninsula the Spartans were cut off from the liberalizing developments in Athens; the Spartans, too, were few and lived among a more numerous earlier people whom they reduced to serfdom. First and last a soldier, the Spartan received an education designed to develop to the full the qualities of courage, endurance, and obedience. This education was described with enthusiasm by Xenophon[1] who, although an Athenian born, looked with sympathy towards the monarchical and aristocratic institutions of Sparta and compared them favourably with the democratic system of his native state. Xenophon was not ill-qualified to write of education; as a young man he had come under the influence of Socrates; his writings have made him an important Greek historian; he was also a man of action who led back to their homeland the 'Ten Thousand' Greeks after the death in 401 B.C. of Cyrus, with whom they had enlisted as mercenaries in his struggle against his brother, Artaxerxes of Persia. After his return to Greece, Xenophon took service with the Spartan king, now the dominant power in the Greek world after the defeat of Athens in the Peloponnesian War. When active service was over Xenophon lived for twenty years the life of a country

[1] Xenophon describes the Spartan education in his *Constitution of the Lacedaemonians*. He also treats of or touches on education in a number of his other works, including the *Cyropaedia*, *Memorabilia*, and the *Economics*. The educational system of Sparta is referred to by many Greek writers besides Xenophon and is described by Plutarch in his *Life of Lycurgus*.

gentleman, hunting, writing and supervising his estates and the education of his sons according to the Spartan system.

In his *Constitution of the Lacedaemonians* Xenophon shows how in Sparta everything possible was done to attain physical perfection. The importance of ante-natal care was realized, and motherhood was regarded as the most important function of freeborn women. These were, therefore, given physical training, while the customary woman's work of spinning and weaving was left to the slave women. Men were to marry, not when they chose, but in the prime of their manhood. If both partners were fit, the offspring were likely to be fit also. These regulations were attributed to Lycurgus. 'Whether he succeeded in populating Sparta with a race of men remarkable for their size and strength anyone who chooses', says Xenophon of the men of his own time, 'may judge for himself'. The training of boys was designed to toughen them by accustoming them to pain and hardship. In the other Greek states the boys were sent under the care of a tutor or guardian to a school 'to learn letters, music and the exercises of the wrestling-ground'. Their feet were softened by wearing sandals, their bodies pampered by clothing and too much food. In Sparta, on the other hand, boys were placed under a disciplinarian—selected from among the leading citizens—with a staff of youths, equipped with whips. The boys went barefoot, wore one garment in winter and summer, and were given enough food to keep them going but not enough to prevent their feeling hunger: in these ways the body was hardened. To develop cunning the boys were encouraged to alleviate their hunger by stealing; if they were caught they were beaten not for the stealing itself, but for stealing badly. When they ceased to be boys and grew older their painful and hard life did not come to an end; 'a ceaseless round of work' and 'a constant round of occupation' were devised. Any shirking of the set tasks was to be punished by exclusion from future public honours. Thus the lads of Sparta preserved decorum and discipline; they were required 'to keep their hands under their cloaks, to walk in silence, not to look about them, but to fix their eyes on the ground'. So quiet and reserved were they that 'when they have taken their place at a public meal, you must be content if you can get an answer to a question'. Lycurgus had held that a man should always 'choose an honourable death in preference to a disgraceful life': this was the ideal of a military state. How far the regulations of Spartan education were strictly adhered to in Xenophon's day is uncertain; in one place Xenophon himself suggests that there had been a falling away from the early strictness. Plutarch, however, though he wrote about five hundred years later, gave a similar account of the old Spartan education; Spartan institutions were, in any case, known among the Greeks for their attention to discipline, and the tradition has survived until to-day in the use which we make of the word 'Spartan'.

The Spartans emphasized the manly virtues at the expense of others, but they were not entirely uncultivated. Whether it was the general practice to learn to read is uncertain; Isocrates said that the Spartans did not learn letters, Plutarch says that they did. They knew Homer; they listened to the recitation of poems, especially poems of war; the laws of the state, set to a tune, they learned by heart; and they loved dancing, of which part consisted of musical exercises of a military type. Much of their educational system has its modified counterpart in modern times. The organization of the boys into packs under the control of the disciplinarian was a forerunner of the English public school: the boys ate, slept, and worked together. Girls were also organized into packs but they were allowed to sleep at home. The Hitler Youth also aimed at the toughening of both boys and girls and preparing them for unthinking devotion to the Nazi state. *Tom Brown's Schooldays* appealed to Nazi education-ists and the English public school was kept in mind in the creation of leadership schools for the National Socialist Party. In the Spartan boys' pack or 'boarding-school' there were elements of the prefect system and of fagging. Expeditions of boys and youths into the countryside, camping, and living an open-air life, all are elements which have reappeared in the Boy Scouts. The frequent sparring and fighting encouraged throughout the Spartan system are recalled by the duelling in

9

2

the student clubs of the German universities and by the fights characteristic of the rougher side of the public school life. The courage, public spirit and devotion to the State developed by Spartan education were admired by one of the greatest of Athenians. Plato himself drew from Sparta his picture of common tables and common meals, the idea of the equality of women and indeed of most of what goes to make the communism of the *Republic*. The true Spartan stood indomitable against fate itself: 'Breakfast here: supper in Hades,' said Leonidas to his soldiers at Thermopylae. They fell before the Persian host; to their duty they were faithful unto death:

> Go tell the Spartans, thou that passest by,
> That here, obedient to their laws, we lie.

It was no mean epitaph; it would describe the self-sacrifice for a great cause of all brave men who have faced overwhelming odds, of the British Expeditionary Force at Mons in 1914, of the French at Verdun, or of the handful of men who defended Calais in 1940 while the main British Army withdrew to Dunkirk.

But if Sparta magnified, perhaps unduly, the virtues of physical strength and courage they were not neglected in the education of Athens and the other Greek cities. What was most remarkable about Greek life as a whole was its admirable sense of balance—that moderation in all things which was a guiding Hellenic principle and was particularly emphasized by Aristotle. Athens sought to achieve that balance in its education as between the physical and the intellectual. 'There can', said Plato, 'be no fairer spectacle than that of a man who combines the possession of moral beauty in his soul with outward beauty of form.' A judicious combination of gymnastics and music, he argued, was the way to form a well-balanced mind and character. In this combination of qualities at which the Greeks aimed lies the origin of the famous Latin tag—*Mens sana in corpore sano*. To suppose that the desired balance was always achieved is, of course, a mistake. The traveller who dreams away an incomparable hour in the stadium at Delphi, or at Olympia with the help of Pindar recalls the glory of the Games, must not suppose that, even at Athens, there was no conflict of educational ideals. The opposition of aesthetes and athletes still known in universities and schools was not unknown in Greece. For Pindar athletic prowess was the supreme good; but Euripides and Plato both denounced exaggerated athleticism—'Of countless ills in Hellas, the race of athletes is quite the worst,' declared the former; Aristophanes again, playing to the gallery, attacked Euripides and the Sophists for turning boys not into men but vociferous pedants. Nevertheless, in Athens men came nearer than at any other time to reaching a balance between mind and body.

Of Greek education Oscar Browning wrote in the nineteenth century that it 'produced the most gifted and attractive nation that ever lived upon earth'. To say that is surely to put the cart before the horse. 'It ascribes', to use the words of Ortega y Gasset, 'to the school a force which it neither has nor can have.[1] . . . Certainly when a nation is great, so will be its schools. There is no great nation without great schools. But the same holds for its religion, its statesmanship, its economy, and a thousand other things. A nation's greatness is the integration of many elements.' The greatness of Greece might be traced to climate, to the racial mixture of the northern invaders with the earlier Mediterranean peoples, to the intimate political and social life of the city state, to the institution of slavery which provided the material foundation for the cultural life of the

---

[1] J. Ortega y Gasset: *Mission of the University*, p. 37. 'The error stems directly from the nineteenth century as a whole. The English rout Napoleon I: "The battle of Waterloo was won on the playing fields of Eton." Bismarck crushes Napoleon III: "The war of 1870 is the victory of the Prussian schoolmaster and the German professor."

'These clichés rest upon a fundamental error which we shall simply have to get out of our heads. It consists in supposing that nations are great *because* their schools are good . . . it is the residue of a pious "idealism" of the past century.'

The same point was made in the Calcutta University Commission *Report*, 1917–19: 'Education of a people is not given by schools and colleges alone. Other influences blend with theirs, the spirit and temper of the community which they serve . . . the conditions under which its daily work for livelihood is done.'

upper class. Certainly the magic of the sun on rock and hill and sparkling shore contributed as did the beauty of temple and theatre and the emotional experience of festival and drama to the moulding of the individual Greek. But only if we regard all these things as part of education—as, in the widest sense, they are—can we say that education produced the greatness of Greece. The work of the schools of Greece was only a part of the necessary 'integration of many elements'. Nevertheless, the aim of the Greek educational philosopher was to produce the best: 'A good education', says Plato, 'is that which gives to the body and to the soul all the beauty and all the perfection of which they are capable.' Beauty and perfection are regarded, however, as social rather than individual. 'Hellenic education,' wrote K. J. Freeman, 'alike at Sparta and at Athens, in theory and in practice, aimed at producing the best possible citizen, not the best possible money-maker; it sought the good of the community, not the good of the individual.'[1]

At the same time, trade and useful manual work were regarded as degrading to the citizen and were often left to slaves. Thus Greek education did not include the branches of commercial and technical instruction so important to-day. The necessary crafts—building, carpentering, ironwork, the potter's craft, and so on—were learnt either in the family of the craftsman or by apprenticeship. With the Greeks originates the unfortunate division in our present society between those who are esteemed and well paid in white-collar jobs and those who perform the manual work in field, factory, and mine. The old view is reflected in the reluctance with which woodwork, crafts, and even science were admitted into the British secondary curriculum during the nineteenth century.

In Athens there was a tradition of literary education about as old as that of physical education in Sparta. Solon, at the beginning of the sixth century B.C., is said to have made a law that every boy should learn to read as well as to swim. His regula-

[1] *Schools of Hellas*, p. 275. Or, as Paul Girard put it, in *L'Education Athénienne*: *'Ce qu'il faut apprendre aux enfants . . . c'est ce qui peut être utile à l'État.'*

tions regarding the conduct of schools show that these already
existed in his time; they must date back to at least some time in
the seventh century. The fifth century saw Athenian education
take definite shape and it is possible to distinguish successive
stages. Up to the age of six or seven children remained at home
under the charge of mother or nurse; then came the primary
stage until fourteen; something like a secondary stage might
follow from fourteen to eighteen; then the young man took
the oath to defend his city and his gods and entered the period
of two years' compulsory military service as an *ephebos* or cadet.
Later, when Macedon established dominion over Athens, the
military duties became voluntary and could be replaced by
courses in philosophy and literature. Thus the institution of two
years' military training changed into something like a university. The lengthy education which was open to the young
Athenian—although only sons of rich parents would be able to
take advantage of the secondary stage—was for boys only. Girls
in Athens spent a much more secluded life than in Sparta and,
living at home, understood only the work of the household.
Thucydides has reported the opinion of Pericles that the
Athenian mother should live such a life that her name would
be neither praised nor blamed among men. But the boys went
to day schools run as private, not state, institutions. The State,
however, sometimes built gymnasia and wrestling-schools where
anyone could exercise himself. Education of the elementary sort
was cheaply obtained and general among the citizens of
Athens, but the teachers who provided the elementary instruction seem not to have been well paid and were poorly
esteemed—as has, indeed, generally been their lot in more
recent ages. A late Greek writer, Lucian, pictures an amusing
scene in which certain great men in this world have had their
fortune reversed in the next; they have been reduced to 'beg-
ging in Hades, selling salt fish for a living, or giving elementary
lessons'.

In the Athenian schools the boys learnt to read, to write, and
to count, and Aristotle remarks that in his time drawing and
painting were sometimes added to the older curriculum. Both

Plato and Aristotle have given an account of the education of their day, and references to education by many other Greek writers help us to fill in the detail here and there. Vase paintings which have survived still picture for us the Greek boy of twenty-three centuries ago learning his letters, practising on the lyre, and exercising his body in the wrestling-school. To learn to write boys used a wax tablet, of which the two parts were hinged and could be folded together with the wax inwards and so easily carried to and from school. They scratched the letters of the alphabet on the wax with a pointed instrument which had at its other end a flat piece for erasing and smoothing the wax surface after use. This writing instrument was the style or stylus, and has given its name in a wider sense to method and manner in writing and speaking. Dictation would come later, and when the boys were able to take down long passages from the poets, ink and parchment may have been used in place of the wax tablets. In learning to read and write the alphabet was probably learnt in the form of a verse—the very word alphabet is, of course, simply the result of joining the first two Greek letters—and it is possible that spelling was practised sometimes with the aid of song and dance, various letters being impersonated by boys who would move into the order necessary to form words. Reading would take the boys directly to the great poets, to Homer and Hesiod and others. The teacher would dictate or recite and boys would learn by heart much of the *Iliad* and *Odyssey*. When boys recited the stirring passages they would give full rein to gesture; drama was in their blood. Counting seems to have been learnt, along with spelling, by counting the number of letters in words; simple counting was done on the fingers and more complicated counting with the aid of an abacus or counting-board. In this way a simple knowledge of arithmetic was imparted which would fit boys for business and the market or for doing the household accounts. Music was an important part of schooling; boys learnt to play the seven-stringed lyre, and sometimes also the flute. To the tune of the lyre the pupil learned also to sing the verses of the lyric poets. The gymnastics teacher instructed the boys in boxing and wrestling, in throwing the javelin and discus, and in running, jumping, and other exercises. A good general description of the schoolboy's day has been attributed to Lucian who wrote in the second century A.D. But whether written by him or not, it would probably cover also the doings of the earlier Athenian schoolboy.

'He gets up at dawn, washes the sleep from his eyes, and puts on his cloak. Then he goes out from his father's house, with his eyes fixed upon the ground, not looking at anyone who meets him. Behind him follow attendants and pedagogues, bearing in their hands the implements of virtue, writing tablets or books containing the great deeds of old or, if he is going to a music-school, his lyre.

'When he has laboured diligently at intellectual studies, he trains his body in manly exercises, riding or hurling the javelin or spear. Then comes the wrestling-school with its labours under the midday sun and its sweats in athletic contests. Then a quiet bath; then a meal, not too large, in view of afternoon school. For the schoolmasters are waiting for him again to imprint on his mind the deeds of antiquity, to teach him who was a great hero, who was a lover of justice and purity. With the contemplation of such virtues he waters the garden of his young soul. When evening sets a limit to his work, he pays the necessary tribute to his stomach and retires to rest, to sleep sweetly after his busy day.'[1]

Such an education had sufficed until the fifth century, but then the great social and political changes in the Athenian state—the growth of maritime trade and with it a wealthy merchant class to challenge the older landed aristocracy, the consequent creation of a political democracy of the free

[1] The description is, of course, somewhat idealized; it occurs in *The Loves*, which is not an educational treatise but one of a very different kind. But Lucian's description would appeal to the educational idealist of many different periods and lands. C. F. Andrews (quoted in W. J. McKee: *New Schools for Young India*) writes in similar vein—and is perhaps half-consciously recalling the above passage—when he describes Rabindranath Tagore's school of Santiniketan. The only marked difference is that the boys at the Indian school do handwork of various kinds, which was excluded altogether from the Greek schools.

citizens, the extension of Athenian power over other Greek territories, and the wonderful intellectual and artistic development—brought changes in the system of education. Most important was the gradual addition to the older education of a secondary stage, which filled the interval between the age of about fourteen and that of eighteen, when the lad entered on his military training. Conservatives, notably Aristophanes in the *Clouds*, denounced the modern tendencies and the loss as they supposed of the earlier simplicity and discipline among schoolboys. But among the lads, or young men, there was a demand for newer forms of education. Some were looking for a training for public life, in which oratory and sound knowledge of human affairs were required; others were impelled by curiosity and sought knowledge of nature and science, turning particularly to geometry, astronomy, arithmetic, and musical theory. Some of the older schools began to run more advanced classes. More important, however, were the teachers known as the Sophists— these were wandering scholars who lectured on every kind of subject. Geometry included some of the propositions to be found later in Euclid; geometrical study was encouraged by the schools of Pythagoras and Plato. Diagrams were drawn in sand or dusty earth, on the ground, with the aid of ruler and compasses. Literary studies took the form of careful examination and interpretation of the poets, criticism of style, and grammar. History, geography, natural history, philosophy, politics, logic, rhetoric, drawing and painting, law and the preparation of speeches for the courts, all found place. Such knowledge regarded as a whole was termed σοφια (wisdom)—hence the name of Sophist applied to these lecturers and teachers who, carried education to an advanced stage, covering the secondary, and often also what we should call the university, stage.

Such courses as the Sophists gave might sometimes be superficial; while they were wandering from place to place they would have little opportunity to get to know their students; lectures were given in any more or less convenient place, in the gymnasium, a friend's house or garden, or in the street. But fixed schools and continuous courses grew up in Athens, and the intense intellectual excitement and the enthusiasm of youth have been well described by Plato. Aristophanes, from his point of view, parodies these teachers and pupils as inhabiting a fantastic thinking-house: there they live, a crowd of dirty, unkempt students, engaged on all kinds of researches and becoming too clever to believe anything. This kind of education, he thought, was sapping the foundations of social life and of the state itself. Academic life, even in Athens, did not, of course, always run smoothly. There were bitter jealousies between the various teachers: Plato attacked much of the teachings of the Sophists; Isocrates criticized his rivals and his criticism is presumed to include Plato. Sometimes teachers made exaggerated claims as to the value of the subjects they taught, sometimes their learning was shallow—one is reminded of the rather pretentious nature of some modern courses in economics or psychology and of some of the various, somewhat grandiose 'institutes' of to-day. Politically, too, in democratic Athens, the work of advanced teachers was a little suspect: their pupils were rich young men whose education might fit them to become tyrants. Socrates aroused the suspicion of the Athenian democrats because he had been the teacher of Alcibiades.

What we know, however, of the great Athenian teachers' work has won the admiration of succeeding ages: Socrates and his discussion method[1] as we perceive them through Plato; Plato himself teaching in the gymnasium called the Academy; Isocrates with his school of rhetoric; Aristotle, the pupil of Plato, with his school in the Lyceum. These schools were established

[1] Discussion as a teaching method and as a rival to the formal lecture or lesson has had an important educational influence; it has been used in the tutorial system at Oxford and Cambridge, in W.E.A. classes, in A.B.C.A. and citizenship classes in the British Army, and by the British Council in explaining British life to foreign groups. Discussion can take three main forms: (1) Questions and discussion after a lecture; (2) The drawing out and balancing against each other of different opinions in a group by the leader but without his giving information or opinion; (3) Where the leader is an expert and can ask such questions as are important and will lead the group towards significant conclusions. The last is probably the most useful and the most Socratic. (See Xenophon: *Economics*, 19.) Plato knew that one does not learn by simply listening or by reading, but by studying—this involves the asking of questions and a painstaking search for the answers.

institutions with continuous courses, and such terms as academy, museum, lyceum (the *lycée* is the secondary school of France), athenaeum (the term *athénée* is given in Belgium to secondary schools), gymnasium (the classical secondary school of Germany) are still used to-day of institutions of learning.

Isocrates has left an account of his school, its objects and methods. He aimed at making philosophy and rhetoric a school for the art of practical living, but he did not condemn mathematics though not including them as part of his course: he thought mathematics would train the mind and make it 'capable of learning more important matters with greater ease and speed' —surely one of the first references to the theory of Formal Training which has since been so often used to defend the learning of Latin. In his school he aimed at teaching good writing and speaking; it was a school of writing and debating: criticism was provided by master and pupils. They discussed current affairs and also questions of historical and political importance. Above all, Isocrates aimed at producing what we should call the gentleman. 'Whom, then, do I call educated?' he asks. 'First, those capable of dealing with the ordinary events of life . . . next, those whose behaviour in any society is always correct and proper . . . treating everyone with fairness and gentleness. Further, those who have the mastery over their pleasures, and do not give way unduly under misfortune and pain. . . . Finally, those who are not spoilt or puffed up by success. . . . Those whose character is in accord with all these things—those I regard as truly educated.'

The discussion of education—what we should call educational theory—figures largely in the writings of the Greeks. The teachings and researches of the Sophists had bred a spirit of destructive criticism. Socrates, although in a sense he was one of them, believed that goodness rests upon knowledge, and that to escape from the uncertainties bred by the spirit of the times, he must lead the youth of his day by question and answer to a deeper, personal understanding of right and wrong. Xenophon, with his admiration for Sparta, emphasized the necessity of teaching good habits: there may not be time to discover by discussion, or people may not be capable of comprehending, the rational basis of society—and if this is the case, then cohesion and loyalty induced by training, habit, and discipline are necessary. Plato's *Republic*—the first blue-print of Utopia except, perhaps, the Genesis story of the Garden of Eden—is both a political and an educational treatise. Plato attempted to combine the best elements of Spartan and Athenian education: he was trying to stop the rot in Athenian life. The whole life of the State becomes a training in citizenship. To achieve the fullest possible unity in the State a communist system is established: private property and separate family life disappear, at least for the rulers. These rulers, or guardians, are selected as a result of a long and arduous training, first in a reformed but recognizable Greek education—music, gymnastics, and the arduous discipline of war, then by an advanced study of mathematics and dialectic. Fitted thus to govern, they are also brought towards the supreme end of education and life itself—the contemplation of the divine or highest good. Aristotle also, though he abandoned Plato's extreme proposals such as the communism, regarded education as a fundamental part of politics. There are, for him, three factors involved in education: nature, habit, and reason. The education of the young inculcates in them the right habits which will lead to the right behaviour in adult life. He, like his master Plato, regarded education as a process leading man from mundane things towards the highest. 'We ought', he said in the *Politics*, 'to choose war for the sake of peace, and business for the sake of leisure, and what is useful for the sake of what is fine . . . . These are the aims we have to keep in view in the education of children and people of every age who require education.'

Aristotle, it so happened, acted as tutor to the son of Philip of Macedon. It was unlikely in any case that the civilization of Greece would remain confined to the city states, but that son—known to history as Alexander the Great—made himself the head of a vast empire which embraced the Near and Middle East and stretched as far as the northern territories of India, and he carried with him on his campaigns of conquest the influence of Greece. New Greek cities were created in different parts of the empire; the most brilliant and most famous was the one which Alexander founded in 332 B.C. in Egypt, and which bore his name—Alexandria. Learning and education were maintained and extended throughout the Hellenic world, and in both Athens and Alexandria something like universities grew into being. When, with the rise of Macedonian supremacy in the fourth century, military service ceased to be compulsory in Athens, many young men found themselves free to study in the philosophical schools, of which, perhaps, the first and best had been that of Plato in the Academy. The schools of Plato and Aristotle, together with those of the Stoics and Epicureans founded at the end of the fourth century, became permanent institutions. For centuries Athens was an international centre of learning; foreigners, including many young Romans, added to the number of its students. During the period of the Roman Empire, the emperors patronized the schools of Athens, and founded chairs. It was not until the classical studies of Athens antagonized the Christian church that the university organization was dissolved by the Emperor Justinian in A.D. 529. New centres of learning had grown up under the Macedonians, at Pergamum, Tarsus, Antioch, Rhodes, and, most outstanding of all, Alexandria. Under the Ptolemies—rulers of Egypt between Alexander's death in 323 and the Roman conquest in 30 B.C.—royal patronage brought into being the famous library of Alexandria, said to have accumulated 700,000 manuscripts, and the museum as a centre for scholars and research workers. The school of Alexandria lasted in some form or other until the Mohammedan conquest swept over North Africa in the seventh century A.D.[1] In Alexandria was concentrated all the wisdom of the ancient world: if its inspiration was Platonic and Aristotelian, it also had traditions drawn from the priestly

---

[1] M. J. Mather in his *Histoire de l'École d'Alexandrie* defines the school as '*vingt à trente générations de savants, dont les travaux, protégés par les Ptolémées et leurs successeurs, les Césars, ont pendant plus de neuf siècles illustré les sciences et les lettres*'. The history of the school is, he says, '*à-la-fois celle des plus célèbres institutions littéraires de l'antiquité et celle du mouvement intellectuel de huit à neuf siècles*'.

colleges of Egypt, at Thebes, Memphis, and Heliopolis, and the considerable body of Egyptian science; its researches laid the foundations of modern mathematics and science—among its most famous students were Euclid and Archimedes, and Hero demonstrated the motive power of steam in his revolving sphere; its literary researches included detailed study of Homer and other Greek writers, translations, histories, and the elements of grammar. Through these schools and their influence, Greek thought permeated the ancient world; no people could escape its effects; Jew and Gentile were affected, although the Jews in spite of it retained their old laws, tradition, and national sense. Most of all the Romans entered into the heritage of Greece: Greece became a Roman province in 146 B.C. but, as Horace put it later, captive Greece by the charm of her civilization took captive her conqueror.

CHAPTER II

IN ROME

'WE must borrow our virtues from Rome and our culture from Greece,' wrote Cicero, and, in the opinion of a Jesuit scholar who has made the education of the Romans his special study, 'those few words express in brief form the whole of Cicero's educational theory'.[1] Cicero was aware that neither Greeks nor Romans had been successful in producing men who possessed all the qualities of character and intellect; he feels a certain contrast and hostility between Roman virtue and Greek culture which it should be the object of a full educational training to overcome. Between Greeks and Romans we can conceive as existing the same broad contrast which the modern world perceives between the French and the Germans or, in the Orient, between the Chinese and the Japanese. On the one hand, there are originality, intellectual development, refinement, manners, culture; on the other, order, discipline, law, determination, industry, imitation and thorough application rather than originality. The Greeks, in fact, had not achieved a lasting solution of the problem of combining the desirable qualities of mind, body, and character; the Greek character was despised by the Romans and, at first, there had been much opposition to the Greek education which was finding its way into the Roman Republic. Cicero knew that the republic was in danger; many of its early characteristics were gone and it was threatened by the rise of autocracy: although himself an admirer of Greek civilization he looks back nostalgically to the virtues of the past when the Roman was simple, hardy, brave, and unspoilt. It is

[1] A. Gwynn: *Roman Education*, p. 120.

22

as if we saw in Rome the history of Greece repeating itself: the courage, discipline, and hardihood of the Spartans, the war-like virtues of the earlier Greeks generally, gave way to refine-ment, sophistry, and sophistication, and in Rome, long before republic turned into empire, a similar process was at work by which power and wealth made the older virtues appear out-moded and replaced them by fashions of luxurious living and moral degeneracy.

Roman education of early times was simple and essentially practical. War and agriculture, as with the early Greeks, were the main business, and consequently the training of hand and eye and the development of physical strength and courage were the most important objects of education. The educational pro-cess was one of learning by observing and doing; it was a preparation for action and not a sedentary application to studious pursuits. The younger Pliny, when he wrote at the end of the first century A.D., described the old Roman provision whereby the young learned from their elders 'not only by ear but also by eye'. The young 'were inured from boyhood to service in camp, that by being accustomed to obey, they might learn to command and by following others, be trained to play the leader'. In the same way they were trained by example for the Senate; young candidates for office were at first spectators and 'the father of each youth served as his instructor'.[1] The father's authority, the *patria potestas*, was indeed supreme in the Roman household, and it was in the home that the early Roman got his first education, a training which was more physical and moral than intellectual. Apart from military exercises and the work of the farm, the boy would learn some-thing of the law—codified in the Twelve Tables at the middle of the fifth century B.C.—and of the customary religious obser-vances. He would learn the necessary offerings to the household gods: to Vesta, goddess of the fire; to the Penates, who watched over the family stores; and to the Lares, who were the guardian spirits of the family and its lands. The seasonal operations of agriculture also were undertaken only after the proper prayers

[1] Pliny: *Letters*, Book VIII, xiv.

and sacrifices—all this was a matter of local tradition and custom and was acquired by the young as a matter of course as they grew up in the family circle with its routine.

The family education of the young Roman has been described by Plutarch in his *Life of Marcus Cato*. Cato (234–149 B.C.) earned as censor a reputation for his stern repression of luxury and extravagance. He was himself 'a man who wrought with his own hands, as his fathers did, and was contented with a cold breakfast, a frugal dinner, simple raiment, and a humble dwelling'. And this was in a time of changing social habits. 'The commonwealth had now grown too large', says Plutarch, 'to keep its primitive integrity; the sway over many realms and peoples had brought a larger admixture of customs.' Cato, who wrote his *De Agricultura* on the basic art of husbandry, wrote also a book, unfortunately lost, on education—*De liberis educandis*. Cato opposed the spread of the Greek education which was growing in popularity, and Plutarch shows him educating his own son on the old-fashioned family lines. 'As soon as the boy showed signs of understanding, his father took him under his own charge and taught him to read . . . . Cato thought it not right, as he tells us himself, that his son should be scolded by a slave, or have his ears tweaked when he was slow to learn, still less that he should be indebted to his slave for such a priceless thing as education. He was therefore himself not only the boy's reading-teacher, but his tutor in law, and his athletic trainer, and he taught his son not merely to hurl the javelin and fight in armour and ride the horse, but also to box, to endure heat and cold, and to swim lustily through the eddies and billows of the Tiber. His history of Rome he wrote with his own hand and in large characters that his son might have an aid to acquaintance with his country's ancient traditions. He declares that his son's presence put him on his guard against indecencies of speech as much as that of the so-called Vestal Virgins. . . . So Cato wrought at the fair task of moulding and fashioning his son to virtue.'

This was the means by which the antique virtue of the Roman of the old republic was nurtured. 'In short,' to quote a modern historian of the Roman Republic, 'the training of the men who led Rome was good and practical within its own narrow range. It served to build up the Roman power at home: it sufficed for the conquest of Italy. The history of the next 200 years will show how insufficient it was for producing men of light and leading to deal with greater struggles, with ever-widening interests, and with new and complicated problems of state. The inability of Rome's generals and statesmen to understand new circumstances and meet new difficulties will often be painfully apparent: the strength acquired in the present period alone enabled her to last through conflicts with inferior powers, in spite of atrocious blundering and the needless sacrifice of hundreds of thousands of men: unconquered by foreign foes, the Republic staggered on, to fall under a Monarchy, merely because of political incapacity within. Whether a true intellectual stimulus, a love of inquiry and learning for its own sake, would have saved the Roman Republic, we cannot tell.'[1]

There was indeed—and we feel it still—a marked difference between the Roman and the Greek spirit in education. The emphasis on physical and moral training is common to both, but the restless, seeking, inquiring genius of the Greek was something alien to the steady and practical Roman. The Roman education was narrow and utilitarian; the Greek went beyond these needs to the imaginative and the intellectual. 'As soon as the boy has learnt his letters', says Plato in the *Protagoras*, 'they put into his hands the works of great poets, which he reads at school . . . and these he is required to learn by heart in order that he may emulate them and desire to become like them . . . and when they have taught him the use of the lyre, they introduce him to other excellent poets, the lyric poets, and they make their harmonies and rhythms familiar to the children, in order that they may learn to be more gentle and harmonious, and rhythmical, and so more fitted for speech and action.' But we must beware of attributing too great an effect to the conscious process of educating the young.

[1] W. E. Heitland: *The Roman Republic*, I, 185.

Greece developed an intellectual training which the Romans could only imitate at second-hand and late. The intellectual character of the Greeks, however, did not save Greece from political disintegration and decline. It was, perhaps, the virtue of the Roman Republic that it did 'stagger on', and when it fell was able to produce the Empire and the *pax romana* which embraced Europe for another four hundred years and passed on to later centuries the influence of both Rome and Greece. And, if we allow the description we have quoted of the short-comings of the early Roman training and outlook to remind us of the greatest empire of recent times, we shall remember that its people also have been thought of as practical, unimaginative, utilitarian, 'a nation of shopkeepers', it too has been accused of sticking to antiquated methods of education and of committing atrocious blunders, but it too has staggered on. Politics is, after all, an empirical art: we do not know its end, and we are uncertain as to its methods. Education also must, therefore, lack finality and perfection.

Contact between Greece and Rome led to a profound modification in the Roman way of life. Greek colonies existed in Sicily and Southern Italy in the earliest days of Rome, and trading contacts encouraged a knowledge of Greek. When Rome extended her sway over the eastern Mediterranean and absorbed the lands of Alexander's empire, Romans found more and more useful a language which was the language of the civilized world. Greek slaves, visitors to Rome, teachers and lecturers of all kinds began to open for the Romans the door to Greek literature; with a knowledge of the language, that literature began to exercise its charm upon even the hard-headed Romans. The translation about 250 B.C. from Greek of Homer's *Odyssey* by Livius Andronicus—himself formerly a slave who had been brought to Rome after the capture of the Greek colony of Tarentum—can almost be regarded as the starting-point in Latin literature. He taught both Greek and Latin to his master's children and with his translation of the *Odyssey* he had a text for his Latin lessons as, with the Greek authors, he had for his Greek. Other Greek teachers followed—

26

Suetonius has described them in *Lives of Eminent Grammarians*
—and in spite of a reaction at the beginning of the second
century B.C. against Greek influences and the occasional expulsion from Rome of Greek teachers, the study of literature—both
in Greek and Latin—gradually became established. Two facts
are outstanding: one is that the Romans at this time possessed
little or no literature of their own, and were therefore forced to
turn to the writings of the Greeks; the other is that the Romans
in so doing based their higher education on the literature of a
foreign nation and written in another tongue. Thus the Greeks
were not only the educational pioneers of Europe in that they
established schools and a curriculum of their own; they determined also a large part of the curriculum to be followed in
schools of the future not their own. For what they passed to
Rome passed on into the European tradition. The place of
Greek to the Romans was taken later by Latin to the nations of
Western Europe: the higher training of the mind did not cease
thenceforth to be composed largely of the study of past wisdom
recorded in an ancient language.

Much that was dross passed also from Greece into the Roman
world. Mommsen has written of Italian Hellenism among the
lower orders as 'a repulsive cosmopolitanism tainted at once
with all the extravagances of culture and with a superficially
whitewashed barbarism'. He has described Roman Epicu-
reanism as 'not so much a philosophic system as a sort of
philosophic mask, under which—very much against the design
of its strictly moral founder—thoughtless sensual enjoyment
disguised itself for good society'. He has explained that the
Greeks who lived and taught at Rome were later than and far
removed from their source, and that their philosophy, 'the
enchanted draught of speculation, always dangerous, is, when
diluted and stale, certain poison'—what the contemporary
Greeks offered was flat and diluted, and accordingly 'the
Romans became in philosophy simply inferior scholars of
bad teachers'. Nevertheless, at the same time, Mommsen
wrote: 'The circle of peoples, which we are accustomed to call
the ancient world, advances from an outward union under

the authority of Rome to an inward union under the sway of the modern culture resting essentially on Hellenic elements . . . the time heralds its approach, when the Roman commonwealth will pass into a bilingual state and the true heir of the throne and the ideas of Alexander the Great will arise in the west, at once a Roman and a Greek.'[1] The fusion of the Greek and Roman cultures was the greatest formative action in the process out of which was to come our later Western world.

The home was, as we have seen, the centre of early Roman education, and it is not certain when schools became common in Rome—they may have originated in the third or fourth century B.C. But as late as the first century B.C., Cicero could still point to an important difference between the effort of the Greeks to provide a general system at least of elementary education and the Roman practice. In the *De Republica* Cicero wrote:' 'Our people have never wished to have any system of education for the free-born youth which is either definitely fixed by law, or officially established, or uniform in all cases, though the Greeks have expended much vain labour on this problem, and it is the only point which our guest Polybius finds neglected in our institutions.' But at this place the text is lacking and the issue between the great Roman lawyer and the Greek historian of Rome cannot be followed up. By about the middle of the first century, however, Roman education, if not fixed and universal by law, was making use of a system of graded teachers or graded schools, a system which lasted without important

[1] Mommsen: *History of Rome* (trans. by W. P. Dickson), vol. IV, chap. xii. What he describes as happening with the Greeks and Romans is a common educational experience—it tends to happen in the life of each individual teacher. 'Even the philosophic activity of the Hellenic mind had, when it began to exert influence on Rome, already left the epoch of productive speculation far behind it, and had arrived at the stage at which there is not only no origination of truly new systems, but even the power of apprehending the more perfect of the older systems begins to wane and men restrict themselves to the repetition, soon passing into the scholastic traditions, of the less complete dogmas of their predecessors; at that stage, accordingly, when philosophy, instead of giving greater depth and freedom to the mind, rather renders it shallow and imposes on it the worst of all chains—chains of its own forging.'

change until the end of the Empire. We can build up a picture of these successive stages of schooling although, of course, some questions must remain unanswered; it is, for example, uncertain whether, or how far, girls attended the ordinary schools with the boys.

Both Quintilian (b. about A.D. 35) and Apuleius (b. about A.D. 125), the author of the famous novel *The Golden Ass*, indicate the stages or grades of schooling. In his *Institutio Oratoria* in which he describes and discusses the whole educational process but especially the training of the finished orator, the teacher Quintilian distinguishes first the nursery stage, then the elementary stage of learning to read either at home or at a school, which latter Quintilian prefers, next 'the turn for the teacher of literature', and finally the school of rhetoric. But there was often, as he points out, some overlap in the functions of the teacher of literature and the rhetorician. Apuleius, in a short essay, writes of education as a series of draughts from the fountain of the Muses: 'The first cup is given by the master that teaches you to read and write and redeems you from ignorance, the second is given by the teacher of literature and equips you with learning, the third arms you with the eloquence of the rhetorician.' But Apuleius suggests how much more might still in his day be had in Greece. 'Of these three cups', says he, 'most men drink. I, however, have drunk yet other cups at Athens—the imaginative draught of poetry, the clear draught of geometry, the sweet draught of music, the austerer draught of dialectic, and the nectar of all philosophy, whereof no man may ever drink enough.'[1] Boastful and superficial, perhaps—but he sets out clearly the stages of Roman schooling; and, himself a Roman from North Africa who had been educated at Carthage and Athens, he suggests the broad difference between the education of Greece and Rome.

To the elementary school, the *ludus* kept by the *ludi magister* or *litterator*, would go the ordinary Roman boy accompanied by the attendant pedagogue. But the father was free to send him or not according to his means, and what we read of Roman education

[1] Apuleius: *Florida*, 20.

is concerned mainly with that of the richer classes. Only to these would the secondary and higher stages of learning be open. The school building might well be a loggia or veranda—with a roof but with sides open to the road. The teacher would sit on his *cathedra*, the pupils on benches; they would rest their wax writing-tablets on their knees (we do not hear of desks or tables). In learning to write the letters a common method was to guide the boy's hand over characters already traced on the wax. At the elementary school the boy learned to read, write, and calculate. In reading and writing use was made of *sententiae*—something like copy-book maxims—such as *Avarus ipse miseriae causa est suae*, or *Audendo virtus crescit, tardando timor*, or *Fortunam citius reperias quam retineas*, or *Gravissima est probi hominis iracundia*.[1] Care was given to the teaching of arithmetic for the sake of its practical value; boys learnt to reckon on their fingers and to use, for more difficult calculations, the abacus. Elementary education in Rome presumably served its purpose, but we know little of it with certainty. Lack of precision in the picture is reflected in the rather vague and even contradictory accounts which modern writers base on their reading of the classical authors.[2]

At about the age of twelve or thirteen the boy would advance to the secondary school kept by the *grammaticus* and here he went through a course of study of language and literature. This study was of both Greek and Latin; Quintilian thought that Greek authors should be studied before Latin, and at first Greek naturally predominated owing to the lack of comparable Latin literature. Later Virgil and Horace took a place beside Homer and Hesiod. The boy had to practise composition and speech in Greek and Latin. A thorough study of the chosen literary texts was made—careful reading and

[1] There is a collection of these in the *Sententiae* of Lublilius Syrus, ed. by R. A. H. Bickford-Smith.
[2] Compare, for example, W. Warde Fowler: *Social Life at Rome in the Age of Cicero*, p. 182, and W. Boyd: *History of Western Education*, p. 66. The former says: 'This elementary work must have been well done.' The latter writes of the *ludus*: 'The quality of the instruction received there seems generally to have been rather poor.'

repetition by the pupil, commentary by the teacher on grammatical points, on style, history and philosophy involved, criticism of the text and study of variant readings, and critical judgement of the author's work as a whole—all of which have reappeared in modern grammar schools and especially in the method of *explication des textes* in the French *lycée*.

At about sixteen the boy reached the official age of manhood and assumed its dress, the *toga virilis* or *pura*. For young men who aspired to careers in public life the final stage in education was that in rhetoric, which meant a thorough study of the theory and practice of public speaking. To speak effectively it was necessary not only to have mastered the art of oratory but also to have a well-stocked mind. The best rhetorical training, therefore, included a study of subjects like law, history, and philosophy, and exercises were set in the composition of speeches on set themes. Cicero and other writers like Varro, Vitruvius, Seneca, and in the second century A.D., Galen, give varying lists of subjects studied in Roman schools— and in these lists we have the beginnings of the subjects later standardized in the seven liberal arts of the Middle Ages, grammar, rhetoric, dialectic, arithmetic, geometry, music, astronomy. But how these subjects were divided between the secondary schools of grammar and the higher schools is uncertain. We can suppose that there was considerable overlap in the schools, and we must remember that the names of these subjects are misleading if we think of the specialized and carefully distinguished subjects of modern schools. The training of the Roman school of rhetoric was essentially one in the art of speech and argument; if the student really desired more, he must go—as many a young Roman did, including Cicero and his son after him—to Athens, or to one of the other schools of the eastern Hellenic world.

Both Cicero and Quintilian dealt at length with the education of the orator. Cicero, successful advocate and statesman and one of the great stylists of world literature, regarded both philosophy and oratory as necessary to the cultivated citizen. *Humanitas*, which combined both, was his ideal. To be a *doctus orator* a man must be trained in rhetoric and also in philosophy, which must be backed by literature and some knowledge of history and law. He was seeking to reconcile the Greek love of speculation and intellectual cultivation with the Roman aim of a practical training in rhetoric, the art of the forum. Which name—philosopher or orator—is used is a small matter. 'To me', he wrote in the *De Oratore*, 'the name matters little, provided it be granted that praise is due neither to the man who knows his matter but cannot give it expression for lack of ability to speak, nor to the man who is never at a loss for words but has no information to give. Certainly, were I forced to choose I would prefer to be wise and unable to speak than to be a talkative fool. But when I am asked what is the highest excellence of all, I give the palm to the cultured orator.'

Quintilian, the most famous of Rome's teachers of rhetoric, followed Cicero in making the perfect orator his educational ideal, although he more sharply accentuated what he felt must be the antithesis between the academic philosopher and the practical orator. Of philosophy he thought that: 'No other mode of life has withdrawn itself further from the duties of civil life and all that concerns an orator. Which of the philosophers ever frequented courts of justice, or distinguished himself in public assemblies?' It is the 'good man skilled in speech,' *vir bonus dicendi peritus*, at which Quintilian aimed. The orator must be a good man, he insisted, so that those who heard him should have complete confidence in him; he must be able also and ready to place his wisdom and eloquence at the service of the state. 'The man who can duly sustain his character as a citizen, who is qualified for the management of public and private affairs, and who can govern communities by his counsels, settle them by means of laws, and improve them by judicial enactments, can certainly be nothing else but an orator.'[1]

But Quintilian, though a good man and a successful teacher, was theorizing about the ideal of education, and, in reality, Roman education had its shortcomings. The early practice of education in the family was sometimes impossible, for fathers

[1] *Institutio Oratoria*, I, 10.

were often absent on campaigns and some never returned; later with a decline in family life and the standards of behaviour father and mother often did not present the best example to the young. Morality reached a very low level under the Empire; divorce was easy and frequent; luxury and ease had replaced the early virtues and the people were encouraged in idleness by public provision of corn and games, while the gladiatorial combats were marked by excesses of brutality and depravity. The fact that the pedagogue or attendant on the schoolboy and the teachers also were often slaves or freedmen meant that they received little or no respect from their pupils. Threats and corporal punishment were the methods of imposing order; Martial wrote of the schoolmaster dealing out 'savage scoldings and blows!' The education given in schools was almost entirely literary; it was concerned with words and writing. The school was not a means of training character; there was lacking for the Roman governing class the training in responsibility, leadership, and corporate life given to the English ruling class by the public school. The exaltation of grammar and the emphasis placed on refinement in style tended to produce a system of education arid and superficial and especially repugnant to the young. In the higher schools, too, the schools of rhetoric, the exercises in declamation seem frequently to have been composed on far-fetched subjects and to have been pompous in style. Among others, Tacitus protested against the unreal nature of the themes chosen for rhetorical exercises, 'which are daily dictated in the schools, and scarce ever in the forum'. Seneca complained that the schools of rhetoric prepared young men 'for the classroom, not for life . . .', a complaint heard many times since against education and containing always an element of truth but one difficult or impossible to determine with precision.

Formal education, in Rome as everywhere else, was only one factor at work producing the man. The Emperor Marcus Aurelius in his famous *Meditations* is influenced by the old Greek view, examined in Plato's *Meno*, that character rests upon inherited capacity, on the early training in good habits, and also upon divine grace as well as upon the kind of instruction usually termed education. Cicero's own son, who had the best tutors obtainable and parental advice and example into the bargain, caused his father considerable anxiety. At the University of Athens he was reported as a drinker rather than a scholar, and there was a rumour that he had robbed Mark Anthony of the reputation of being the hardest drinker of his time. But perhaps he was little different from many students then and since. A letter written home from Athens has survived in Cicero's correspondence, and of it an American classical scholar has said: 'It is a student's letter *par excellence*, with its excuses for neglect in writing home, its anxiety to appease an angry father, its regret for the past, its glowing account of work at present, its brilliant literary hopes for the future, its solicitude for the health of the recipient. Even a suggestion of financial difficulties and a hint for further advances find a plea in it. Change the scene from Athens to Princeton or Cambridge, the date from B.C. to A.D., the name to Robinson or Brown, and the student's letter of to-day is complete.'[1]

Marcus Aurelius, however, who was emperor from A.D. 161 to 180, might appear as an outstanding product of Roman education although it was the education of the old family type, still possible for a man of high estate, to which he gave partial credit for his successful career. Among the gifts for which he was grateful he included: 'From my mother's grandfather: not to have attended public schools but enjoyed good teachers at home.' He describes how he received from the elder members of his family the best example: from his grandfather 'the lessons of noble character and even temper'; from his memory of his father 'modesty and manliness'; from his mother 'piety and bountifulness, to keep myself not only from doing evil but even from dwelling on evil thoughts, simplicity, too, in diet and to be far removed from the ways of the rich'. From his various tutors he had learned discipline of body and mind; he was thoroughly at home in both Greek and Latin, and wrote works in each; he studied rhetoric and law, but turned most warmly to philosophy.

[1] F. F. Abbott: *Society and Politics in Ancient Rome*, p. 211.

He thanks the gods for his good family background and general good fortune; as a practical Roman he thanks them also that 'although in love with philosophy I did not meet with any sophist or retire to disentangle literary works or syllogisms or busy myself with problems "in the clouds". For all these things require "the gods to help and Fortune's hand".'

Just as Alexander the Great had hellenized the east, so the Romans carried their institutions to the conquered peoples. In the towns which were the administrative centres of the Roman Empire schools for the teaching of grammar and rhetoric were created. The system of education seems to have been a regular —and a popular—part of the way of life the Romans introduced. It was a great civilizing force among the barbarians embraced by the Roman power and it appears to have been marked by considerable uniformity throughout the extent and duration of the Roman Empire. St. Augustine, who was born at the middle of the fourth century A.D., went through, in North Africa, a course of education similar to that already described as existing at Rome in the first century B.C. He has left a full account of his life in the *Confessions*, and in it we can trace the familiar stages of education: at the school of the *primus magister* he learnt to read, write, and count; next came the study of literature at the grammar school in a nearby town; finally, at Carthage, a course in rhetoric. Then he became himself a teacher of rhetoric, but continued to study, proceeding to philosophy and the other liberal arts. Long before Augustine's time, however, the Roman emperors had commenced a policy of state endowment for education; in the first century A.D., chairs of Greek and Latin rhetoric were endowed in Rome—with Quintilian as the first to hold the Latin post—and funds were set aside to provide annual allowances for boys and girls to complete their education. Alexandria had flourished under Augustus and the emperors who followed immediately. Under Hadrian (117–138) further steps were taken: he patronized teaching in both Alexandria and Athens, and founded in Rome the Athenaeum as a centre of Graeco-Roman higher education.

Antoninus (138–161) organized education systematically

35

throughout the Empire by making it obligatory on the cities to pay salaries to teachers: each must support a stipulated number of physicians, sophists, and grammarians. Marcus Aurelius endowed chairs in each of the four established philosophical schools in Athens. But while Roman education was extending its sway and becoming more systematized and better endowed than ever before, it was losing its moral foundation in the hearts of men. Marcus Aurelius, the 'stoic-saint', stands out as a lonely figure of excelling worth in the degenerating pagan scene. A new moral force—that of Christianity—was beginning to find its way to influence in the Roman world.

CHAPTER III

IN CHRISTIANITY

THE Romans bequeathed to Europe a system of language and literature study which never altogether ceased to determine the character of education. The Greeks, as Mill remarked, 'were the beginners of nearly everything, Christianity excepted, of which the modern world makes its boast'. But in that modern world—of the nineteenth century—Squire Brown, as we have seen, expected of education that it should make Tom a Christian. Christianity indeed, in one form or another, has, ever since its rise to a position of pre-eminence in the declining years of the Roman Empire, influenced the development of European education. Like the cultures of Greece and Rome, Christianity is one of the three main sources in which that education originates: Christianity dominated the cultural life of the Middle Ages; it supplied in the New Testament, the writings of the Fathers, and the works of the medieval theologians a new Latin literature for the studies of the student; it organized the system and determined the form of European schools for centuries; and, when its sway was challenged by the claims of a new social institution, the national state, and a new source of learning, natural science, it did not cease to maintain or to claim a partial control of education. If we can make out of the many and diverse events which have marked the passing of the centuries in the continent of Europe a continuous, homogeneous narrative which we think of as European history, if we can still find among the different states of Europe a certain, abiding similarity of life which we can regard as European unity, these things are to be traced to the common

37

background in Graeco-Roman culture and to the common Christian Church which made, for so long, religious unity a reality. It is not coincidence that the countries of western Europe which cling to-day to the democratic way of life in the world struggle between Communism and the West are countries in which Christianity is still, more or less firmly, established.

To say that, however, is to anticipate. In its nearly two thousand years of life Christianity has endured for a period far longer than that of either Greece or Rome. Like them, with the passage of time, it has itself undergone changes in form and character; it has, in different ages, been differently interpreted. An other-worldly faith, which grew up in the Roman world with its already existing system of education, had at first no direct influence on that education. A spiritual message to the individual soul did not necessarily make impact on the state or its institutions. Christ did not preach opposition to Rome—although Jewish nationalists had looked for it. Christ's political teaching was perhaps summed up in 'Render unto Caesar the things which are Caesar's, and unto God the things which are God's'. To the apostles the Christian message was a spiritual message, and the social and political life of the individual was subordinate to the spiritual life. 'Let every soul be subject unto the higher powers,' wrote St. Paul in the Epistle to the Romans, 'for there is no power but of God: the powers that be are ordained of God.' These words are of the first importance in the history of political thought; they are quoted constantly from the second century onwards. They represented civil government as of divine institution, and disobedience to the magistrate as not only a political but also a religious misdoing. St. Paul held this view because he saw the state as existing in the main for the end of justice—as Plato and Aristotle had seen it, though there is nothing to show that St. Paul had studied their writings. The magistrate, said Paul, is 'God's servant for the infliction of wrath as a punishment on him who does evil'. Within the framework of the state a quiet and peaceful life might prove possible.

St. Paul, unlike many of the simple people who joined the

Early Church, was an educated man. In his native city of Tarsus, he was reared in the strict Jewish tradition and studied the Hebrew law and scriptures; he also learnt the Greek of Cilicia, and may have made some slight study of rhetoric, though he does not appear to have had any deep acquaintance with Greek literature. As a Jew he had been taught the trade of tent-maker—for the learning of a trade was enjoined by the rabbis. The *Talmud*—a collection of their writings—states, amid a number of educational maxims, that 'Just as a man is bound to have his son instructed in the Law, so also should he have his son taught some handicraft or profession. Whosoever does not teach his son a handicraft teaches him to be a thief.' The teaching of a handicraft was something which clearly marked the difference between the Jewish and the old Greek outlook on the training of the young. Christianity with its doctrine of the fatherhood of God and brotherhood of man—'There can be neither Jew nor Greek, there can be neither bond nor free, there can be no male and female: for ye all are one man in Christ Jesus', as Paul stated it in Galatians—had in it the promise of equal educational opportunities for all, but this was, for long enough, nothing more. Christ Himself had admonished His disciples: 'Suffer the little children to come unto me, and forbid them not: for of such is the kingdom of God.' But this could be taken as springing from a natural goodness of heart and did not need to be given any direct educational application. The apostles were concerned with the great questions of the faith and the children were cared for in the family or in the existing schools. At first, therefore, Christian educational precept was of a general character, as appears in St. Paul's Epistles. Parents were counselled to bring up their children 'in the nurture and admonition of the Lord'. The bearers of office in the church were to be men who ruled their households well. Fathers were not to vex their children lest they should be discouraged, though such admonition did not rule out punishment, 'for what son is he whom the father chasteneth not?' Mothers were to love their children and attend to their proper upbringing. Children, in their turn, were bidden to obey and honour their parents.

But Christianity eventually found itself in open conflict with paganism. The Christians were persecuted by the Roman Empire as disloyal citizens, because they refused to sacrifice to the old Roman gods. And even if Christians did not hesitate to give their bodies to torture and death, they could not escape a real dilemma in the problem which confronted them in the matter of education. The existing Roman education was a pagan one; the literature which was the principal subject of study in the schools was a pagan literature. Was the Christian to send his son to the pagan school or was he to let him go uneducated?

Christian writers hesitated between their aversion for pagan literature as pagan and the need for that literature as a means of education. So far as the teacher was concerned, it seems to have been considered well for him to abandon that calling as being too closely bound up with the old way of life; but if he knew no other trade, then he might continue to teach so long as he made plain to his pupils the existence of one God and that the old gods were demons.[1] Christians sometimes condemned the pagan writers, sometimes found in them points of agreement with the Scriptures, and sometimes accused pagan writers of having taken their material unacknowledged from Moses and the Old Testament authors. Zealous Christians of an unintellectual kind might despise learning itself. 'Do not examine but believe' was reported to be the attitude of Christians by the Platonist, Celsus, about A.D. 180. 'The wisdom of the world is an evil thing.'[2] Tertullian (b. about 160) attacked, Clement and Origen criticized more mildly, the pagan writers. These Christian apologists were thoroughly educated in Greek and Latin, yet Tertullian, when he became a Christian, condemned secular literature as folly—*doctrinam saecularis litteraturae ut stultitiae apud Deum deputatam*.[3] Clement, however, found much to value in the ancient philosophers and regarded some of their writings as fitting preparation for Christianity.

---

[1] This view of the teacher's duty is expressed in the so-called Canons of Hippolytus. See Cadoux: *The Early Church and the World*, p. 323.
[2] Quoted *ibid.*, p. 238.   [3] *De Spectaculis*, XVII.

In any case, so long as Christians lived in a pagan world
and had to defend their position against criticism, so long
as they sought to convert others to the Christian faith, so long
must they acquaint themselves with the older Hellenic philosophies in which the pagan world was steeped. Thus the
Christians came to accept the schools of their time and to
attend them; in this way a compromise of some sort was reached
in practice. Inside the Church catechetical schools were set up
for the preparation of adults for baptism. In the first centuries
infants were not baptized, and these schools were simply courses
of preparation by catechesis, or oral instruction, of grown-up
people who wished for baptism, which was a serious matter of
moral responsibility. At Alexandria in the second century the
catechetical school under Origen—followed by Clement in
202—developed into a school of higher learning which gave
something like the old education but with a Christian instead of
a pagan foundation. Other similar schools came into existence,
like that at Antioch and that at Edessa, and in these Near
Eastern centres of education higher study continued for some
time after the collapse in the West of the Roman power and
its educational system with it.

But whatever might be the compromise in practice between
Christianity and paganism it was an uneasy one. Within the
political framework of the Roman Empire two great spiritual
systems or ways of life were silently struggling for the ascen-
dancy. In the outcome neither would achieve complete victory,
although one would become dominant: meanwhile the whole
situation would be altered by the collapse of the framework
itself. Before that happened, before the fall of the Roman
Empire, we should find, if we were to trace the story in detail,
that both paganism and Christianity were marked by successive rises and falls, although looking at the first four Christian
centuries as a whole we observe the decline of paganism and the
rise of Christianity to a position of dominance. One outstanding
event in the long struggle between them was the action of the
Emperor Constantine in 313 which legalized Christianity: it
put an end to the persecutions and gave the Christians the same

civil rights as were enjoyed by the adherents of the older religions. Christianity was soon to be the official religion of the Roman Empire, and Church and state were to be closely associated. Constantine did not, indeed, discourage the existing schools: he was anxious to develop in every way the new capital he established at Constantinople, and to this end he granted endowments for the teaching of grammar, rhetoric, law, and philosophy. Constantinople now took its place as a centre of learning alongside Athens, Alexandria, Rome, and the rest. It might have seemed that the old educational order was renewing its strength. But, in fact, the recognition of Christianity was, in the long run, a serious blow to the older culture. In spite of the continued existence of pagan faiths and their occasional renewal, as in the combination by Plotinus and Porphyry of the Platonic philosophy with an Oriental mysticism based on faith rather than reason, in spite of the attempt of a later emperor, Julian the Apostate, to restore paganism, the vitality of the ancient world was waning. The challenge of Christianity was causing a decline of interest in the old subject matter of education; at the same time, the increasing taxation to meet the costs of imperial administration tended to lead to a reduction of salaries to teachers by the provincial towns, and the growing centralization of administration reduced the number of local people appointed to the available posts in the provinces, so reducing the demand for the education which had fitted them for such posts.

Christianity, however, was not ready with a bold policy of educational reconstruction. Christian leaders still hesitated in their attitude to the old learning, some took one view, some another. St. Basil, in the East, took a favourable view; he came of a Christian family in Cappadocia, and his father was a teacher of rhetoric and a lawyer. Born in 329 at Caesarea, Basil studied at Constantinople and Athens, and returned as a teacher of rhetoric himself to Caesarea. He showed high esteem for ancient letters, especially in one of his works on *The Value to the Young of the Reading of Ancient Authors*; he regarded the study of these authors as a preparation for a study of Scripture and

Christian writers. Just as the soldier prepares himself by exercises and manœuvres for warfare, so must the Christian. 'We have a struggle to wage,' he wrote. 'To prepare for it we must make ourselves acquainted with the poets, historians, orators.' The Christian student must read these pagan works as the bees make use of the flowers—to take only the honey. Basil could compare Plato with St. Paul; and, in his admiration for the ancients, St. Gregory of Nazianzus, St. John Chrysostom, and others thought like him.

But in the West, some Christian leaders like St. Jerome took a narrower view. In their writings, for the most part, preoccupation with their religious faith triumphs over their love of letters. St. Jerome (331–420), though he had been a pupil of the famous grammarian Donatus, could write in a letter to the bishop of Rome of 'poetry, worldly wisdom, the vain eloquence of rhetoricians. Their agreeable cadence flatters the ear and enchants the heart, but after a careful reading of books of this kind one finds that they are empty.' And although 'we do not give credence to the fables we find in them, this is no excuse, for we scandalize other people who think that we approve what they see us reading'. But in the same letter he says that the study of these authors is necessary for the young. He makes a distinction between pleasure and study, and blames grown-up people and particularly certain priests 'who always had Virgil in their hands, and made a criminal pleasure of something which was a necessity in their youth'.[1] And this came from a man of whom Erasmus was to say that the Latin world held no one more learned. It was Jerome who provided the Latin translation of the Bible, known as the Vulgate from its common use in the Roman Catholic Church. Even when he had withdrawn to the Syrian desert Jerome still had his books with him; he alternated between them and remorse for his sins. 'Wretched man that I was!' he cried. 'In the midst of my fasts I read Cicero.' Still undecided, all Jerome does is to point to the classics as necessary for youthful study but undesirable for older people who should have something more serious to do. The outcome of

[1] Letter XXI, *Ad Damasum de Duobus Filiis*.

the extreme attitude to education, as of the extreme attitude to sex, marriage, property, and the world in general, was retirement from the world. The depth of conviction as to the sinfulness of man accounts for the rise of monasticism and the even more extreme isolationism of the hermits and anchorites: to escape the sins of the world they withdrew altogether from the world.

St. Augustine favoured a rhetorical training for the clergy: 'Rhetoric can be used to enforce either truth or falsehood. Who then will dare to say that the defenders of truth must take their stand unarmed against falsehood?'[1] But he suggested that the content of the training in grammar and rhetoric should be that of Scripture and Christian writings rather than of the classics. 'You have', he said, 'in the Church men who have explained the divine word not only with wisdom but also with eloquence. For your studies you will find that time is too short rather than that the proper books are lacking.'[2] Christian writers with the older education behind them were attempting to provide Christian literature on classical lines. Latin hymns and versions of the Gospel story in verse appeared which could be used in schools. Augustine also suggested that compilations might usefully be made of knowledge, historical, geographical, and so on, which would enable the reader to acquaint himself easily with things mentioned in Scripture. Augustine mentions that he himself wrote a number of introductions to the liberal arts, but the work appears never to have been completed.[3] Martianus Capella, however, a rhetorician of North Africa, early in the fifth century wrote a compilation which became famous. His *De Nuptiis Philologiae et Mercurii* by its very title illustrates the

[1] Augustine: *De Doctrina Christiana*, IV, ii.

[2] *Ibid.* IV, v. *Sunt ergo ecclesiastici viri qui divina eloquia non solum sapienter, sed eloquenter etiam tractaverunt.* Of this work Lalanne wrote: '*C'est dans ce livre même que saint Augustin nous paraît avoir le plus mérité, je ne dis pas le reproche, mais à notre point de vue, l'éloge d'avoir détaché les jeunes chrétiens des études littéraires, telles qu'on les pratiquait de son temps.*' Here we observe a French ecclesiastic of the nineteenth century defending the Fathers' attitude of reserve towards the study of pagan authors.

[3] *Retractationum libri*, I, vi. Only the *De Musica* appears to have survived. Others under Augustine's name on grammar, dialectic, etc., have been published, but the authorship is doubtful. See Alfaric: *Évolution intellectuelle de Saint Augustin*, p. 410.

fantastic nature of the allegory used as a framework for his treatment of the seven liberal arts. Practically nothing is known of the author's life; he makes no mention of Christianity, and was almost certainly not a Christian. Yet his book was to become a standard work during the Middle Ages; when once a boy had mastered the elements of Latin in another standard work—the *Ars Grammatica* of Donatus—he would find a summary of knowledge in Capella. The marriage of Mercury and Philology was but an allegory, but the seven maidens attendant upon them represent the seven liberal arts, and a book was devoted to each, grammar, dialectic, rhetoric, geometry, arithmetic, astronomy, and music. It was not an original composition—it was apparently based on the work, since lost, of the Roman writer Varro—but it provided a handbook for generations of teachers. The very fact is indicative of the decline of letters: original works of value were disappearing into oblivion while a compendium such as the *De Nuptiis* survived.[1]

Yet when one surveys the considerable literary output of the Fathers of the Early Church—collected in the 221 substantial volumes of Migne's *Patrologia Latina* and the 161 volumes of the Greek series—it does appear that the writers of the Church were indeed creating a new literature with its own Christian content of theological writing, commentary on Scripture, letters, and other works, a material for the education of a new age which was imperceptibly coming into being. Graeco-Roman civilization with its literature was slowly perishing. Only the lawyers, like Gaius, and the Christian Apologists show a vigour which can add something of the creative spirit to literature. A modern classical scholar goes so far as to say that 'not only are the Christian writers of this age far above their pagan contemporaries; they can stand comparison with the greatest authors of classical times. There is nothing in Roman oratory finer than

[1] See the opinion of H. O. Taylor in *The Medieval Mind*, I, 71. 'Possibly some good Christian of the time could have composed a worse book, or at least one somewhat more deflected from the natural objects of primary education. But the *De Nuptiis* is astonishingly poor and dry. The writer was an unintelligent compiler, who took his matter not from the original sources, but from compilers before him.'

Tertullian's *Apologeticus*. There is nothing in Roman philosophy so original as Augustine's *City of God*. And there is no work of Roman scholarship in any way equal to Jerome's translation of the Bible. Nietzsche with something more than his usual perversity maintained that Christianity had a weakening influence on men's minds; but it is plain that nearly all the strongest intellects in this age turned to the Christian faith, and from that faith drew vigour and inspiration.'[1]

A careful reading of Augustine's *De Doctrina Christiana* suggests that a constructive educational compromise between the old and the new might not have been impossible. The Fathers who created the new literature were learned men; some had been thoroughly trained in the old grammatical and rhetorical schools. Augustine clearly indicates the value to the Christian of knowledge, and he contrasts 'useful study' with 'the dull sloth of ignorance'. The *De Doctrina Christiana* begins with the assertion that: 'There are certain rules for the interpretation of Scripture which I think might with great advantage be taught to earnest students of the word, that they may profit not only from reading the works of others who have laid open the secrets of the sacred writings but also from themselves opening such secrets to others.' Thus the object of education is new—it is the understanding of the Scriptures, the basis of the Christian faith. But the method is old—it is the understanding of written texts and for their interpretation 'there are certain rules'. It was necessary, however, to defend the educational process itself against those Christians who regarded it—as they regarded almost everything else—as worldly and superfluous. This defence Augustine offered: 'As to those who talk vauntingly of Divine Grace, and boast that they understand and can explain Scripture without the aid of such directions as those I now propose to lay down . . . I would such persons would remember that it was from human teachers they themselves learnt to read.' Augustine was dealing specifically with those who maintained that God would bestow directly what knowledge was necessary without human intervention; he was thinking, too, of a society,

[1] Professor F. A. Wright in his introduction to *Fathers of the Church*.

the Christian society, in which many members were illiterate, for he speaks of an Egyptian monk who, 'not being able to read himself, is said to have committed the Scriptures to memory through hearing them read by others', and of a barbarian slave who was reported to have 'attained a full knowledge of the art of reading simply through prayer that it might be revealed to him'. Should we therefore not teach our children languages 'because on the outpouring of the Holy Spirit the apostles immediately began to speak the language of every race'? 'No, no; rather let us put away false pride and learn whatever can be learnt from man . . . lest, being ensnared by such wiles of the enemy and by our own perversity, we may even refuse to go to the churches to hear the gospel itself, or to read a book, or to listen to another reading or preaching, in the hope that we shall be carried up to the third heaven . . . .' He points out that those who claim direct knowledge of the Scriptures generally set about expounding by speech or writing what they claim to know to others—why do they not send their pupils 'direct to God, that they too may learn by the inward teaching of the spirit without the help of man'? The fact is, as Augustine realized fully, that the arts of reading and understanding are acquired only by diligent study, and 'the man who lays down rules for interpretation is like one who teaches reading, that is, shows others how to read for themselves'.

Men communicate by means of signs, mainly spoken or written. 'Conventional signs are those which living beings mutually exchange for the purpose of showing, as well as they can, the feelings of their minds, or their perceptions, or their thoughts.' Because sounds pass away at once, the art of writing was developed and it has come about that Scripture has been interpreted into various tongues and spread far and wide. In reading them 'men seek to find out the will of God', but to read them a knowledge of the written signs must be first acquired. 'And men who speak the Latin tongue need two other languages for the knowledge of Scripture, Hebrew and Greek, that they may have recourse to the original texts if the endless diversity of the Latin translators throw them into doubt.' In

Christian studies, 'no help is to be despised, even though it come from a profane source'.[1] The Christian must avoid superstition and idolatry, but he must not spurn the truths and virtues which were existent in the pagan world. 'We ought not to give up music because of the superstition of the heathen, if we can derive anything from it that is of use for the understanding of Holy Scripture . . . we ought not to refuse to learn letters because they say that Mercury discovered them; nor because they have dedicated temples to Justice and Virtue, and prefer to worship in the form of stones things that ought to have their place in the heart, ought we on that account to forsake justice and virtue. Nay, but let every good and true Christian understand that wherever truth may be found, it belongs to his Master; and while he recognizes and acknowledges the truth, even in their religious literature, let him reject the figments of superstition.' The ordinary knowledge of the everyday world is also necessary to the Christian, such as of dress, means of communication, and of 'arrangements as to weights and measures, and the stamping and weighing of coins, which are peculiar to each state and people. . . . This whole class of human arrangements, which are of convenience for the necessary intercourse of life, the Christian is not by any means to neglect, but on the contrary should pay a sufficient degree of attention to them, and keep them in memory.'

History also is a valuable aid, for 'anything we learn from history about the chronology of past times, assists us very much in understanding the Scriptures, even if it be learnt without the pale of the Church as a matter of childish instruction'. Thus a knowledge of the successive Olympic Games and of the names of the consuls could be of assistance in dating other events. History itself, though it describes the institutions of men, is 'not reckoned among human institutions; because things that are past and gone and cannot be undone are to be reckoned as belonging to the course of time, of which God is the author and governor . . . . History narrates what has been done, faithfully and with advantage.' Augustine also included what we might

---

[1] II, xviii, *Profani si quid bene dixerunt, non aspernandum.*

call natural science as useful to the Christian—'all that has been written about the situation of places, and the nature of animals, trees, herbs, stones, and other bodies'. A knowledge of the stars, of the course of the moon, of useful arts employed in making, 'for example, a house, a bench, a dish', of medicine, agriculture, navigation, even of dancing, racing, wrestling— all this may serve in the work of life if 'some duty compel us' but assists especially the Christian student 'that we may not be wholly ignorant of what Scripture means to convey when it employs figures of speech derived from these arts.' Dialectic, or the science of reasoning, 'is of very great service in searching into and unravelling all sorts of questions that come up in Scripture, only in the use of it we must guard against the love of wrangling, and the childish vanity of entrapping an adversary'. Logic is not something made by, but only observed by, man: 'it exists eternally in the reason of things, and has its origin with God.' Rhetoric, or eloquence, is a means of 'setting forth the meaning when it is ascertained', and of 'moving men's minds to desire and aversion'. It is rightly used when employed to set forth the truth. The science of number also 'was not created by man, but was discovered by investigation'. All these things have a place in the Christian education. 'If those who are called philosophers, and especially the Platonists, have said aught that is true and in harmony with our faith, we are not only not to shrink from it, but to claim it for our own use from those who have unlawful possession of it.'

Thus, in spite of the many doubts and hesitations of the Fathers on the subject of pagan learning, Augustine does not, in effect, reject the fruits of human experience, investigation, and learning. He turns them towards a new objective: he uses them as useful worldly means to an other-worldly, spiritual end. As he put it himself in his preface, in considering man's place in this mortal life: 'We have wandered far from God; and if we wish to return to our Father's home, this world must be used, not enjoyed, that so the invisible things of God may be clearly seen, being understood by the things that are made[1]—

[1] Quoting from the Epistle to the Romans i, 20.

49

that is, that by means of what is material and temporary we may lay hold upon that which is spiritual and eternal.' 'Two great roads lead to wisdom,' he wrote elsewhere, 'authority and reason. One is for the ignorant, the other for the educated. Although reason is the greater, authority comes first for ignorance precedes education.'[1] He knew, too, like Xenophon, that mere knowledge was not enough. Man needs not only to know what is right; right habits also are important. To move men to act rightly rhetoric may be employed,[2] but Augustine warned the educated Christian against presumption in looking down on the uneducated who might know better how to keep themselves 'free from vices of conduct than from faults of language.'[3] Augustine lived in a world which still possessed the Roman system of schools and educational tradition was strongly conservative; it would seem as if he, and many of the Fathers like him, largely accepted the existing system of education as they found it, for the young, although the adult must turn his eyes to Scripture rather than the old authors and use his education to achieve understanding of the Christian faith. But had the Roman system of schools endured, they might have been given a Christian content and turned to a Christian end. It was the collapse of the Roman Empire, and with it of its schools, that left the Christian Church as the only surviving cultural institution and imposed upon it the task of erecting new, and Christian, schools.

Christianity triumphed in the Roman world: at the close of the fourth century the adherents of the old religion found their sacrifices forbidden by law and their endowments confiscated, only in Athens and Alexandria did pagan philosophy in the form of Neo-Platonism linger on. Christianity brought to the decadent pagan world a new moral force. The great days of the ancient Greek civilization were long gone by; the Roman creation of a Latin literature in its own right was a thing of the past. If these things were still studied, the life had gone out of

---

[1] *De Ordine*, II, ix.　　　[2] *Ibid.*, II, xiii.

[3] *De Catechizandis Rudibus*, I, xiii. Educated Christians also *cordi casto linguam exercitatam nec conferre audeant.*

them. The new faith brought new life. Whence and from what cause come those vitalizing movements of the human spirit which create fruitful and influential civilizations, who can say? But into the old, decaying chambers of the once magnificent civilization of the ancient world blew the strong keen wind of the Christian faith. The emptiness of scepticism, the barren and superficial brilliance of mere style, the great void of Roman spiritual life was filled by the sense of divine purpose in life which Christianity had brought. Here, then, was a new force at work among men. Hardly, however, had Christianity been established in the Roman Empire than that Empire itself collapsed. This, like the loss of its life-giving power by the antique culture, is another of the profound human mysteries; Rome which, while a poor and insignificant republic, had conquered Italy, and then the Mediterranean world, now in the days of its wealth and power succumbed to the pressure of the Northern barbarians. Were the causes economic, racial, psychological, who can say? The collapse was gradual and not fully perceived by those living at the time—the rhetorical schools were, as Augustine described them, still 'alive with the noise of students through the whole world'—but Augustine himself in the *De Civitate Dei* was obliged to answer the accusation that Rome had fallen in Christian times and to answer that the true city was the city of God; he thought it expedient also to get the young and studious Orosius to write his seven books of histories *Adversum Paganos*, in which he enumerated, with a wealth of lurid detail, the many calamities which man had suffered in the pagan world *before* the advent of the Christian faith.

The collapse of the Roman Empire was accompanied by the decline of the schools. There was no sudden break, perhaps, but profound change in the social and political conditions of Europe necessarily brought a change also in education. The invading barbarians were often illiterate, and uninterested in the education of the schools; the breakdown of the vast administrative machine of the Romans removed a powerful incentive for the acquisition of education. By the sixth century many of the schools must have disappeared. They had been an essential part of the old Roman system of life. Although Augustine had shown that the Christian must make use of education in order to understand the Scriptures, in the vastly changed conditions the Christian Church was not ready and able to take over the schools wholesale and turn them to its own uses. A great darkness settled down over Europe: the only bright signs for the future were the message of Christianity with its hope of a better way of life, and the strong, clean, virile, if savage and barbarous, energy of the newcomers—an energy which was, after all, the energy of youth. But, intellectually, Europe had fallen back. Gregory, Bishop of Tours towards the end of the sixth century, confessed his own incorrectness in grammar. 'The cultivation of liberal studies', he wrote, 'is declining, or rather dying out, in the cities of Gaul.'

Another political factor which helped to determine the future of European education was the establishment of the new Roman capital by Constantine in the Greek city which he called after himself, Constantinople. From this there followed a division of the Empire into two, an Eastern and a Western Empire, and when the Roman Empire collapsed in the West, the Eastern half continued to have an independent existence. The Eastern Empire continued, in some form or another, until the Ottoman Turks captured Constantinople in 1453. The political separation of East and West was paralleled by a division in the Christian Church. Political and ecclesiastical was accompanied by linguistic division; Greek was the language of Constantinople, Latin of Rome. Greek now gradually disappears in the West; the influence of Greek on Roman education becomes but a memory. The Christian civilization of Europe was to be a Latin civilization. To the Christian Church there passed the task of saving what it could from the wreck of the Roman Empire. Slowly, out of the ruins, developed the new culture of the Middle Ages, a culture which was dominated by the church. And with it was created a new education to serve the ends of the faith.

PART TWO

Medieval Education

CHAPTER IV

THE MEDIEVAL DICHOTOMY: CHIVALRY AND GRAMMAR

IF there is still in modern society a certain gulf and antagonism between affairs and scholarship, between study and games, between thought and action, it is in the Middle Ages that we see this division most clearly marked. There was indeed a dichotomy in medieval education. Although it is often said that that education was a training for the clerk, in fact a large part of the training of the young man was that of action. Education, if we take the term broadly, was of two kinds: one was book learning, the other was the training of the knight. The difference has been well put by a modern historian who was himself a product of the oldest English public school and also Lloyd George's President of the Board of Education: 'In the ancient world culture and high birth went together. It was the grave misfortune of Europe in the Middle Ages that these two qualities admired of man were sharply dissociated. The business of the knight was to fight and hunt; the duty of the clerk was to pray and learn.'[1] Differentiation of social class was

[1] H. A. L. Fisher: *History of Europe*. The dichotomy was, of course, not complete, and it was sometimes possible to transfer from one career to the other. Abelard says that his father had had some education before turning to arms and that he himself, though educated first, was intended for a military career but he 'abandoned the court of Mars to enter the bosom of Minerva'. *Historia Calamitatum* in Migne, CLXXVIII 114–15. Medieval university students sometimes found their inability to learn and asked their fathers to transfer them—*ab officio clericali removendo et ad decus milicie . . . transferendo*. Munich MS. quoted by C. H. Haskins: *Studies in Medieval Culture*, p. 21, note 1.

55

sharper and clearer than to-day, and beneath the clergy and the knights were the peasants whose humble but essential function was to produce the wherewithal for society as a whole. For the peasants, formal education of one kind or the other was not thought to be necessary, and attempts to pass from one social stratum to another might meet violent opposition. Dr. Coulton draws a parallel with the opposition to popular education in modern times: 'That jealousy of primary education, which remains one of the vividest political pictures in the minds of those who remember the struggle of 1870 and the following years, must be multiplied fourfold when we think ourselves back to the Middle Ages.'[1] Late in the fourteenth century Parliament in England petitioned the king that no bondman should be allowed to send his sons to school in order to advance them by the avenue open to the clergy. And the privileged position of the clergy would not encourage them to exert themselves overmuch to make easy the narrow way of learning. In fact, the three strata of medieval society were distinct and different and educational preparation of the young was patterned accordingly.

The Middle Ages, as historians call the period between the collapse of the Roman Empire in the fifth century and the renaissance of classical learning and the fruition of the new political institution of the national state in the fifteenth, was a period in which the principal cultural influence was Christianity as interpreted by the Roman Catholic Church. The earlier centuries of the Middle Ages are sometimes, not inappropriately, termed the Dark Ages: the brilliance of classical civilization had departed, and Europe was in the hands of the illiterate tribal leaders of the Northern barbarians themselves pushed on by even more savage peoples from central Asia. Goths, Franks, Vandals, Huns remade the face of Europe; the separation of the Eastern Empire from the West accentuated the isolation and the novelty of the life of European West and North; and, finally, the great territorial expansion of Moham-

---

[1] *Medieval Village*, p. 254. This position is further explained in *Medieval Panorama*, p. 389.

medanism in the seventh century completed the destruction of what had been the Roman world and threw Europe on to its own resources. The Moslem invasions, which detached from the Eastern or Byzantine Empire the richly hellenized or romanized provinces of the Near East and North Africa, were, in Pirenne's striking phrase, 'thrown across the path of history with the elementary force of a cosmic cataclysm'.[1] The *orbis romanus* had already lost its oecumenical character; the Mediterranean now ceased to be a Roman lake; the new religion of Mohammed with its own system of Moslem law and its Arabic tongue replaced the Christian culture in the East. The medieval civilization of Europe—of western and northern Europe—was a localized civilization. Politically, Europe came to be organized under the systematized anarchy of feudalism, an emergency regulation under which society was arranged on the basis of the tenure of land (at that time the most important form of wealth) and military service (the most important form of service). Each small district or fief looked to its military holder for leadership and protection in troubled times, and he in turn looked to his feudal superior. Economically, each district, or farm or manor, must be largely self-sufficing. The interdependence of the Roman world, the wide Mediterranean commerce, were things of the past, and the manorial system is simply a name for an agricultural, self-sufficing economy. Yet the new, barbarian world of Europe could not fail to be impressed, when it could understand, by what it found among the ruins of Rome: a synthesis of old and new took place. Town life, though it greatly declined, did not altogether disappear; the Church based its ecclesiastical districts on those of Roman administration, the diocese generally corresponding to the old *Civitas*. Though new Germanic tongues were to be heard there was one language of learning, Latin. The Roman Catholic Church imposed one faith and one attitude to life throughout the territories which adhered to it. The pope, as head of one Church, preserved the idea of a central authority

[1] Henri Pirenne: *Medieval Cities* (translated from the French by F. D. Halsey), p. 23.

57

5

and the idea of Roman imperial power was not forgotten. It was revived, though in a shadowy form, by popes and Teutonic rulers working together. Their Holy Roman Empire of the German Nation revived the name, though not the reality, of Roman authority. Men spoke of the 'two powers', or 'two swords', pope and emperor.

The great task of the Church, whether consciously felt or not, was to civilize the barbarian: chivalry in its essence represents the christianization of the Teutonic fighting man; grammar the Church's training of its own future servants, which also incidentally equipped them for administrative service in the feudal states. The subtle invitation or challenge of unknown things just beyond their comprehension exercised its effect upon the uneducated: the fierce chieftain or ruthless feudal baron might despise the clerk, yet find himself dependent upon him as soon as it came to a matter of business or the keeping of a record. Education would appear to have its uses; the new man would come under an old influence. Similarly, in the nineteenth century the successful industrialist or business man might speak with contempt of the bookish education he had done without in 'making his pile'; yet he might use a part of his fortune to help in the endowment of a school, and send his son to be educated. The appeal of the things of the mind does not completely lose its force, even if that appeal has to be discovered again and again. The Church came to provide schools for its own servants, but the means of book learning were in Latin. To teach boys Latin to turn them into priests was to introduce them, however slightly, to the older civilization: a first step taken might well lead to others. Sooner or later human curiosity would lead once more to a study of Latin authors. Potential in the needs of the ecclesiastical system was the development of a system of literary education.

But an education in letters was not the lot of the layman, and for long enough no education at all, in any formal, conscious sense, must have been the general rule. Even monks and priests were often but poorly educated and mumbled through the Latin services without properly understanding the meaning of the words.[1] A scholar king like Alfred was an exception; Charlemagne, who founded the medieval empire in 800, although he spoke Latin, and understood some Greek, as well as his Germanic tongue, made little headway in his attempts to write. His biographer Einhard described how the great Charles kept writing materials under his pillow and in moments of leisure would practise the characters of the alphabet. Popular ignorance was the natural concomitant of the squalor, poverty, and disease of medieval life. Salimbene in the thirteenth century described the services in the heat of summer when the churchmen were tormented and distracted from worship by the vermin; in the next century a writer who is urging the proper care of books speaks of the careless boy who will 'at the prick of a biting flea, throw aside his precious volume'. Attention was also necessary 'that no sooty scullion reeking from his unwashed pots touch the leaves of books'; nor should the illiterate handle them for they 'view a book with the same interest whether it is upside down or right side up'.[2] For an impression of prevailing squalor, filth, and universal lack of sanitation one must go to-day to the materially backward East. With all this went a savagery and barbarism in war and personal feud which we supposed, until 1939, Europe had outgrown. The chroniclers have left a lurid account of the troubled Merovingian period on the Continent and of the feudal barbarities of Stephen's time in England. In the fourteenth century Froissart described in a cold-blooded way the slaughter of prisoners, only regretting the large sum in ransom money which was thereby lost. It does not do to romanticize, or sentimentalize, the Middle Ages. Human greatness there was, as in every age: medieval culture showed itself in the cathedrals, in the scholastic philosophy, in the Flemish and Italian painting of the fourteenth and fifteenth centuries. But there were a cruelty, a roughness and a lack of finer feelings which were symptomatic

---

[1] See the examples given by G. G. Coulton: *Europe's Apprenticeship*, chap. iii. He suggests that the majority of priests learned their job by practical apprenticeship.

[2] *Philobiblon* of Richard de Bury (ed. A. F. West).

of an underlying barbarism. The personal endowment of greatest value in that rude age was the possession of physical strength and courage.

How, then, was the young man of good birth prepared for adult life in the feudal age? It is difficult to give a detailed account of the early life of any single figure, but the story in general has been largely pieced together by historians. Until the age of seven the boy was under his mother's care. At home he learnt to speak—whatever might be the language of his neighbourhood. In England, after the Conquest, it would have been Norman-French; later, in the fourteenth century, English. If the mother could read herself she might teach her son. In any case, a lot would depend upon the character and education of the mother, which must have varied widely. If she were so inclined she might gain the assistance of some priest in the boy's early lessons. The mother would in all probability give the boy his first religious instruction as well as his first introduction to behaviour and manners. At seven or thereabouts the boy might be sent to the castle of some great noble—probably the feudal superior—and there trained with the lord's own children and others of good family from the neighbourhood. Girls would be similarly trained in the household for their domestic duties. For the next six or seven years the boy served as a page in the household and came particularly under the influence of the ladies. Much in the formation of his character would depend upon them; if they were shallow, fickle, and concerned with nothing save personal adornment and the scandals of illicit love which the troubadours encouraged, then the moral development of the pages must suffer in consequence. In general, perhaps, the women introduced a civilizing influence into the castle; they were, after all, the stay-at-homes while the men were out at the chase or the wars, and it was in their own interest to find diversions to pass away the long hours of seclusion. Singing, music, the making of verse were all means of doing this, and good manners with all their ceremonial courtesy had also some effect in producing at least a veneer of civilized behaviour. Dancing and playing at indoor games, like chess, were also indulged in, and the page who was adept at them and willing to please would be popular.

During this period of his upbringing the boy might also learn some Latin and perhaps a foreign language. How much he learnt would depend very largely on aptitude and inclination. Certainly not all medieval chronicles were the work of churchmen. The anonymous *Gesta Francorum*, the history of the First Crusade, appears to have been put together by a knight who took part. Villehardouin, a knight of Champagne, described the Fourth Crusade, as did also Robert de Clari; Joinville, who wrote the history of St. Louis, and the writer of the *Histoire de Guillaume le Maréchal* were also laymen. And the same must have been true of the troubadours and trouvères. It is not inconceivable, however, that some of these lay chroniclers may have dictated their narratives to a scribe without being able to write themselves. Some of the nobles and knights learnt to read and write; others did not—especially in the earlier centuries.[1] Much more important, however, was the training in arms from about the age of fourteen to twenty or twenty-one. In this next stage of his training the young man, now a squire, hardened his body by wrestling, jumping, and swimming, learnt to hunt, to hawk, and to joust, and practised himself in the use of the necessary weapons, in wearing armour and in the management of the heavy war-horse. The squires also waited upon their lord, attending his horse and armour, carrying out personal duties in his household, and waiting upon him at table. Thus the training in deportment and manners which had commenced under the women's care was continued. Of the squire in the *Canterbury Tales*, for example, Chaucer said:

> Curteys he was, lowly and servisable,
> And carf biforn his fader at the table.

By the fourteenth century, too, one can suppose that the young man also acquired rather more literary education.

---

[1] Léon Gautier: *La Chevalerie*, p. 143, poses '*le grave problème: le jeune noble du XIIe siècle savait-il lire et écrire*'. He considered that while some remained ignorant, many learnt enough to read a romance, and to write a letter.

Chaucer said also of this squire that he could read and write. The final ceremony of knighthood came at about twenty-one, although a man could be dubbed knight on the battlefield. When fully carried out, the ceremony was most elaborate: it included purification by bath, symbolic clothing, fast, and vigil, as well as the accolade or dubbing knight by king or noble. The vows to serve God and maintain the Christian faith, to honour women, to fight for honour and the welfare of all pointed to an ideal, but one only too frequently unachieved in practice. But the ceremony represented admission to full manhood: we can discover the essential core of this procedure in primitive initiation ceremonies, in the Teutonic investiture with arms of the young freeman of the tribe which Tacitus described in his *Germania*, and in the admission to citizenship among the Greeks and Romans.

Personal glimpses of the training of the young knight can be gleaned from the life story of one of the most famous knightly warriors of the twelfth century. William Marshal, though born a landless younger son, became through his prowess and good fortune one of the greatest feudal barons of England and ruled the country as regent during the first years of the minority of Henry III. His life was recorded in a rhyming chronicle[1] soon after his death, and the story lays the emphasis in his youth on bodily strength and training in arms. There is little or no reference to what nowadays we should ordinarily call education. Whether the Marshal learnt to read and write is uncertain, though his name appears as a witness on charters. A younger brother became Bishop of Exeter. But most of William's boyhood and youth were spent in disturbed conditions and in the life of castle, camp, and field. The chronology for this period of his life is not certain but he seems to have been sent about the age of twelve to the court of a relative, the chamberlain of Normandy. More turbulent than England, Normandy was more suitable for knightly adventures. William served for eight years as a squire, and received knighthood about the age of twenty. He now began to make a name for himself as a warrior both in

[1] *L'Histoire de Guillaume le Maréchal.*

the feudal warfare of his time and in the many tournaments. His training in arms stood him in good stead; he captured so many horses and so much armour in the affrays that he was able to maintain himself until he won the royal favour and the hand of the great heiress of Pembroke. Thus a 'specialized' knightly training led to high fortune, and, in this case, to real service in later years to English kings.

Apart from arms, the Marshal had also learnt to sing well. At tournaments the ladies sometimes asked him to entertain them with a song and this he willingly did.[1] In the story of the Marshal we are reading history and not the romantic concoction of some *chanson courtoise*; we see a real figure and not merely a *chevalier français idéal, galant et adventureux*. The tournament was the school of war: in the *ludi militares* and *militaria exercita*[2] the young knight kept himself in training, practised his arms, and won his maintenance. He could also make his name by giving largesse to trouvères and heralds. On one occasion as a tourney was beginning, a young herald stepped out with a new song:

Mareschal,
Kar me donez un boen cheval.

William straightway unhorsed one of the opposing knights and presented the horse to the herald. All present declared it a charming exploit. So grew the young man's fame in the twelfth century as might in our own that of athlete, cricketer or footballer, more skilled on the field than in the classroom.

A modern writer, a professor of medieval history in the University of London, has described the word *education* as 'a cardinal word in respect of the institution of Chivalry. For the strength and the permanent importance of Chivalry lay in the fact that it was a complete way of life, moulding the character and determining the destiny of its subject from the cradle to the grave. As a type of training, as a code of honour, as a standard of good form, as a school of courtesy, as a norm of piety, ceremonious but not enthusiastic; in all these respects, Chivalry

---

[1] *L'Histoire*, l, 3477. '*Li Marischals qui bien chantout.*'
[2] Du Cange: *Glossarium*, Dissertation VI.

made an enduring mark, not only upon the later Middle Ages, but also upon all the subsequent centuries of Western civilization. In England, particularly, it set the tone which has been perpetuated in the great Public School tradition. Freed from ephemeral accidents, and purged from its absurdities and impurities, the system of education established and developed in the baronial castles and knightly hostels of the twelfth century is precisely that system which has been continued and enlarged in the splendid curricula of Winchester, Eton, and the later members of the great group of which they were the pioneers. They did but graft the classical learning of the monastic schools upon the chivalric training in honour, in sport, in military exercise, in social intercourse, in courtesy and generosity, in reverence and devotion, of the schools of Christian knighthood.'[1] Thus once more we observe in an institution long departed something that strikes us as familiar; the institution of chivalry like the Spartan pack provided a hard training for the man of action. Chivalry, we know—and the fact is emphasized by the writer quoted—had its bad side. Dr. Arnold, the famous headmaster of Rugby and creator of the modern public-school system, did not in fact recognize a kindred spirit in medieval chivalry. 'If I were called upon', he wrote, 'to name what spirit of evil predominantly deserved the name of Antichrist, I should name the spirit of Chivalry—the more detestable for the very guise of the "Archangel ruined" which has made it so seductive to generous minds.'[2] Yet as the wild savagery of the earlier medieval centuries was brought under control by a more settled form of society, the element of courtesy, the idea of a gentleman, became stronger. 'He is gentle that doeth gentle deeds', wrote Chaucer in the *Wife of Bath's Tale*; 'Thou wert the kindest man that ever struck with sword', said Malory of Sir Lancelot in the *Morte d'Arthur*.

As it was the task of the Church to provide an ideal aim in the service of God for the knightly training, so also was it the task of the Church to provide a means of education for those

[1] F. J. C. Hearnshaw, in *Chivalry*, ed. Professor E. Prestage (1928).
[2] *Life and Correspondence*, I, 255.

who were to serve it as priests. It thus turned—since its own service was in Latin, the most accessible translation of the Bible was St. Jerome's Latin translation, and the works of the Western Fathers were also in that tongue—to Latin.

There was an inevitable connexion between the education of the Church and that of the Roman schools of grammar. The Roman schools had disappeared; the Church had, therefore, to create afresh a system of education to serve ecclesiastical needs. It is a mistake, however, to attribute—as has often been done—this process of providing education to the monasteries. Sometimes the monasteries were centres of learning; at St. Gall Greek was studied as late as the ninth century. The Benedictine rule fixed for the daily routine, in addition to manual labour, two hours of reading. Monks, too, were often employed in copying manuscripts, and monasteries have in this way been instrumental in preserving a certain amount of ancient literature. But it has been disputed whether the monasteries really provided education in a general sense. They doubtless educated their own novices, but it does not follow that they also educated boys from outside their walls. It is also doubtful how far monastic education went: whether it was simply instruction in the Psalms and the rule of the particular Order or whether it went beyond this. The general ignorance of the times must be remembered, for this affected the monks themselves: often they would not be educated men. They were men who had retired from the world; the monasteries were often in lonely, secluded places and therefore not within easy reach of people who might be wishing education for their children.

In one country, however, the monasteries did make a great contribution to cultural life during the dark sixth, seventh, and eighth centuries. That country was Ireland, to which Christianity had come in the fourth century; and, while the barbarians were over-running continental Europe and Britain, Ireland escaped and her Church developed on independent lines, for the monks performed also the functions of secular clergy. There was among the Celts, in Gaul and Britain, an educational tradition: Caesar mentioned the schools of the Druids in Gaul.

After the conversion of Ireland monks and lay teachers appear to have replaced the Druids. We hear of the study of Latin and Christian literature, of Irish literature, and of Irish law; we hear also of the large number of students, including students from overseas, attending the courses at the monastic schools. Laymen attended the schools as well as men in orders: the exact curriculum is not known, but theology was doubtless important, and Latin and Greek appear to have been carefully studied. Missionaries to Europe from Ireland in the sixth century were better read in the classics than their contemporaries elsewhere. Some of these missionaries founded monasteries and schools—of which St. Gall is one—on the Continent, and this was the Irish contribution to the slow growth of a new life of letters. But at home the light of learning was extinguished. A new barbarian invasion—this time the invasion of Ireland by the savage and pagan Vikings from Scandinavia at the end of the eighth century—destroyed the bright and promising culture in the western island.

The schools which had in them the seed of future educational development were the bishops' schools; the cathedral school was the parent of modern grammar school and university. Schools are heard of in France and England somewhere about the end of the sixth century. Bede in his *Ecclesiastical History* tells of the king of East Anglia establishing in 631 a school to teach boys grammar, and in this the king was helped by what he had, while in exile, seen 'well arranged among the Gauls'; Bede also referred to the school already existing at Canterbury. It appears, therefore, that once more schools were springing up to teach Latin grammar; this time they were created by the Church to serve its needs. It had both to train its own priests and, in the case of the English, to introduce the language of the Church to a people ignorant of it. It had to teach choristers to sing psalms and hymns. From an early date the teaching of church singing made a song school a necessary adjunct of the grammar school. The cantor, or preceptor, who directed church singing and the training of the choir, became an important dignitary in the medieval cathedral. In the seventh and eighth centuries church canons[1]—at first in the East, then in the West—stated the obligation of priests to keep schools of grammar without fees except for voluntary payments, and in the ninth century a canon enjoined every care in the appointment in bishops' sees of 'masters and doctors to teach faithfully letters and the liberal arts, because in them especially the divine commands are declared and made manifest'. The fact is that during these centuries the Church was rebuilding a system of education: song schools and grammar schools were becoming a normal provision of a cathedral, the former entrusted to the cantor, the latter to a *scholasticus* or *magister scholarum*, later known as chancellor.

The efforts of the Church to provide education were not altogether unaided, even in the earlier centuries, by the laity; even some of the early Teutonic kings interested themselves in encouraging schools. Later the emperor, Charlemagne, and in England the king, Alfred, were shining examples of royal determination to use education as well as they could to improve the intellectual and spiritual condition of their subjects. Charlemagne used the Palace School—which had flourished already under his father, Pepin—to educate the court circle. This school, attended by Charlemagne himself and by his wife, sons, and daughters, educated the young nobles from whose number would come later leaders in state and Church. As head of the school, Charlemagne obtained the services of the Englishman, Alcuin, who had been both pupil in, and head of, the school at York—a great educational centre in the eighth century. With the help of Alcuin, Charlemagne issued edicts exhorting bishops and abbots to press on with the study of the Scriptures and the teaching of grammar, and with the great emperor's vigorous backing behind these edicts we can suppose that they had some effect. Charlemagne seems to have had an idealistic faith in education, which culminated in 802 with a proclamation bid-

---

[1] See Mansi: *Sacrorum Conciliorum* . . . *Collectio*, XI, 1007, for a canon of 680—*Presbyteri per villas et vicos scholas habeant*. Repeated in Capitulary of the Bishop of Orleans, 797 (Mansi, XIII, p. 994). Canon 34 of the Council of 853 (Mansi, XIV, p. 1007).

ding everyone send his son to school to study grammar and keep him at school until he should be well instructed. This was an ideal quite impossible of realization in the conditions of the time, and it is in any case probable that Charles in fact thought of the term 'everyone' in a much narrower sense.[1]

From these beginnings there grew up during the Middle Ages what seems to have been a widely spread system of schools. 'That all bishops cause the art of grammar to be taught in their churches' appears in the record of a synod held at Rome by Gregory VII (1073–85).[2] The fairly frequent repetition, however, of such injunctions makes one wonder a little if they were always carried out. In western Europe the Church assumed, at least in theory, the responsibility for teaching not only its own members but also others; this was recognized by canon law. In 1189 the Third Lateran Council laid down: 'Since the church of God, like a loving mother, is bound to provide for the needy both the things which concern the maintenance of the body and which tend to the profit of souls, in order that the poor who cannot be assisted by their parents' means may not be deprived of the opportunity of reading and proficiency, in every cathedral church an adequate benefice shall be bestowed upon a master who shall teach the clerks of the same church and poor scholars freely, so that both the necessities of the teachers shall be relieved and the way to learning laid open for the learners.'[3] Throughout the Middle Ages the various schools, those attached to cathedrals, to collegiate churches, or, in some cases, to monasteries, and those endowed in connexion with an alms-house, or by a gild or chantry, gave an education in Latin and one which, in its main outlines, did not change.

There was not, at least at first, the fairly sharp dividing line

[1] One is reminded of the confusion caused by the interpretation of the Magna Carta feudal term *liber homo* in later centuries simply as freeman and its consequent association with democratic sentiment. It is still quite easy to slip into such an error. Atticus in *The Sunday Times* (16 Jan. 1949) wrote of the average Englishman being influenced by his public school. In sober fact, however, the average Englishman does not go to a public school.

[2] A. F. Leach: *Educational Charters and Documents*, p. 23.

[3] A. F. Leach, *op. cit.*, p. 122.

which there is to-day between school and university study, and education was still based on foundations in which the remains of classical antiquity are discernible. The medieval course of study was founded on the seven liberal arts:

The Trivium: Grammar, Dialectic, Rhetoric.

The Quadrivium: Music, Arithmetic, Geometry, Astronomy. Alexander Neckam, English scholar of the twelfth century, described them as illuminating knowledge as the seven planets light up the world—*Artes ingenuae sunt septem lumina mundi*.[1] But naturally the first, and main, preoccupation of the grammar-school boy was the learning of Latin and this must be mastered before much else could follow. The standard grammar book of Aelius Donatus, the *Ars Minor* (or *De Octo Partibus Orationis*) was much used from the fourth century onwards, and editions were printed in the sixteenth century, which fact in itself is witness to the long domination of Latin in the schools. Priscian's treatise on Latin grammar, written at Constantinople at the beginning of the sixth century, was studied in the medieval universities. To a modern schoolboy—to any modern reader, indeed—the layout of Donatus is forbidding. The eye and memory are not assisted by the setting out of the parts of a word in tabular form. Declensions and conjugations do not look familiar to the modern eye. The content was indeed intended more for the ear than the eye; the master read, and the pupil recited after him. Much of it was in the form of question and answer, e.g., *Partes orationis quot sunt? Octo. Quae? Nomen pronomen verbum adverbium participium coniunctio praepositio interiectio. Nomen quid est? Pars orationis cum casu corpus aut rem proprie communiterve significans. Nomini quot accidunt? Sex. Quae? Qualitas conparatio genus numerus figura casus.*[2]

Other text-books which were much used and helped to keep alive some of the learning of the ancient world were compilations, of varying degrees of value and worthlessness. Such books were the *De Nuptiis*, already referred to, the *Origins* or *Etymo-*

---

[1] *De Laudibus Divinae Sapientiae* (*Distinctio Decima*, l. 37) and *De Rerum Natura*, chap. clxxiii. See also John of Salisbury's *Metalogicon*, I, xii.

[2] *Ars Minor*, in Keil: *Grammatici Latini*, IV.

logies, an encyclopaedic work by Isidore of Seville (570–636), the histories, *Adversum Paganos*, of Orosius, and the *De Arithmetica* of Boëthius.

As for method, there was much repeating in chorus and learning by heart. For learning to write the method of the stylus and wooden tablet smeared with wax was still used. Discipline was severe and beating frequent, for it was after all a brutal age. Most pictures of the schoolmaster show him with a birch and many illustrations survive of a beating in process. This was regarded as an inevitable part of the business of learning. 'Will you be flogged while learning?' the master asks the boys in Aelfric's *Colloquy* (1005). And the boys reply—an astonishing reply for boys who were English—'We would rather be flogged while learning than remain ignorant.'[1]

[1] Printed in A. F. Leach: *Educational Charters*, p. 39. Aelfric was Abbot of Eynsham about 1005; in addition to the *Colloquy* he wrote an Anglo-Latin grammar and a glossary.

CHAPTER V

ENGLISH MEDIEVAL SCHOOLS AND SCHOOLBOYS

To the English Christianity and schools came together. It is true that Christianity had been brought to Roman Britain and that Roman schools had doubtless been created there as elsewhere in the Empire, but with the withdrawal of the legions and the Anglo-Saxon conquest all this vanished. A darkness thicker than elsewhere settled down over the island; only the slightest historical evidence can be gathered for the events of the next two centuries, and historians still dispute as to the facts and exact character of the English conquest. The English were pagans. It was the pope, Gregory the Great, who sent Augustine (not to be confused with the famous Bishop of Hippo) to convert them, and with the missionaries from Rome there returned to the island something of Rome, although a changed Rome. The pagan English were brought for the first time within the orbit of the new Christian Europe, and if that Europe no longer shone with the lustre of imperial Rome it was at least brighter by far than the barbarous English kingdoms. Of the coming of Christianity to the early English the greatest of modern English historians has said: 'The Christian conquest of the island was the return of Mediterranean civilization in a new form, and with a new message . . . . Christianity meant, also, the return of learning to the island, and the beginning among the barbarians of a political and legal civilization based on the arts of reading and writing in the practicable Latin alphabet . . . . It is with the arrival of the Christians in Saxondom that we begin to get *written* laws, chronicles, and poems. One source, however, the historian loses—the weapons and ornaments which the heathen Saxons buried with their dead, but which Christian custom omitted. "Graveyards", all-important for the heathen period, are of much less service in the Christian epoch.'[1] From the historian's point of view we move in those years from a period in which he depends for his information on the spade of the archaeologist to one in which the written record enters once more into its own. English culture is becoming literate, and with letters we find the beginnings, in a fuller sense, of education. As a result of the efforts of the Christian missionaries there was introduced to the island a system of education which was basically the same everywhere, whether it was among the English or the Franks, whether it was in Spain, beyond the Rhine, or in Rome itself: its object was the training of priests to conduct the Church service, and to read the Bible and the patristic writings, and its method was the learning of Latin grammar.

The first English school was the school in Canterbury. Augustine was sent in 597 to Ethelbert, king of Kent, whose Frankish wife had disposed him towards Christianity. Unlike missionaries of to-day, who would use the native language, Augustine imposed the Latin service of the Roman Church; his missionaries came 'with the Latin-service book in one hand, and the Latin grammar in the other'.[2] They created both church and school. Bede, describing the foundation in 631 of the school at Dunwich, implies the existence of the earlier one at Canterbury.[3] In each case the school was attached to the bishop's see, and in each we observe the foundation of a grammar school; the Canterbury school, founded about 598, refounded by Henry VIII, continues to-day as King's School. The schools attached to the sees of St. Paul's, London, and Rochester may date from the foundation of those bishoprics in 604. Bede refers to a song school as existing at York in 633, and in this we see an early example of the institution for teaching church singing. Song schools and grammar schools, henceforth, generally existed side by side, attached to cathedrals and other great churches. Grammar schools, so attached, can be

[1] G. M. Trevelyan: *History of England*, p. 49.
[2] A. F. Leach: *Schools of Medieval England*, p. 3.   [3] See also p. 66.

postulated as having been founded during the next seventy or eighty years at Winchester, Sherborne—perhaps by the learned bishop Aldhelm—Hereford and Worcester.[1] It is the grammar schools—the *scole gramaticales* or *ludi literarii*—which are the pattern of medieval education because they taught the all-important subject of Latin grammar. These schools in essentials find their origin in the ancient world, and the old tradition was perhaps recalled when Theodore of Tarsus, a Greek from the home of St. Paul in Cilicia, was sent to England to become Archbishop of Canterbury in 669. He was assisted in his work by Hadrian, a monk from North Africa, and Bede, writing about 730, could say that 'even to this day some of their pupils survive who know Latin and Greek as well as their own language'. Both were 'abundantly learned in sacred and profane literature'; both, it appears, probably taught in the school at Canterbury.

The north of England also produced scholars and the great school of York. The foundation of the latter can be attributed to Paulinus, the first bishop, about 630, and later in the century must have originated Hexham and Ripon. It was Bede (b. about 672–735) who made the joint monastic establishment of Wearmouth and Jarrow famous as a centre of learning. The author of the *Ecclesiastical History*—almost a unique source for its period—was brought up from childhood there. 'I passed the whole of my life living in that monastery,' he said, 'and gave my whole life to the study of the Scriptures; and in the intervals of the observance of the regular discipline and daily singing service in church, I have always held it a pleasure to learn or teach or write.' Bede, then, taught the monastic school. But what exactly this meant it is difficult to say, and it would be unwise to assume that he taught others than the younger inhabitants of the monastery. Of the cathedral school at York, Alcuin (735–804), both boy and master there before he went to Charlemagne's court, has left a fairly full description.[2] From

[1] A. F. Leach, *op. cit.*, pp. 36–45.
[2] *De Pontificibus et Sanctis Ecclesiae Eboracensis Carmen*, in *History of the Church of York*, I, 390 (Rolls Series). Also in Leach: *Educational Charters and Documents*, pp. 10–7.

this we can learn what kind of education Alcuin himself had had at York.

Alcuin spoke first of his master, Albert, who 'was sent to the Minster to school in his boyish years and became a priest quite young, and was made advocate of the clergy and preferred as master in the city of York'. This became common practice: the cathedral chancellor acted as its lawyer and was also master of the school. The fact that Alcuin mentioned the city suggests that the school was indeed a city school, for sons of the laity as well as for young clerks. There were, it seems, boarders in the school, for 'whatever youths he saw of eminent intelligence, these he joined to himself, taught, fed and loved'. Among the subjects he taught—and we can picture Alcuin diligently attending his classes—were grammar, rhetoric, law, singing, playing on the flute and lyre, natural history, the church calendar, and theology. Albert became archbishop, and when he retired from active duties two of his chief pupils succeeded him, one as archbishop, the other as master of the school. The schoolmaster was Alcuin himself, and with the school went the store of books which Albert had collected. What these were Alcuin tells us, although it would be more interesting to have greater detail. The narrative is written in verse, rhetorical in style, and refers to Latin, and to what 'famous Greece passed on to the Latins', and also to Hebrew. It is interesting to note that Alcuin understood the relationship of Greek and Latin letters but from the list of names given it appears that most of the books were actually in Latin. There were some of the works of the Fathers; Boëthius and Cassiodorus; two of the popes, Leo and Gregory; Aldhelm of Sherborne and Bede; Pliny, Pompeius Trozus, 'keen Aristotle himself and the mighty orator Tully' (Cicero); Virgil, Statius, Lucan; a number of Christian poets, like Juvencus (about 330), who turned parts of the Bible into verse; a number of grammarians including Donatus, Priscian, and Servius (the great commentator on Virgil); and also, said Alcuin, there were 'many other masters eminent in the schools, in art, in oratory, who have written many a volume of sound sense, but whose names it seemed too long to

74

write in verse'. Alcuin himself added to these by writing dialogues on grammar, rhetoric, and dialectic. Later in his life when established at Charlemagne's court, Alcuin did not lose all touch with England. He wrote in 796 to the Archbishop of York recommending that he should divide the school and have different masters for grammar, song, and writing.[1] This appears to have been done; later a division became common practice in secular cathedrals and the song school is generally found under the cantor or precentor while the grammar school is distinct and under the chancellor. On another occasion Alcuin sent a pupil to the King of Mercia, Offa, to act as master in his school. Whether this was a school at Lichfield—or where else it may have been—we do not know.

Of the difficulties with which students like Alcuin had to contend we gain a glimpse about seventy years earlier from another source. The serious student, then as now, had to apply himself diligently. 'No small time must be spent in the study of reading,' wrote Aldhelm, later Bishop of Sherborne, 'especially by one who, influenced by the desire of knowledge, wishes at the same time to explore Roman law to the marrow, and examine in the most intimate fashion all the mysteries of the Roman lawyers; and what is much more difficult and perplexing, to digest the hundred kinds of metres into prose rules, and illustrate the mixed modulations of song in the straight path of syllables. And in this subject the obscurity is so much the harder for the studious reader to penetrate because of the small number of teachers to be found.' The eager student went on to speak of how 'the secret instruments of the art of metre are collected in letters, syllables, feet, poetical figures, verses, accents, and quantities . . . . All this methinks and other like learning cannot be grasped in a mere interval of time and a momentary application.' And as for arithmetic—*De ratione vero calculationis quid commemorandum?* 'The despair of doing sums oppressed my mind so that all the previous labour spent on learning, whose most secret chamber I thought I knew already,

[1] Letter to Archbishop Eanbald II, quoted in Leach: *Educational Charters and Documents*, p. 19.

75

seemed nothing, and to use Jerome's expression I who before thought myself a past master began again to be a pupil, until the difficulty solved itself, and at last, by God's grace, I grasped after incessant study the most difficult of all things, what they call fractions. As to the Zodiac and its twelve signs, which circle in the height of heaven, I think it better to say nothing . . . the mysteries of things cannot be understood without long and frequent study.'[1]

The invasion of the Danes played havoc, as one would expect, with education. King Alfred complained that when he came to the throne (871) 'so general was its decay among the English people that there were very few on this side of the Humber who could understand their services in English, or translate a letter from Latin into English'; the king also remembered 'how I saw, before it had been all ravaged and burnt, how the churches throughout the whole of England stood filled with treasures and books'. But even in the good old days to which Alfred looked back 'the great multitude of God's servants had very little knowledge of the books, for they could not understand anything of them, because they were not written in their own language'. Alfred therefore set himself to the task of translation from Latin into English; among his translations were works by Bede, Boëthius, Orosius, and Pope Gregory the Great. The king also expressed the hope 'if we have peace, that all the youth of our English freemen, who are rich enough to be able to devote themselves to it, should be set to learning, as long as they are not fit for any other occupation, until they are well able to read English writing: and further let those afterwards learn Latin who will continue in learning, and go to a higher rank'.[2] Alfred, it is clear—in spite of the mythical stories which have gathered round his upbringing—was a man who knew Latin as well as English, and therefore, even in those troubled times, had found the means of education available to him. He did what he could to revive education in Wessex, and in the

---

[1] Letter to Bishop Haeddi, c. 680, in Leach: *Educational Charters and Documents*, pp. 9–11.
[2] From the preface to the Anglo-Saxon translation by King Alfred of Gregory's *Pastoral Care*, in Leach: *Educational Charters and Documents*, pp. 22–5.

story of his life—written about a hundred years later and falsely attributed to one of his bishops, Asser—there is in the description of the supposed schooling of Alfred's son the use of a stock phrase for sending a boy to a grammar school (*ludis literariae disciplinae*), which is evidence for the existence of a grammar school about 1001 (the alleged date of the 'Asser' manuscript) and its use as a matter of course.[1] By that time English education must have revived; as Alfred's son and grandson had extended English power further and further over lands retaken from the Scandinavians, schools restarted. Dunstan, Archbishop of Canterbury, was famous as a scholar. Nor did Alfred's tradition of *English* learning altogether disappear. Aelfric, Abbot of Eynsham, writing about 1005, translated parts of Priscian's Latin grammar into English for the use of 'little boys'—a notable step, for later in the Middle Ages Latin grammar was generally studied in that language. When the Scandinavians triumphed again and the Danish Canute became king in 1017 he was already a Christian; a good ruler, he is reputed to have encouraged schools and learning.

With the Norman conquest of England a new influence entered the country. Its effect on the schools was to strengthen the Continental character of their education by reducing the part previously taken by English. Norman-French was the vernacular of the upper and governing classes and schoolboys began to translate Latin into it instead of into the older language of the English.[2] Apart from this the schools continued to give, as before, a Latin education suited largely to the needs of the Church. Of Henry I—the youngest son of the Conqueror, which fact, combined with his nickname *Beauclerc*, helps to confirm the supposition that he had been intended for the priesthood—the chronicler William of Malmesbury said that he was well educated and received his early teaching in a grammar school—in *scolis litteralibus*. To such good effect was he supposed to have learnt that William used of him a striking if somewhat rhetorical reference 'to that saying of Plato:

[1] See A. F. Leach: *Schools of Medieval England*, pp. 73-4.
[2] Higden's *Polychronicon*, II, 158.

"Blessed is the state in which philosophers are kings or kings philosophers." [1] In the twelfth century the memory of the Greek philosopher had not completely disappeared. It would not be a bad guess to suppose that the young Henry went to school in Winchester—that city rather than London was still the residence of kings. In this same century or soon afterwards we hear of the school—in conjunction with the cathedral—at Salisbury, York, London (St. Paul's), Exeter, and Lincoln; at the two latter advanced teaching in law and theology was also available.

Thus we observe the continuation of a system of cathedral schools of which we saw the beginning with the first introduction of Christianity among the English: 'at the end of the eleventh and the beginning of the twelfth century, the normal state of things in the Cathedrals was that the bishop had delegated to the dean and chapter the supervision of the schools, and that one of the chief canons, the second or third in rank, was called schoolmaster, and personally taught the cathedral school himself; and, if he allowed other schools in his districts, himself issued the licence without which no one was allowed to teach school'.[2]

Other similar schools, attached to collegiate churches, are heard of during the same period; among these are Shrewsbury, Beverley, Pontefract, Hastings, and Gloucester. 'There can be no manner of doubt', wrote the greatest authority on English medieval schools, 'that all the cathedral and collegiate churches kept schools, and that the schoolmaster was one of the most important of their officers.'[3] But this statement may go too far; true of the cathedrals, it cannot be proved of all the collegiate churches. And although the decree of the Lateran Council of 1215 that grammar-school masters should be appointed 'not only in the cathedral church but also in others which can afford it' might seem to justify it, the mere existence of a rule on paper is no guarantee of its general observation.[4] Cathedrals

---

[1] William of Malmesbury: *De Gestis Regum Anglorum*, V (Rolls Series).
[2] A. F. Leach: *Schools of Medieval England*, p. 113.   [3] *Op. cit.*, p. 115.
[4] See on this A. G. Little in *English Historical Review*, XXX.

and collegiate churches 'were not the only source of schools in the eleventh and early twelfth, any more than in later centuries. On the contrary, in every town of considerable population there was a demand for, and consequently a supply of, schools.'[1] Among such schools were those at St. Albans—taught by a secular and in the borough, not in the abbey, although the appointment of the secular to teach depended on the abbot—and Bury St. Edmunds, outside the monastery but under its patronage. Monasticism became very powerful in the twelfth century and a number of cathedrals and churches passed into the control of monks; in this way certain schools were placed placed under their care, and monks began to play a part previously taken by secular clergy. The abbot of Reading Abbey, founded in 1125 by Henry I, was given by the Bishop of Salisbury the same control of the school and of the licence to teach in Reading as a bishop possessed in his diocese. At Gloucester and also at Bristol the appointment of the teacher of the grammar school passed into the hands of the monks.

What were these medieval grammar schools really like? In spite of the many books which have touched on the subject of medieval education it is impossible to form a really clear picture. In contemporary sources references are frequent but detailed description almost entirely lacking; secondary accounts are too often vague and made up of wide generalization. But that the means of education were there for those who were able to make use of them, is made evident by the survival of the many Latin chronicles printed in the Rolls Series and by the emergence in medieval England of great scholars like John of Salisbury, Neckham, and Roger Bacon.

There is one contemporary record which does give a lively account of some aspects of education in London about the middle of the twelfth century. Fitzstephen, cleric in the archbishop's household and later very probably one of the king's justices, wrote a life of Thomas Becket,[2] Archbishop of Canterbury, whose murder in his own cathedral made him one of the

---

[1] A. F. Leach: *Schools of Medieval England*, p. 115.
[2] *Vita Sancti Thomae* with its *Descriptio nobilissimae civitatis Londoniae.*

most famous ecclesiastical heroes of the Middle Ages. Thomas was born a Londoner—*utramque harum urbium sanctus Thomas illustraverit, Londoniam ortu, Cantuariam occasu*—and Fitzstephen prefaced his life with a description of the city, its churches, people, commerce, amusements, and—its schools. Thomas's education was dismissed in three lines—he passed his boyhood at home, in the city school, and, later, studied at Paris.[1] The common medieval habit of finding supernatural omens of future greatness marks the story of Thomas's birth and early years. His mother, before her son was born, dreamt that she carried in her womb the whole archiepiscopal church of Canterbury; his father did homage to the boy before the astonished prior of Merton, who seems to have cared for the boy's earliest education, explaining his action by the words: 'I know what I am doing: this boy will be great in the sight of God.' These stories do not add clarity to the educational picture, but the description of London does. The surroundings described by Fitzstephen were those in which the young Becket grew up. His father was a London official and sent his son to one of the London grammar schools, perhaps to St. Paul's. We can make a picture, even if it be a hazy one, of the kind of education which filled the boyhood of the future archbishop.

Of the London education in Becket's boyhood Fitzstephen wrote: 'The three principal churches have celebrated schools of privileged position and of ancient dignity; sometimes more schools are allowed. On feast days the masters hold assemblies, in festive garb, at the churches. The scholars make disputation, some by way of demonstration, others by question and answer. Certain of them make use of enthymemes; certain of syllogisms. Some speak for show; others to find the truth . . . . Those who learn oratory make their speeches rhetorical in order to persuade, and take care to follow the rules of their art.' There is, in this description, something which reminds us of the student rather than the schoolboy, and we see vividly illustrated the possibility—what, in fact, did happen in Paris—of a university

---

[1] *Vita*, p. 14. *Annis igitur infantiae, pueritiae et pubertatis simpliciter domi paternae et in scholis urbis decursis, Thomas adolescens factus studuit Parisius.*

developing out of the studies among the older pupils in a grammar school. These three schools, the principal schools, of twelfth-century London were the cathedral school of St. Paul's, St. Martin's-le-Grand, and the Arches or St. Mary-le-Bow. The two latter disappeared in the time of Henry VIII. For the younger boys the main concern was, of course, with Latin grammar. These boys would 'compete in verse, or contend with each other on the principles of grammar or the rules of preterites and supines'. And it must be remembered that they were learning to speak easily and freely in Latin, not only to read or to write it. Other boys, the narrator continues, 'make use of epigrams, rhymes and metres, with licence and eloquence, to hammer their fellows; they hurl epithets and jeers; they condemn their faults, and even those of their elders, touching their words with Socratic salt; and they bite in bold dithyrambics with the tooth of Theon'. The passage makes one sure that the author had himself spent many a youthful hour in a grammar school. The classical references suggest the attainment of no mean level of education. And, although the rhetorical style does not make for precision in the educational picture, there is in it, nevertheless, a life and energy which create an impression of reality. But it is difficult to go further. We do not know exactly what authors were read in the English medieval schools although by the beginning of the sixteenth century boys were reading a variety of the great writers as Wolsey's statutes for Ipswich school indicate. The books range, for different forms, from Aesop (*quis facetior?*), Terence (*quis utilior?*), to Virgil, Cicero, Caesar, Horace, and Ovid. In addition to their reading and study of grammar the boys were also to do verse tasks, write précis and essays, and, in the top form, make some study of the life and style of their authors.[1] By the middle of the fourteenth century boys were translating their Latin into English instead of French, which was unfortunate if they travelled, for they knew 'no more French than their left heel'.[2] Apart from this the curriculum was exclusively

[1] A. F. Leach: *English Schools at the Reformation*, p. 107.
[2] John of Trevisa's English version of Higden, *Polychronicon*, II, 161.

Latin; there were as yet none of the familiar sciences and mathematics, history, geography, and the modern languages of the school time-table of to-day.

But the concentration on Latin in the school curriculum did not prevent the acquisition incidentally of a certain amount of other knowledge. Books did exist, although before printing copies were few and expensive. The *Polychronicon*, or universal history, written by Ranulph Higden, a Benedictine monk of Chester, who died in the second half of the fourteenth century, gives one a fair idea of the extent of historical and geographical knowledge of the time and of the sources available. Higden's work was probably much used, for the Latin manuscripts surviving are estimated at over one hundred. He describes the various parts of the world, and its history to his time. There is much information of value, but much which is inaccurate and valueless, depending on the worth of the author he is quoting, because the *Polychronicon* is, like so much medieval work, uncritical compilation from earlier writers. Fact and fanciful story are mixed; in his description of India (vol. I, chap. xi), for example, there are dragons and griffins, but he mentions correctly polygamy and the funeral of the widow with the husband. Among the authors whom he lists in his second chapter—something like the bibliography in a university thesis of to-day—are Josephus, Pliny, Eusebius, Jerome, Augustine (*De Civitate Dei*), Orosius, Isidore (*Etymologies*), Paul the Deacon (*Historia Longobardorum*), Cassiodorus, Suetonius, Priscian, Gregory, Bede, Gildas, William of Malmesbury, Giraldus Cambrensis (*Itinerarium Walliae* and other works), John of Salisbury (*Polycraticus*), Vincent of Beauvais.

Fitzstephen gave also a picture of the schoolboys at recreation—'for we were all boys once'. On Shrove Tuesday each year 'all the boys in the schools bring their game cocks to their masters. The holiday is spent watching the cock fights, in the morning; in the afternoon, the whole youth of the city goes into the suburban level for the famous game of ball.' What this was like anyone can perhaps guess who has taken part in the Shrove Tuesday football still played in the village streets of

Ashbourne, Derbyshire, or who reads the following words of Fitzstephen. 'The grown ups, the fathers, and rich men come on horseback to see the struggles of the young, and with them they become young again; by looking on at so much activity they become hot with excitement and participate in the pleasure of the freeborn youth.' If it froze in winter, boys, and population generally, went out to skate and slide on Smithfield marshes; in summer boys exercised with the bow, and in running, jumping, wrestling, and stone-throwing; on fine summer evenings, schoolboys and youths congregated at the principal springs, Holywell, St. Clement's Well, and Clerkenwell—the well of the scholars or clerks. But it was at the Christmas feasts—although not described by Fitzstephen—that schoolboys found their greatest opportunity for relaxation. On these occasions they could satisfy something of their desire for acting, movement, and pageantry; and they could—to use a metaphor, strictly speaking, anachronistic when applied to the Middle Ages—let off steam. Something of the Roman festival of the Saturnalia may have been handed down; and from these feasts—mixed up as they came to be with the cult of St. Nicholas, an Eastern saint, patron of children and boys because of his abstinence in babyhood, on certain fast days, from his mother's milk and on account of his reputed resurrection of three students murdered on their way to the University of Athens—from these feasts descend the modern cult of Santa Claus, and the pantomime in the Christmas holidays. The special boys' service with the boy-bishop commemorated the slaughter of the innocents by Herod. On the eve of Holy Innocents' Day the boy-bishop (previously elected for the occasion) took service in the cathedral or church; processions and collections took place and were sometimes taken out into the neighbouring countryside in the following days: special suppers were eaten on Innocents' Eve and Innocents' Day. Although the more serious of the clergy occasionally attacked the drinking and frivolities of the festival, it survived until the Protestant Reformation.

Festivals such as that of the boy-bishop and the relaxations of Shrove Tuesday represent the lighter side of the medieval schoolboys' life. But many questions arise. Who were these boys —from what class did they come? How numerous were they— how big were the medieval grammar schools? Were the schools free or were fees paid? It is not possible to give short, precise answers to these questions.

Fitzstephen spoke of the 'freeborn youth'. In theory the sons of serfs or villeins were excluded but occasionally they did find through the grammar school the way open to a career in the Church. Grossetete, the thirteenth-century scholar and Bishop of Lincoln, was 'of humble origin'. Boys at grammar schools would generally be, however, the younger sons of nobles and gentry—the elder sons destined for knighthood would not as a rule go to the grammar school—and also the sons of merchants and officials in the towns. As to the numbers at the schools, two of the greatest of the later medieval schools—Winchester and Eton—had seventy scholars each; they had, in addition, commoners paying fees, and these at Winchester numbered a hundred before the end of the fourteenth century. Schools at Worcester, Taunton, and other places are said to have had over a hundred scholars. At the other end of the scale were very small schools like Wotton-under-Edge, founded in 1384 for a 'schoolmaster and two poor scholars', the latter to act as pupil teachers to those coming for instruction. With regard to fees, again, no single answer is possible: some schools provided free education, some did not A 'free grammar school', where the term is used, probably denoted a school which did provide education free. In many cases the endowment in lands of a school provided the living of the master and for the livelihood of so many scholars. Otherwise tuition fees were payable, and in any case there might be entrance fees and various extras to be paid for. In the early centuries, it appears, the cathedral schools were intended to give free education. But even then voluntary payments or gifts might be made to the teachers. The fierce contentions which went on between the Church authorities and outsiders accused of keeping unlicensed schools, which took boys from the official ones, indicate that the keeping of a school was a profitable source of income.

The twelfth and thirteenth centuries were marked by great educational activity—some would say progress. The most spectacular development, at least to the modern historian who surveys the series of events stretching down the centuries behind him, was the rise of universities. But the human love of rearrangement and of organization showed itself also in changes in the school system. Codification of the customary law of cathedrals and collegiate churches took place—for example, at Elgin, at St. Paul's, and at Chichester in the thirteenth century. These cathedral statutes show that there were now three types of school attached to important churches: the theological school under the chancellor (generally a master in theology), the grammar school under the schoolmaster (generally a master of arts) appointed by the chancellor, and the song school under the song schoolmaster appointed by the precentor. This differentiation of school types indicates, or at least suggests, a growing power to analyse the different kinds and functions of education; it indicates a growing specialization in theology which was the principal scholastic preoccupation of the Middle Ages, at least in northern Europe. And it indicates also that something very like university studies were developing at certain centres, notably in London, at Hereford and at Salisbury.[1]

Not only were the old schools being rearranged and systematized, but new foundations were being created. The establishment, in the thirteenth century, of colleges at the universities was followed up and down the country by the founding of a number of new colleges or collegiate churches of secular canons; to these collegiate churches schools of grammar and song were attached. These foundations were frequent until the Reformation, and they do not seem at first to have differed from the colleges at the university; in the case of the collegiate church its function was primarily religious, in that of the university colleges the function was primarily educational. 'The collegiate church was

---

[1] See K. Edwards, *English Secular Cathedrals*, pp. 192–5.

ad orandum et studendum, the house of scholars at the university *ad studendum et orandum.* Both were indifferently spoken of as colleges.'[1]

The fourteenth century saw the great collegiate foundations of William of Wykeham—a school at Winchester and a college at Oxford; the fifteenth saw the foundation by Henry VI of Eton and King's, Cambridge. These establishments, though patterned on those characteristic of their times, are like the universities outstanding creations to the educational historian. He sees in the medieval *studium generale* the beginnings of a development which was to lead to the setting up of universities in later centuries all over the world; in the foundation of Winchester and Eton the beginnings of the public schools to be so influential in British education and not without influence on education in other parts of the world. In the fourteenth and fifteenth centuries, too, the monasteries made a small contribution to English education. The monastic almoner—whose daily duty it was to distribute broken meats from the monks' table to the poor at the gate— was given the task of keeping an almonry or choristers' school. Such schools existed in the priories at Norwich, Ely, and Winchester. 'There were no doubt many other monasteries which maintained Almonry schools, or at least Almonry boys, whom they sent to school. Taking them all together, and putting the average number of boys at ten for a monastery, upwards of a thousand children of the lower classes altogether may have received their board and lodging in the monasteries during the last century of their existence; and most of them learnt to read and sing and some got a more or less good grammatical or general education there.'[2]

At the end of the Middle Ages, then, the many grammar schools were dependent upon various different institutions. The careful study of the official records of the reigns of Henry VIII and Edward VI has shown this to be the case. 'In the records,

---

[1] A. F. Leach: *Schools of Medieval England*, p. 167. For a fuller account of the changes briefly mentioned here see his chap. viii, 'University Colleges, Collegiate Churches, and Schools'.
[2] A. F. Leach, *op. cit.*, pp. 229–30.

specimens of all the kinds of schools then existing in England appear, from the ancient Cathedral Schools to the not yet completed foundation of Berkhampstead; from Winchester and Eton, with their well-paid masters and 70 scholarships apiece, to Cirencester with two scholarships, and Launceston, where an old man is paid 13s. 4d. a year by the mayor, to teach young children the A. B. C.' But these many kinds of schools can be roughly divided into groups. 'There were seven classes of schools at that time, classifying them according to the institution with which they were connected. There were schools connected with Cathedral Churches, with Monasteries, with Collegiate Churches or Colleges, with Hospitals, with Guilds, with Chantries, and lastly, independent Schools, existing ostensibly and actually for themselves as independent entities.'[1]

Of the number of schools available in England and Wales before the Reformation an approximate calculation has been made.[2] For a population of about $2\frac{1}{4}$ million there were some 400 grammar schools—allowing ten on the average in each of forty counties. One county, Hereford, seems to have had seventeen schools for a population of 30,000; London had five, York and Bristol several each, and almost every town probably had at least one. Some of the schools were small, but some appear to have had numbers reckoned in scores. England may well have been better provided with education then than in the nineteenth century when there were, in 1864, 830 secondary schools of all grades for a population of 19 millions. 'The contrast between one grammar school to every 5,625 people, and that presented by the Schools Inquiry Report in 1864 of one to every 23,750 people . . . is not to the disadvantage of our pre-Reformation ancestors.' It was the great pioneer work of A. F. Leach, which must be the foundation of any account of the English medieval schools, to show how ancient were the grammar schools of England and that they did not date for the most part, as had often been supposed, from the reign of Edward VI. The results of this long and laborious research

[1] A. F. Leach: *English Schools at the Reformation*, p. 7.
[2] A. F. Leach: *Schools of Medieval England*, pp. 329–32.

have now found their way into general history, although echoes of the old misconceptions are still to be heard.[1] England had, then, in the Middle Ages in its many grammar schools the means to the Latin education of the day. But a curriculum largely composed of Latin grammar had in it not much hope of progressive development; and the fact that the educated priestly class was celibate prevented the perpetuation and handing on of knowledge and intelligence from father to son and so prevented the formation of a class from which initiative might spring.

[1] For a clear statement of the position of English schools at the end of the middle ages, see G. M. Trevelyan: *English Social History*, p. 52 and pp. 74–7. But in Edith Rickert: *Chaucer's World* (O.U.P., 1948) the editor of Miss Rickert's materials refers (p. 114) to Trevisa's expression of the fourteenth century—'in all the grammar schools of England'—and makes the comment: 'This is interesting in view of the fact that many of the famous grammar schools of to-day are believed to have been established in the following century. Perhaps there were more in the fourteenth century than we have been supposing.' A study of Leach would have made this suggestion unnecessary!

CHAPTER VI

THE GROWTH OF UNIVERSITIES

ONE of the most extraordinary social institutions of the modern world is the university: organizations under that name exist in every, or almost every, country of the world, and, in so far as intellectual life is organized, the universities embrace and represent that intellectual life, yet it is at the same time true that ninety-nine people out of a hundred would have but little conception of the place and function of the university in society. That function can be briefly described as teaching and research at the highest levels—those processes which prepare for the professions, public life, scholarship, scientific investigation, and the pursuit of truth, in every sphere, up to and beyond the frontiers of knowledge. Of these things the great majority of people in most countries have only the vaguest idea, although their lives are touched at many points by the work of the university: those who govern them, both the politicians and the civil servants, will in many cases have been educated there, the lawyers will have studied there, the doctors will have passed through the university medical schools, the teachers in the secondary schools will be graduates in the faculty of arts or of science. For the purpose of higher teaching and research the university will possess often enough magnificent buildings, well-equipped science laboratories, libraries, playing-fields, colleges or hostels, and all the organization and paraphernalia of social living. Many of these things were lacking until the present age when industrial and technical progress have made possible the development of the university as a great business machine for the advancement of learning: London, for example, at which in 1948 5,000 different examination papers were set, or Harvard (by no means the largest even if the greatest of American Universities) which in the same year paid to its permanent academic staff salaries amounting in aggregate to nearly four million dollars. Vast as are the budgets and imposing the number of students at many of the universities of to-day, and strange as many of the studies in them would be to students of the past, the origin of the modern university is to be found in the Middle Ages.

'We may be tempted to smile', said a great American chemist and president of Harvard, 'at the antiquarian zeal of anyone who wishes to define a modern social institution by an appeal through seven centuries of turbulent European history. Yet I suggest that the essence of a university has remained unchanged through all that period of time and is far too little understood to-day.' The university in origin is, he said, 'a juridical and social concept of the Middle Ages; it is a special type of corporation, an association of professional men for a definite purpose'.[1] It is that corporate autonomy, that freedom of association, that makes possible the concentration of scholars upon learning and the pursuit of truth. It is that freedom which has been one of the first victims of dictatorship in the modern world, whether that dictatorship came from right or left; and, with the disappearance of that freedom, universities in the true sense cease to exist and become simply the training colleges of political 'yes-men'.

It is, indeed, not surprising that universities sprang up in the Middle Ages as soon as life became sufficiently settled to allow of organized study. In the ancient world, in both Greece and Rome, there had been the advanced schools of philosophy and rhetoric. The disintegration of that world had reduced intellectual life to a low level, but by the twelfth century that life was being renewed. There was an intellectual ferment; historians speak of the twelfth-century renaissance. And once more scholars were able to organize intellectual life within a con-

[1] J. B. Conant, President of Harvard University, in his report for 1948 to the Board of Overseers.

venient framework which they created for the purpose. But whereas in the ancient world, at least in Greece, there had been a disinterested attention to intellectual pursuits which is the origin of the idea of a liberal education, in the Middle Ages the study of the liberal arts was generally not for their own sake but for the sake of the Christian faith. A future archbishop of Canterbury lecturing in 1200 at Oxford on arithmetic was warned in a dream, so it was reported, to turn from that study to theology.[1]

The medieval universities came silently into institutional existence amid the pandemonium of spontaneously developing student life. The outstanding facts in the situation as we can reconstruct it are the existence of this revived intellectual life and its eventual organization by means of the institutions in which we see the beginnings of universities. For such developments the time was now ripe: the barbarian invasions were over; the menace from Norseman, Magyar, and Saracen was gone; England had settled down after the Norman conquest; Frankish Europe was now in the Crusades hitting back against the Mohammedan East, and the new menace of the Ottoman Turks had not yet appeared; there was in the medieval cities both the time and the opportunity for the life of scholarship. Nor in the darkest of dark ages had the questing mind of man been ever completely still. Intellectual life could not remain at a standstill; positions once accepted might need to be reconsidered; faith in the revelation of the divine truths might be sufficient for the simple Christian, but reason was necessary to deal with criticism; contradictions in the patristic writings called for resolution, and the arguments of heretics, Jews, and Mohammedans might call for answer. At the same time the gradual recovery of the works of Aristotle and the renewed study of Roman law made available a new material and a new stimulus.

The quality of the intellectual life of the twelfth century appears in the wealth of literary material which has survived, in

---

[1] In a letter (of 1243) from the University to the pope, Innocent IV, quoted in *Educational Charters and Documents*, p. 136.

addition to the historical chronicles and the official records of chancery and exchequer. If we consider the court of Henry II of England, under whom such centralized organs of government together with the system of itinerant justices were growing up, we shall find there evidence of wide and varied talent. Bishop Stubbs was perhaps the first historian to point out 'the fact that the same age that originated the forms in which our national and constitutional life began to mould itself, was also an age of great literary activity; of very learned and acute men, and of culture enough to appreciate and conserve the fruits of their labours'.[1] And this was all the more remarkable in an age when literary activity was secondary to something else. A man was not primarily a writer; he could not make a living by writing in the days before the press. The literary works of the circle around Henry II were by men who were primarily ecclesiastics, court chaplains, officials. There were Peter of Blois, whose many letters show attention to style though they are somewhat verbose and sometimes full of inappropriate references to classical figures; Walter Map, whose *De Nugis Curialium* (*The Trifles of the Court*) throws much light on the constitutional development of the reign; Giraldus Cambrensis, a prolific writer on Wales, Ireland, and many topics of the day.[2] These men had not studied at a university, perhaps, for the university had not yet taken formal shape; but, somewhere, somehow, they had certainly been students. Perhaps most outstanding was John of Salisbury. Born in that city, or rather in its predecessor now called Old Sarum, somewhere about 1115, he died as Bishop of Chartres in 1180. He served two archbishops, Becket and his predecessor; he was a great scholar, Latin stylist, and philosopher, and the central figure of the English learning of his time. His letters[3] show that he was

---

[1] *Lectures on Medieval and Modern History*, VI, on 'Learning and Literature at the Court of Henry II'. See also *Essays presented to Professor Tout*, chap. by C. H. Haskins on 'Henry II as a Patron of Literature'.

[2] For Peter of Blois, *Opera* (ed. J. A. Giles)—to be used with caution, see E. S. Cohn in *English Historical Review* (1926). Map's *De Nugis Curialium* (ed. M. R. James). Giraldus Cambrensis, *Opera*, in the Rolls Series.

[3] Those on the Becket affair in the *Becket Materials* (Rolls Series).

as an ecclesiastical secretary, in close touch with the relations going on between the archbishop's see, the Roman curia, and the royal court; a letter from Peter of Blois addresses him as *Vos qui estis manus Archiepiscopi et oculus ejus*; of his two principal works one, the *Policraticus*, was an important contribution to political theory. Dedicated to the chancellor (that is, to Becket), it early asserted the supremacy of the spiritual power: using the analogy of the soul and body, it argued that the clergy represents the soul, and the king the head; as the soul rules the head and the rest of the body, so must the king be subject to God and to those who hold His place on earth. This principle was involved in the fatal clash that brought about Becket's murder by the king's knights; nor is the problem of Church and state yet resolved. It was raised again in Nazi Germany; it has appeared once more in acute form in the condemnation in Hungary of Cardinal Mindszenty and the attack on the evangelical churches in Bulgaria by the Communist government.

How did a great ecclesiastic and scholar like John of Salisbury acquire his education? Unfortunately John says nothing of his early education, except a mere mention in the *Policraticus* that as a boy he was entrusted to a priest to teach him the psalms and that this priest also tried to use him as a crystal-gazer. But he has left a fascinating account of his higher studies at Paris and at Chartres.[1]

As a youth, he says, he went in 1136 to France to study, and so famous must Paris and Abelard have become in his time that he does not need to mention their names but simply says that he took himself to the Palatine Peripatetic, the famous lecturer on the Mont Ste. Geneviève. There in the future *Quartier Latin*, on the left bank of the Seine, John of Salisbury found the greatest teacher of the day and refers to him by the name of his birthplace of Palais in Brittany, and by the epithet attaching to him by reason of his great master Aristotle, whose disciples had been known by the term peripatetic probably from Aristotle's habit of walking to and fro, while teaching, in the gymnasium. Thus eighteen years before

[1] *Metalogicon*, especially II, x, and I, xxiv.

the young William Marshal was sent to Normandy to undergo the arduous training of knighthood, the mental warriors of book and gown were already at work in Paris. From another source we hear that students flocked to Abelard from all parts: from the provinces of France, from Rome, from Flanders, and beyond the Rhine, and not even the peril of the Channel crossing prevented the English, when once they had heard his name, from attending his lectures.[1]

Under Abelard, John of Salisbury studied dialectic. 'At his feet I acquired the first rudiments of this art, and seized with my full attention, so far as my moderate talent allowed, whatever issued from his mouth.' Next, for two years, he studied under a certain Alberic, 'a noted dialectician and a sharp opponent of the Nominalist sect', and Robert of Melun, an Englishman and later Bishop of Hereford. The description of these two men goes far to re-create the atmosphere of the medieval lecture, of scholars engaged in attack and defence by the processes of argument. 'One sought out in every matter something to question, so that however polished a plane surface might be he would find some little blemish . . . whatever needed explanation he would explain. The other, however, prompt and ready to answer, never avoided a proposition by taking refuge in a subterfuge; either he chose to contradict it or, by explaining how complex the question was, he showed that there could be no single answer. Thus one was a subtle asker of many questions; the other in answering a proposition was acute, clear, and to the point. If the qualities of these two could have been joined in one man, no equal disputant could have been found in our age.' But they were a little too pleased, John thought, with their own ingenuity; they might have relied more upon the great tradition of letters. Alberic, indeed, 'went afterwards to Bologna and unlearnt what he had taught; he returned and untaught it. Whether this later course was the better, those may judge who heard him both before and after-

---

[1] *Anglorum turbam juvenum mare interjacens . . . non terrebat . . . audito tuo nomine, ad te confluebat.* Letter to Abelard from Fulk, prior of Deuil, in Abelard's *Opera* (ed. V. Cousin), I, 703.

wards.' What their judgement was we cannot tell; the students who could trace the intellectual development of Alberic have long been silent, and in what way he and Robert were ingenious and original we shall never know. Robert turned later, as John says, to theology; this was doubtless a safer course and he finished his career with a bishopric.

No definite or prescribed order of studies appears yet to have existed. John had started with Abelard's lectures on dialectic; after describing the dialectical abilities of Alberic and Robert, John says that 'under these men I grew accustomed to the assigned passages, the rules and rudiments with which boyish minds are filled, and in which the above-mentioned doctors were expert'. Perhaps John's early schooling had been slight; if so he soon made up for lost time. Next he went off, on the advice of his teachers, to the grammarian William of Conches and followed his courses for three years. He read much, and mentions other teachers who helped him; he says that he studied the Quadrivium and made, in addition, a re-study of rhetoric. It is not possible to be quite certain of John's movements during these years, but he was probably in Chartres where William of Conches had followed Bernard as head of the cathedral school.

The school at Chartres was one of the cathedral schools, which by reason of its higher studies was particularly distinguished, and might, though it did not, have grown like Paris into a university. John, though he only experienced the teaching method of Bernard of Chartres at second-hand, has given a special description of it; the school at Chartres was marked by a love of ancient letters, rather than dialectic, somewhat in the later Renaissance fashion; it is clear that close attention was given to what was grammatically correct in writing and to style. 'Bernard of Chartres *exundantissimus modernis temporibus fons litterarum in Gallia* used to show, in the reading of authors, what was without art and what was suitable as a model; he pointed out grammatical figures, rhetorical decorations, sophistical quibbles, and any point where the matter read touched on other subjects of learning; at the same time he taught according to the capacity of his hearers and gave them a certain measure of doctrine. And because effective expression depends upon either being appropriate, that is the neat associating of adjective or verb to its noun, or metaphor, that is the proper transfer of a word from its ordinary sense to a new use—these things he especially impressed on his hearers' minds . . . .' Bernard and William appear to have had a clear procedure: the pupils were made to explain to-day what they had read and listened to the day before. Each day also they practised the writing of prose and poetry and exercised themselves in mutual comparison. A year's course of these lessons in grammar, John says, would give one a familiarity with writing and speaking Latin. In addition to the training in grammar itself, in correct writing and speaking, religious literature was placed before them; and to encourage a love of the classics, certain of the classical authors. Bernard urged each pupil to commit to memory some passage every day, but he also taught the value of economy of words, where necessary. 'He used to say that what was superfluous might well be allowed to fly away: those things were sufficient which had been written by famous authors . . . to examine and turn over every piece of literature, not perhaps worth the reading, was of no more use than old women's stories.' In other words, just as all that glitters is not gold, so all that litters is not literature.

John also undertook, to help maintain himself, the instruction of the children of certain nobles much as, in more modern times, many a clever university student has done. Then he returned to Paris and added theology to his studies. His student years had been long. 'Almost twelve years had thus elapsed in different studies, and so it seemed pleasant to revisit my former companions whom dialectic had detained on the Mount, to talk over our early ambiguities, and to measure what progress we had made. I found them still where they had been; they appeared to have advanced not a hand's breadth. To the old questions they had not added a single tiny proposition . . . . And so I experienced, what can easily be shown, that just as dialectic furthers other subjects, if it remains alone, it is bloodless and sterile, and cannot fertilize the soul to bring forth the fruit of philosophy.' Nor was John of Salisbury the only contemporary to have a dig at dialectic. Peter of Blois, in one of his letters, twits his correspondent on a love of disputation, and his dislike of dialecticians appears to be founded on his respect for the classical authors.[1] But dialectic—coupled with philosophy and theology—was destined to triumph over the more liberal tendency of the school at Chartres; it was dialectic which was the foundation of medieval scholasticism and which stamped itself on the studies of Paris and the northern universities generally. It may be doubted, however, if medieval dialectic at its best was more sterile than Roman rhetoric in the later schools of the Empire or, indeed, than much which passes as research in the arts at modern universities. Argument did at least provide an exercise for the mind, but the compilation of long theses containing too often second- and even third-hand material scarcely achieves even that end.

It was out of the intellectual ferment of the twelfth century that the universities grew: in northern Europe higher studies developed, not unnaturally, from the existing cathedral schools where the teachers were themselves sufficiently gifted and energetic to carry their curriculum beyond that of the grammar school; in Italy, where learning had lingered on after the collapse of Rome and where law and medicine had survived as lay professions, the Church had never exercised the same monopoly as in the barbarian north, and the universities as they grew into life were almost lay organizations. It is impossible to find an exact date for the origin of universities. But in the early twelfth century, long before actual university organization had come into being, students were engaging in higher study at certain definite centres. Paris was frequented especially for philosophy and theology, Bologna for law, and Salerno for medicine, and only a little later Oxford also became a centre of the new intellectual life. To each of these centres of learning the term

---

[1] See M. Grabmann: *Geschichte der Scholastischen Methode*, II, 120. He speaks of Peter's love for the classical authors '*deren Studium durch die Vorherrschaft der Dialektik in der Artistenfakultät immer mehr zurückgedrängt wurde*'.

studium generale was applied, a term which indicated a place to which students came from all parts. The word *Universitas*, meaning 'a whole', which later was to describe the organized university,[1] could be used of any group or association, such as the council in a town or a cathedral chapter or a trade gild. The organization of corporate bodies—cathedral chapters, city communes, orders of monks, knights, and friars, merchant gilds, craft gilds—was a great medieval preoccupation, and not without reason. An association offered, in troubled times, protection to the individual. The *Universitas* of the learned was a particular kind of gild to regulate a particular kind of craft and to protect its members in their contacts with the outside world, and the student must pass through certain determined periods of study and pass certain tests, like the apprentice to any other trade or even the aspirant to knighthood undergoing the chivalric training, before he could gain full membership of his gild with his master's degree just as the journeyman might on successful presentation of his masterpiece become a master craftsman. The university gild was, however, of two kinds: in northern Europe, generally, it was a gild of masters; in Italy and southern Europe a gild of scholars.

Paris achieved a lasting fame as a centre of study, before the formal organization of its university, by reason of the brilliant lectures of Peter Abelard (1079–1142); he immortalized himself in the great and tragic love story of Abelard and Heloise. The cathedral school of Paris was not outstanding before this time; the schools of Bec and Chartres, of Tours and Rheims were famous, and there were several schools in Paris itself. The chancellor of the cathedral of Notre Dame licensed the Paris masters, and they taught on the island in the Seine where the city originated and on or near the southern bridge, the Petit-Pont. Sometimes they taught on the south bank where the university was finally to take root—the future *Quartier Latin*—around the Mont Ste. Geneviève where Abelard himself lectured and where the library of the same name and the

[1] The term is so used at Oxford in a statute of 1253 and one of possibly even earlier date, see *Statuta Antiqua*, p. 49 and p. 107.

Pantheon stand to-day. In the middle years of the twelfth century Paris was certainly well established as a centre for students; we hear that many famous men, including Becket, John of Salisbury and Walter Map, had studied there in their youth. Alexander Neckham, English scholar and Abbot of Cirencester, was as a boy at the grammar school in St. Albans. About 1173, although he had feared the Channel crossing, he was in Paris. Neckham says that he studied at the Petit-Pont, he refers to the divers subjects, the arts, theology, medicine, the canon and civil law, and speaks of the fame of Paris:

> I find than Paris no more noted town,
> Where at the Little Bridge I sat me down;
> There faithfully the arts I learnt and taught,
> To Scripture's sacred page made my resort,
> Galen, Hippocrates I found and more—
> I heard the civil and the canon law.[1]

In Abelard's day there were already indications that the Paris teaching was to be brought within a formal system. The *Licentia docendi*—the licence to teach—which the scholar received from the cathedral chancellor was coming to be insufficient as a qualification; the new teacher, to become a master, must go through a ceremony of inception into the masters' gild, and this gild or association of masters became the university and established a monopoly of higher education. Membership of this new organization became as indispensable for the would-be lecturer at Paris as the chancellor's licence was for the teacher in the grammar school of the cathedral. Stages, grades, or degrees became recognized—Bachelor (applied also to the young knight), Licentiate, Magister. But Master, Doctor, Professor were at first synonymous terms.

Towards the end of the twelfth century the university organization was taking definite shape: the first documentary testimony is in 1200 in a charter of Philip Augustus, the king of France, to the University of Paris; university statutes are first heard of in 1209.[2] As a new organization the university had to

[1] *De Laudibus Divinae Sapientiae* (Rolls Series), p. 503.
[2] For these documents see the *Chartularium Universitatis Parisiensis*, I, 59 and 67.

assert its independence as against the established authorities for education—the chancellor and behind him the bishop and chapter. The university, however, received support from the papacy and, with the help of a series of papal bulls, established itself, the granting of the bishop's licence to teach being reduced to a formality. In any case, the masters who taught on the left bank, the south side, of the Seine were outside the episcopal jurisdiction and could obtain the licence to teach from the abbot (or his chancellor) of the Abbey of Ste. Geneviève; they could play off one authority against the other. By the middle of the thirteenth century, or thereabouts, the university organization had taken shape. There were four faculties: Arts, Theology, Canon Law, Medicine. The Faculty of Arts was sub-divided into four groups or nations—France, Normandy, Picardy, England—each under its Proctor. Each of three superior faculties was under a dean. The head of the Arts Faculty was the rector and he, after a long struggle sometimes leading to blows between the partisans of different faculties, made himself head of the whole university.

The medieval university was, at first, without endowments. It had no buildings of its own, and borrowed a neighbouring church or its chapter-house. The Paris Faculty of Arts used to meet in the little church, which is still to be seen, of St. Julien-le-Pauvre, across the river from Notre Dame; the nearby Rue de Fouarre, the street of straw, took its name from the straw used to carpet the floors in the rooms hired for lectures. This lack of permanent buildings and equipment made the medieval student—and the university itself—extremely mobile, and a university could always use, in its conflicts with ecclesiastical or civil authority, the threat of a migration to a new centre of study which would deprive the old centre of its fame and business. It is supposed—though it is not certain—that in such a way the university came into existence in Oxford. Why Oxford was chosen remains, when all is said and done—and plenty has been said ever since Camden inserted into his edition of Asser a spurious account of the university's foundation by Alfred the Great—a mystery. Why did not a university spring up at the cathedral school of St. Paul's in London, or even in the north at York, or at England's oldest school, on the route to the Continent, at Canterbury? Any one of these famous schools would seem to have offered a more likely ground than Oxford for the growth of a university. Little was heard before about 1170 of the Oxford schools to suggest their future fame. For the year 1185 there is in the writings of Giraldus Cambrensis one isolated reference to Oxford. He says that he read there his *Topographia Hibernica* and refers to 'the doctors of the different faculties'.[1] Oxford was already, it appears, a *studium generale*. Either its development was rapid, or the organization may have sprung full-grown to life as the result of the expulsion of foreign students by the French king in 1167 and an order, about the same time, of Henry II bidding English scholars return to this country. The scholars who found themselves forced to leave Paris, if they found their way to Oxford, would bring with them the scheme of organization as they knew it in its place of origin.

But, although the new University of Oxford imitated that at Paris, local conditions from the first imposed also important differences. There was at this time no bishop of Oxford, which formed part of the diocese of Lincoln; there was thus a much greater freedom from episcopal control than at Paris, and it is possible that the first masters were incepted without a licence to teach or that they themselves made the arrangements for the grant of the licence. In the first quarter of the thirteenth century the chancellor appears. But, whereas in Paris the chancellor was the bishop's officer and it was against his authority that the university struggled to assert its independence, in Oxford the chancellor, although deriving his authority in theory from the Bishop of Lincoln, was in fact elected by the masters. At length in the fourteenth century the Oxford chancellor became independent of the bishop and acquired, as the result of grants from pope and king, great power in Oxford over the scholars and even over the citizens. Thus the Oxford chancellor was the real head of the university: 'He was, in fact, the

---

[1] *De Rebus a se gestis* in his *Opera* (Rolls Series), I, 72.

Parisian Chancellor and the Parisian Rector in one—and a good deal more besides.'[1] Another interesting development at Oxford, which differentiated it from Paris, was in the organization of students into nations. At first at Oxford there were probably four as at Paris; by the mid-thirteenth century there were two only, the Northern and Southern Nations. But faction fights were bitter between the rival students, and as a result the University in 1274 put an end to the nations though not, altogether, to the fights between their members. Two proctors remained, originally one for each nation, and became an important part of the university's executive machinery. The superior faculties had no deans and little organization of their own, and at Oxford the Faculty of Arts was, and has continued, predominant.

If Paris and Oxford appear prominent among the first of the medieval universities there were others also of great interest. Salerno had its school of medicine, reputed already early in the twelfth century as 'existing from ancient times'. But medicine, we must remember, was medieval medicine, without anatomy but tinctured with astrology and founded on Hippocrates and Galen. Salerno was largely isolated from the rest of Europe and does not appear to have exercised any influence on the constitutional development of universities elsewhere. But it was an interesting centre where many influences, Graeco-Roman, Jewish, and Arabic met. Throughout the twelfth century Bologna was a centre for the study of law; eminent jurists who lectured there drew to them students from all over Europe. During that time the formal organization was growing up, and early in the next century we hear of two colleges of doctors, one of civil law and one of canon law. Here the admission to the body of doctors must have been arranged by that body itself for there was no traditional control of education by the Church as in northern Europe; a papal bull in 1219 did, however, give to the archdeacon of Bologna a merely formal share in the conferment of degrees. Though the doctors had their gild, the Bologna University was otherwise, as were most of the Italian universities,

[1] Rashdall, in *Cambridge Medieval History*, VI, 589.

unlike the organization at Paris and in the north. At Bologna the students themselves organized gilds; by the end of the twelfth century they had acquired dominance and had virtually established a students' university or universities, for there were several university organizations linked together, each one sub-divided into groups somewhat analogous to the nations in the northern plan. Student organizations reduced the doctors or teachers to subservience: a student committee—*denunciatores doctorum*—kept them under surveillance, and fines were imposed for late arrival at lectures or for going on too long. The teachers of law depended, too, upon the fees paid by their students. Later on, however, the city began to provide salaries, and in this way something like a modern paid professoriate grew up. Although the lawyers exercised a dominant influence, Bologna was not without other branches of study: the ordinary arts faculty and medicine also flourished there in the thirteenth century. A migration from Bologna led to the foundation of Padua in 1222; the Emperor Frederick II, himself an extraordinary figure of great intellectual curiosity, founded Naples two years later, a university governed by a royal chancellor. Most later Italian universities were founded by papal bulls and, by the end of the Middle Ages, almost every Italian state of any importance possessed its university.

The supply of universities evidently met some real European need, for universities were founded everywhere. In France besides the famous University of Paris, Montpellier was a centre rivalling Salerno for medicine even in the eleventh century. Many other universities soon sprang up, at Orleans and Toulouse in the thirteenth century, and between 1303 and 1464 in most of the substantial cities of France. In England, Cambridge originated with a migration from Oxford in 1209; it followed the Oxford pattern but was never, in the Middle Ages, so famous. But despite the attempts of seceders no other English universities became established until London and Durham in the first half of the nineteenth century; in Scotland, however, St. Andrews, Glasgow, and Aberdeen all date from the fifteenth. The first Spanish university organization was a royal foundation in 1212, but the first to become permanent was the University of Salamanca, founded about 1220; others followed. Germany came late into the field. The first German university was not, strictly speaking, in Germany; it was at Prague, founded by the Emperor Charles IV in 1348. Vienna was founded in 1365. Erfurt, Heidelberg, and Cologne date from the same century; in the next century other universities followed in north and south of the German dominions. In the lesser countries of Europe, Cracow dates from 1364, Hungary had two in the fifteenth century; Upsala and Copenhagen both date from the second half of that century.

The curriculum pursued in the medieval universities originated, like the university itself, in the intellectual renaissance of the twelfth century and was closely associated with the rediscovery of Aristotle and the revived study of Roman law. By the mid-twelfth century Aristotle's logical work, by the mid-thirteenth almost the whole body of his surviving writings were available in Latin translation. Aristotle's works had found their way into the Arab world which had embraced so much of the hellenized East: contacts with Latin scholars in Spain, the south of which had succumbed to Arab conquest, and some translation directly from the Greek by scholars in Venice, brought Aristotle back to men of learning and gave them something stronger to deal with than the compilation of Martianus Capella and the translation of a small part of Aristotle by Boëthius. At the same time there reached Paris the commentary upon Aristotle of the Arabic scholar Averroës (1126–1198). From then on the influence of Aristotle on medieval thought and higher study can scarcely be exaggerated: it runs through the Realist-Nominalist controversy of the scholastic philosophers and the work of the greatest theologian, Thomas Aquinas, whose task it was in the *Summa Theologica* to reconcile philosophy with theology, or, as one might say, reason with revelation. Apart from the knowledge of Latin grammar and the reading of certain Latin authors, chiefly Ovid and Virgil, required for the university examinations but acquired mostly in the grammar school, and some attention to the subjects classified in the earlier centuries as Trivium and Quadrivium, apart from these things, Aristotle becomes the foundation of the curriculum in the Faculty of Arts. The list of books[1] used for the examinations (largely by public disputation) at Paris in 1366 illustrates this fact. Similar books were in use in the arts course at Oxford, which included also the grammatical works of Priscian and Donatus. The educational tradition of the study of the subjects of the Quadrivium was more closely observed than at Paris, with greater attention to mathematics and astrology. 'Text-books, no doubt, might vary, but Aristotle held the field.'[2]

How then did the student at medieval Oxford fill his days? For his B.A. he had to hear lectures on certain specified works of logic, by Porphyry, Boëthius, and Aristotle; in grammar, he took Priscian and the *Barbarismus* of Donatus; he also attended certain mathematical lectures, on arithmetic, the calculation of the date of Easter, and on the *Tractatus de Sphaera*. For licence and inception (M.A.) he continued his attendance at lectures, adding to what he had already heard further courses on the seven liberal arts: grammar was based on Priscian; rhetoric on Aristotle, Boëthius, and Cicero—and by 1409 Ovid's *Metamorphoses* and Virgil are set down for hearing, an indication, perhaps, of a coming literary renaissance; logic on Aristotle and Boëthius; arithmetic and music were based on Boëthius; geometry on Euclid; and astronomy on the *Theorica Planetarum* or Ptolemy's *Almagesta*. In addition, the student heard the three philosophies made possible by the rediscovery of Aristotle: in natural philosophy Aristotle's *Physica* or *De caelo et mundo* (or other specified works); in moral philosophy, Aristotle's *Ethica* or *Economica* or *Politica*; and in metaphysical philosophy, Aristotle's *Metaphysica*. During the years of his attendance at these various lectures the candidate for a degree had several times to dispute publicly on some question. This was a means of testing his knowledge of the set books and his

---

[1] *Chartularium Universitatis Parisiensis*, III, 145. See Rashdall, I, 443–62, and a tabular summary in the article in *Cambridge Medieval History*, VI.
[2] C. E. Mallet: *History of the University of Oxford*, I, p. 183.

facility in logic or dialectic. As for the final examination, at Oxford at least, it seems conspicuous for its absence. For the licence in arts (M.A.) the student appeared before the chancellor and swore that he had studied the required books while ten of the resident masters testified to his knowledge of them.[1]

Of university studies from a personal point of view we know little. The students' letters surviving have been surveyed by one of the greatest of American medievalists, but as he says: 'What a pity that out of such a mass of letters there are none that tell us in simple and unaffected detail how a young man studied and how he spent his day!' Of this material 'much of it would be almost as representative of the Harvard or Yale of to-day as of medieval Orleans or Bologna . . . money and clothing, rooms, teachers and books . . . the fundamental factors in man's development remain much the same from age to age.'[2] We are reminded of another American scholar's comment on Cicero's son at the university of Athens.[3]

The course of study lasted five or six years at Paris, longer perhaps at Oxford; but students entered on their university career much earlier then than now, sometimes about fourteen.[4] The course leading to M.A. would generally be taken by students intending to proceed to higher faculties, like theology or medicine. But it is known that, of those who began, many never graduated, and the ordinary priest did not proceed to the long and specialized training in theology. This further course—at Paris, of about twelve years, though actual residence may not have been insisted on throughout the period—was based

[1] For summaries of the Oxford arts course, and also those in medicine, law, and theology, see Rashdall, III, 153–60.

[2] Quotations here are from C. H. Haskins: *Studies in Medieval Culture*, pp. 34–5.

[3] See p. 34.

[4] There is difficulty as to the age of entry—perhaps it varied considerably. Rashdall (III, 353) gives it as between 13 and 16 years, but the Winchester statutes said that boys were to remain in the school until 18. N. Schachner: *Medieval Universities*, p. 228, referring to New College, Oxford, says: 'The scholars who came up from Winchester were lads of about fifteen', a statement which seems simply to be based on Rashdall's general estimate.

upon lectures on the Bible and Peter the Lombard's *Sentences*, a book which had introduced some order into the conflicting writings of the Fathers, many of whose contradictions had been pointed out by Abelard.

Law, as we have already observed, was a principal study in Italy. Indeed, it seems that as a practical subject important to statesman and administrator, the study of the subject had never entirely died out. In Italy, also, certainly in the early fourteenth century, lectures were to be heard on the classics of Latin literature, on Virgil, Ovid, and Cicero—and this in the Middle Ages. For Italy that period appears to have been, like a luminous summer night in the far north of Europe, one in which the last brilliance of antiquity blended with the early glow of Renaissance. At the very beginning of the twelfth century Irnerius was making Bologna famous as a centre of study of the civil law, based upon the *Digest* of Justinian, a codification carried out in Constantinople in the sixth century by the lawyers of the greatest of the Eastern emperors. Then, between 1142 and 1151, the *Decretum* of the Bolognese monk Gratian appeared, which made a text-book of church, or canon, law out of the mass of existing conciliar canons and papal decretals. But it was above all the Roman civil law which turned men's minds towards a study worthy of the hardest intellectual effort. From that moment in twelfth-century Bologna, says a great historian of modern Europe, 'From that moment it would be difficult to overestimate its power as a factor in the moulding of intellectual, social, and political life. The Roman law expressed the ideas of a society more civilized and mature than the Western Europe of the early Middle Ages. It was a society which had evolved clear-cut ideas about private property and possession, family rights and the sanctity of contract, and had come to regard law as a reasoned and intelligible system adapted to the needs of humanity as a whole . . . .

'And so as western Europe emerged from medieval darkness it found in the *Corpus Juris* of Justinian a revelation of the great thing which European civilization had once been and might again become. The ferment of the mind thus occasioned was immense. Perhaps a faint analogy may be found in the exciting influence at a later stage of human development of Rousseau's *Contrat Social* or Darwin's *Origin of Species*.'[1]

One important medieval university development remains to be mentioned—the growth of colleges. The boarding and lodging of students in the university towns was at first at their own will and pleasure; they found accommodation where they could in the squalid lanes and streets. This created all kinds of difficulties, moral and economic, including brawls over failure to pay the rent of lodgings. To support poor students endowed hostels were set up, and in these it soon became clear that there were great advantages to the students in the common life: the college, in its chapel, provided for prayers for the founder's soul; it could also provide books and tuition for its student-inmates. Thus there came into existence the endowed college, itself a corporation with its own statutes and perpetuating itself by the election of new members to fill up vacancies among its permanent fellows. The first college to be created was between 1256 and 1270 in Paris—'the House of Sorbonne' founded by Robert de Sorbon, chaplain to the king of France, St. Louis. Soon afterwards, in England, Walter of Merton, Bishop of Rochester and Chancellor of England, founded the first Oxford college—'the House of the scholars of Merton'. Many other colleges were to follow—amounting in Paris to the number of sixty. Cambridge followed Oxford in making its colleges the foundation of university life. But the future of the colleges in England and France was to be very different, a future which a famous Warden of New College, Oxford, has briefly described: 'The visitor to Paris may still see on the left bank of the Seine the Rue de Fouarre where Dante may have heard lectures. He may still enter the curious little church of St. Julien-le-Pauvre, where the first Masters of Arts of the Paris University used to hold their meetings. But only a name attached to an uncouth modern building recalls the memory of the Sorbonne, and of the sixty medieval colleges of Paris not a stone remains.

[1] H. A. L. Fisher: *History of Europe*, p. 133.

England has been more fortunate, and in the splendid collegiate foundations at Oxford and Cambridge preserves a memorial of the munificence and piety of a vanished age.'[1]

[1] H. A. L. Fisher: *History of Europe*, p. 249.

CHAPTER VII

MEDIEVAL MISCELLANY: WINCHESTER, ETON, ELEMENTARY AND GIRLS' EDUCATION

I T is not only in the preservation of the Oxford and Cambridge Colleges that England has been fortunate to inherit the splendid educational establishments of an earlier period. For the later Middle Ages saw not only the creation of the noble residential colleges at the two universities but also the foundation of the two greatest English schools—Winchester and Eton. These schools were grammar schools, not at first very different from many existing schools, and, like the universities and the colleges, they were products of the medieval way of life. In the education of university and of, what we call to-day, secondary level there is a certain continuity between the Middle Ages and modern times; and, indeed, the tradition of grammar schools and higher education goes right back as we know to Roman and to Greek origins. The special instruction and training of a section of the community is nothing new in history; it is the forerunner of the secondary and higher education of to-day. But to-day we find, in addition, two kinds of education of which, so far, little has been said: popular or elementary education for the masses and education for girls as well as for boys. Did nothing of either kind exist in the Middle Ages? In this chapter we shall say something of the creation of the great schools and something of, such as it was, elementary and girls' education.

Winchester College—as the famous school is known—is an outstanding example of the continuity, the unbroken thread, which runs through English life. For more than five and a half centuries the school has stood; it is still housed in its fourteenth-century building and in all the lengthy period of its existence it has never failed to be in the front rank among schools. 'It is', wrote A. F. Leach of his own old school, 'certainly a strange, and one may perhaps claim it as a characteristically English, phenomenon that the Public School which is the oldest, and in which the Public School spirit was first developed, should still retain its position among the most vigorous and successful of its exponents, whether judged by the more ancient test of success in the schools, or the more modern test of success in the cricket field. The secret of England's success as a political body lies in its gradual development of the old to meet the needs of the new, instead of making a clean sweep of the ancient to clear the field for the modern. In no sphere of life, in no institution, is this more profoundly shown than in this school.'[1] Those words were written fifty years ago, but they are still true; Wykehamists continue to gain their many 'firsts' in the Oxford examination schools and to win distinction on the sports field and in every walk of life. Old and new have often mixed in striking fashion; in 1918 a Wykehamist, H. A. L. Fisher, as President of the Board of Education, was responsible for the Education Act which marked a considerable advance in popular instruction; in the late twenties he was Warden of the sister foundation of New College, Oxford, when its association football team had in it ten Wykehamists but a captain who came from a country undiscovered when Wykeham 'invented' the public school; two decades later a Wykehamist Chancellor of the Exchequer (Sir Stafford Cripps) was presiding with his Labour colleagues over the transformation of the British Empire into a commonwealth and the transition of English society from an age of free enterprise to one of socialism and austerity. Nay, more, some of the extremists of the Labour movement—Mr. D. N. Pritt and Mr. R. H. S. Crossman—are also products of Winchester.

William of Wykeham founded Winchester College in 1382— that year is the date of the foundation deed; the College register beginning in 1394 calls the new foundation *Sanctae Mariae*

[1] A. F. Leach: *History of Winchester College*, p. 5.

Collegium, or, in the vulgar tongue, *Seinte Marie College of Wynchestre*. About the same time Wykeham founded in Oxford what was later to be known as New College: the date of its foundation charter, of *Seinte Marie College of Wynchestre in Oxenforde*, was 1379; the buildings, in the north-east corner of the city wall, were formally entered in 1386. But whatever else he did, and astute and able though he was, Wykeham could not have produced ready made, in the fourteenth century, a modern public school. What Winchester is to-day is the result of its five hundred and fifty years of changeful existence, as well as of the intentions and labours of its founder. But Wykeham had laid firm foundations on which the future could firmly build. What then were the characteristics of the new school which Wykeham founded and what his intention?

Wykeham's school was a grammar school, and in that was like other schools of its time. The earlier educational history of the town of Winchester is obscure, but it appears that there was another grammar school there both before and after 1382. Wykeham's own early life and education are also obscure; but he rose from a humble origin to a position of national eminence. As a clerk in the king's service and overseer of the workmen at Windsor Castle, it was the plague of 1360, second only to the Black Death of 1349, which brought him fortune by removing so many clerical competitors. Many benefices were heaped upon him—he held numerous canonries before he actually took priest's order in 1362—until he finally became Bishop of Winchester and Chancellor of England. Thus he came to hold the richest bishopric and was what would correspond to-day to prime minister. It was almost a duty for so great an ecclesiastic to devote part of his wealth to pious ends; in an earlier age he might have established a monastery, but now it was the fashion to endow collegiate churches or colleges. The Winchester statutes of 1400 show that they were framed on the model of those of Merton and Queen's, Oxford, and on the College of Navarre in Paris, founded in 1304 by the Queen of France and Navarre. In his foundation deed of 1382 Wykeham refers to having 'lately erected and founded a perpetual college of seventy poor scholars, clerks, to study theology, canon, and civil law, and arts in the University of Oxford', and goes on to explain his reasons for adding a school in Winchester. For 'as experience, the mistress of life, already teaches, grammar is the foundation, gate, and source of all other liberal arts, without which they cannot be known, nor can anyone arrive at their pursuit.' Thus school in Winchester and college in Oxford were linked; one was to supply the other with scholars. The two colleges, as Wykeham said in the statutes, 'though situate in different places, issue from one stem . . . . They are next-of-kin, and are called by one name.'

The statutes dating from 1400—there are statutes from that year for both Winchester and New College—state a reason for and object of the new foundations. The New College statutes suggest as a reason the shortage of priests, referring to 'the general disease of the clerical army, which through the want of clergy caused by pestilence, wars, and other miseries of the world, we have seen grievously wounded'. As an object the statutes speak of the desire to spread Holy Scripture, but refer also to the need for civil and canon law and philosophy—perhaps one can infer that Wykeham as a great ecclesiastical statesman was not blind to the importance of such subjects to the priest who might also have before him a career in the royal service. But the expressed intention is primarily religious:'that Christ may be more fervently and frequently preached, and faith and the worship of God's name increased and more firmly maintained . . . that so the praise of God may be spread, the church ruled, the strength and fervour of the Christian religion grow hotter, and all knowledge and virtue be increased in strength'.[1]

What was novel about Wykeham's foundation was its size, splendid buildings, and large measure of independence of external control (of that, for example, of the bishop). The school itself was a substantial one, and New College with its seventy scholars was almost equal in number to that of the scholars of all the other Oxford colleges put together. Winchester with its

[1] The extracts from foundation deed and statutes are from Leach: *History of Winchester College*, chap. vi.

warden and fellows was an independent corporation—a school existing for itself—though closely allied with its sister house at Oxford. New College elected the Warden of Winchester, and fellows of Winchester were to be, for preference, fellows or former fellows of New College. The seventy scholars at Winchester were to lead a community life. An arrangement was made for supervision in each room by 'three scholars of good repute'—an early example of something like a prefect system. A schoolmaster and his assistant made up the teaching staff.

Admission was, apart from founder's kin, for 'poor and needy scholars, of good character and well conditioned, of gentlemanly habits, able for school, completely learned in reading, plain song and old Donatus'. They entered school between the ages of eight and twelve, and left at about eighteen or nineteen; they were to have the tonsure, that is, to be clerks. The school, too, looked for boys beyond its immediate locality; although the districts where lay the estates of school and Oxford College and the diocese of Winchester had preference in the admission of scholars, next came a number of neighbouring counties and finally the kingdom at large. In addition to the scholars there were also to be some commoners paying their own cost—'the sons of notable and influential persons'. In these latter features we see, perhaps, the germs of the public school: it was to draw boys by its fame from all over the country, and the wealthy were to pay fees to send their sons to such a school. It is above all the fact that persons influential in State and Church have come to send their sons to the great public schools that has made those schools what they are and given them a privileged position in society. There has been great discussion as to what Wykeham intended by the expression 'poor and needy scholars'. It has been suggested that he was providing an education for the 'poor' in the modern sense. But it must be remembered that a vast working-class population in large towns did not exist in those days, and that the serfs of the countryside were, as a rule, far away from any grammar school and quite illiterate. It is much more probable that the term applies to the younger sons of comparatively poor nobility and gentry. It is not likely that

Wykeham would have sent his own relations (founder's kin), nor that the notable and influential persons would have sent their sons, to school with the children of the poor.

Of the actual life of the medieval schoolboys at Winchester practically nothing is known. School conditions were doubtless hard enough; there was no fireplace in the old schoolroom, though it did at least face south. It has been supposed that the boys slept on straw, but Leach maintains that the straw was sewn into canvas to make a mattress and has found mention in the accounts of blankets, sheets, and pillows. Of the way the boys learnt their Latin nothing is known. On admission, as we saw above, they could read and were expected to know the elements of grammar as set out in Donatus. The books read in school were, Leach suggests on the basis of general information about medieval schools, Virgil, Ovid, some of the Christian authors, Boëthius, the *Moralia* of Cato (so called), and Cicero's *De Oratore*. The last named was a standard for rhetoric, and it is probable that the older boys who were competent in grammar gave some of their time to that and to dialectic, the other subjects of the Trivium. Thus, perhaps, the boys practised the art of disputation, so important a part of university education in the Middle Ages, and the lack of which is compensated for to-day by the activities of school debating and dramatic societies. But in fact very little indeed is known of the life which went on in medieval Winchester and, as Leach says, 'an attempt to reproduce a "Day of my life at Winchester in the fourteenth century" would be wholly guess-work'.[1]

In 1440 Eton was founded, the other great school which, as in the case of Winchester, was to see its history closely interwoven with that of the nation. Its historian, Sir Maxwell Lyte, himself posed the question of how the history of such a school should be written: 'According to some, it should be a biographical register of successive Provosts, Fellows, and Masters, who have guided a great national institution through more than four centuries of almost unbroken prosperity; according to others, it should trace the continuous existence of an ecclesias-

[1] *History of Winchester College*, p. 168.

tical corporation, richly endowed and boasting a picturesque pile of medieval buildings; some think that it should follow the careers of a vast number of England's greatest men from the cradle to the grave; others that it should be a record of educational progress, a treatise on grammars and exercises; while yet another class would wish to see in it a faithful picture of school life at different periods, with long accounts of popular games and boyish adventures.'[1] The history of Eton, indeed, embraces all those things, and the splendid medieval buildings testify still to the unbroken continuity of a school which like Winchester became a great national institution. In fact Eton came to outstrip the earlier school in both size and importance, and in modern times, as the leading school of the dominant nation in the world, it achieved a reputation which was universal. It has filled the most famous regiments and the ranks of the diplomatic service, it has seen many of its boys become illustrious in both houses of parliament, it has provided a long series of prime ministers and some of the most outstanding, like Walpole, Chatham, and Gladstone.

Eton was like Winchester, although a magnificent foundation, completely medieval in character and in keeping with the times. It was indeed closely modelled on Winchester, and its establishment was the greatest possible tribute to the success of the earlier school. The young king, Henry VI, who created Eton and the sister foundation of King's College, Cambridge, was surrounded by those who knew the works of Wykeham. That great ecclesiastic's successor, Cardinal Beaufort, the king's uncle, was the official visitor of the two Wykehamist establishments. A fellow of New College, Henry Chichely, was Archbishop of Canterbury, and another was the king's secretary. Thus it was, perhaps, that the king adopted Wykeham's idea of arranging for a continuous supply of scholars to a college at the university from a great grammar school established with that end in view. Since Eton was a royal foundation its charter, of the year 1440, opened with the official phraseology of a state document: *Henricus, Dei gracia, rex Anglie et Francie, et dominus*

[1] *History of Eton College*, original preface.

Hibernie, omnibus ad quos presentes litere pervenerint, salutem.[1] The expressed object of the new foundation is, once more, a religious one: 'To the praise, glory and honour of the same Crucified One, to the exaltation of the most glorious Virgin Mary his mother, and the establishment of most holy church, His spouse . . . we found . . . a college to be ruled and governed according to the tenor of these presents, in and of the number of a Provost and ten priests, four clerks and six chorister boys whose duty it shall be to serve divine worship there daily, and 25 poor and needy scholars whose duty it shall be to learn grammar, and moreover 25 poor and weakly men whose duty it shall be always to pray in the same place for our good estate while we live and for our soul when we have passed from this light, and for the souls of the illustrious prince Henry our father, late King of England and of France, also for the Lady Katherine, of most serene memory, his late consort, our mother, and of all our ancestors and of all the faithful departed; also of a master or teacher in grammar, whose duty it shall be to teach the said needy scholars, and all others whatsoever and whencesoever of our realm of England coming to the said college, the rudiments of grammar gratis, without exacting money or anything else.' The new body thus created, declared the royal charter, 'for ever shall be called the Provost and College Royal of the Blessed Mary of Eton by Windsor'.

Thus came into existence the great foundation with its aims of the furtherance of the Christian Church, prayer for the founder's soul, alms-giving, and the keeping of a grammar school. It was the keeping of the school, the means to achieving the other objects, which was to be the dominant feature of the new institution. After a visit to Winchester in 1441, the king remodelled his foundation: Eton and King's were made of the same size as Winchester and New College. Thus Eton was to have its seventy scholars besides Provost and Fellows; commoners were added; and a close relationship established

---

[1] Printed in full, with translation, in *Educational Charters and Documents* (ed. Leach). An analysis of the statutes, issued in 1447, is in Maxwell Lyte, Appendix A.

between Eton and the Cambridge college. William Waynflete, who had been headmaster of Winchester since 1430, was called upon by the king to organize the new school of Eton. Whether he acted as headmaster at Eton or not is uncertain, but he was Provost (i.e., head of the governing body of fellows); many of the Eton headmasters who followed were Wykehamists. Winchester can justly claim to be the mother of public schools, and although Wykeham, in establishing his school, was not acting otherwise than a great medieval ecclesiastic could be expected to act, his work did establish firmly in the educational life of England an institution which was to be of the very first importance. The public school of to-day traces many of its characteristic features back to Wykeham and his times: the corporate life, the education in Latin grammar, the close connexion with the older universities, the prefect system, and the religious character of the training given as a basis for formation of character. Its object is, perhaps, summed up in the famous Wykehamist motto—*Manners makyth Man*.

Just as Wykeham's action was not in its essence something new, so it was not without imitators, great and small. Some of the new creations were great, like Eton, others were small like that at Wotton-under-Edge, founded in 1384 with a master and two scholars in a small country town in Gloucestershire. William Waynflete, when Bishop of Winchester, created in the great tradition Magdalen College, at Oxford (the date of the foundation charter is 1448 although the college was not fully established in its present buildings until 1480), with a Wykehamist as its first president. Magdalen College had also its school, at first inside the college buildings and always closely controlled by the college. Waynflete was perhaps the first of the great schoolmaster-bishops: he has had great successors, in Wolsey, once headmaster of Magdalen College school, and in a succession of modern archbishops of Canterbury who have also, earlier in their careers, been the heads of important schools. Especially interesting, however, are two foundations in Yorkshire which, while imitating Winchester and Eton, provided also for elementary instruction, and this brings us to the question of what instruction there was for the ordinary man in the Middle Ages.

The topic is a difficult and obscure one. What we know of medieval education is principally the training in chivalry and grammar, and even the education of the grammar schoolboy is difficult to describe with any certainty. From all the industrious researches of A. F. Leach, the greatest authority on the English medieval schools, no clear picture emerges of the daily life of the schoolboy. What we do now know, thanks to his continued labours over many years, is that grammar schools existed in close connexion with important churches in the medieval towns; in those grammar schools boys, the majority of whom were destined for the Church, learned Latin—to read, write, and speak it. The position with regard to elementary or popular instruction is much more obscure. It is clear, of course, that there was no general system of elementary education either in Latin or in the vernacular. The ordinary person was a peasant or, to put it in other words, the mass of the people who did the ordinary manual labour in the fields upon which medieval society depended were peasants. They needed no formal education in letters for their agricultural tasks. They were illiterate as were, before recent educational advances, the peasant masses of China, India, and parts of Russia and the Balkans. Nevertheless, by the end of the Middle Ages, and indeed long before, a new civilization had grown up: England had its wealthy merchants with their important wool trade to Europe; in Italy and north Germany there were flourishing cities with merchant and banking houses and ships plying to the Levant or in the Baltic. Merchants, bankers, the higher craftsmen, and their clerks and accountants would need for their undertakings some elementary education, at least in reading, writing, and the operations of arithmetic. How did they get it?

Information on which to base an answer to this question is scanty. It is supposed that chantry priests gave instruction and also that unlicensed song schools may have taught reading and writing in the vernacular, and solitary women or anchoresses may also have given lessons of this kind. At any rate, we hear of ecclesiastical warnings and prohibitions of such practices. In the twelfth century, for example, the Abbot of Rievaux in Yorkshire warned anchoresses, for spiritual reasons, against keeping school; in the fourteenth century, the Archbishop of York forbade the continued keeping of unlicensed song schools by 'chaplains, holy water carriers and many others of that kind . . . in the parish churches, houses and other places within the said city of York'.[1] There must, therefore, have been such schools in existence; they do not appear to have been schools of grammar, and they may have given elementary instruction in the vernacular. Certainly schools for this purpose existed on the Continent, at least in the fourteenth century. In 1338 the chronicler Villani when describing the city of Florence mentions boys and girls learning to read, and also boys who were learning calculation; these were mentioned as distinct from those learn-ing grammar and logic.[2] Popular schools, sometimes private concerns, sometimes run by a town council, existed in Germany in the fourteenth and fifteenth centuries, for the purpose of teaching reading and writing in German. The Lübeck *scho-lasticus*—the established ecclesiastical authority—complained that he lost income because of the new school of the town council. At Brunswick in 1420 we hear of a school curriculum limited, after a conflict with the Church, to 'writing and reading the alphabet and German books and letters', and in Hamburg such schools were found from the beginning of the fifteenth century and there were the same conflicts between Church and town council.[3] At the same time the city schools were probably at first largely the result of a growing city life and not the result of any very clearly felt need for elementary or vernacular education. They were often Latin schools, sometimes gave a better Latin education than the older schools, and were not in the general sense anti-clerical. The quarrels with the Church authorities were of local importance only, and were simply due to the disturbance caused to the old

[1] A. F. Leach: *Early Yorkshire Schools*, I, 22.

[2] G. Villani: *Historie Fiorentine*, Book XI, cap. xciii (in *Rerum Italicarum Scriptores*, ed. Muratori, vol. xiii).

[3] See W. Rein: *Encyc. Handbuch*, II, 47–9. Also *Schulordnungen der Stadt Braunschweig*, in *Monumenta Germaniae Paedagogica*, I.

ecclesiastical monopoly in education by the new schools of the city councils. *Melius malum latinum quam bonum teutonicum.*[1] But the use of the German language was increasing and in the thirteenth century German was sometimes employed in official documents.

The two Yorkshire foundations, referred to above, at Acaster and Rotherham, were important establishments and, had their later fortune been different, might have survived as great colleges. Robert Stillington, Bishop of Bath and Wells and chancellor, founded, probably between 1467 and 1475, a college at Acaster with 'three divers Masters and Informators in the faculties under written; that is to wit, one of them to teach grammar, another to teach Music and Song, and the third to teach to Write and all such thing as belonged to Scrivener Craft'. Similarly at Rotherham, but on a grander scale, Jesus College was founded in 1483 by Thomas Rotherham, who had been born in that town and who had risen to be Archbishop of York. In remembrance of his own early difficulty as to education, which he would not have acquired 'had not by the grace of God a man learned in grammar come there', he founded the college with provost and fellows in the approved style, and with rooms in college for chantry priests of Rotherham church and for other commoners who might live there at their own expense. The provost was to be a theologian who would preach throughout the York diocese. The three fellows were to be teachers: one was to teach grammar, a second a song school—so far everything was as one would expect. But the third fellow was to turn his hand to elementary instruction: 'because that county produces many youths endowed with the light and sharpness of ability, who do not all wish to attain the dignity and elevation of the priesthood, that these may be better fitted for the mechanical arts and other concerns of this world, we have ordained a third fellow, learned and skilled in the art of writing and accounts.' All this—save the grammar school which still exists—perished during the Reformation.[2]

---

[1] See Paulsen: *Geschichte des gelehrten Unterrichts*, I, 18–24.
[2] A. F. Leach: *Early Yorkshire Schools*, II.

9

Another interesting foundation—though a small one—was that of a chantry in 1489 at Aldwincle in Northamptonshire, with a chaplain who 'shall teach and instruct, in spelling and reading, six of the poorest boys of the town'. Such instruction, however, may have been in Latin, not English, especially as the boys 'when they have been so instructed and taught were to say in the church every night the psalm *De profundis* and the prayers *Inclina Domine* and *Fidelium*.[1] But it seems that, in some places at least, elementary instruction was becoming available, and the means to this end grew, perhaps, with the increasing use of English as the ordinary language of the country. The *Paston Letters* (1422–1509) are those of a family—and a fair number of people took part in this correspondence—who could write in 'English tongue'. In the closing decades of the fifteenth century Caxton's printing-press at Westminster produced many works in English—Chaucer, Gower, Lydgate, Malory's *Morte D'Arthur*, and translations of Cicero and of Aesop's *Fables*. Where there were books there were presumably readers: where there were readers there must have been some means of learning to read.

If information on the subject of elementary instruction in the Middle Ages is scanty that on the education of girls is more scanty still. The reverence for the Virgin Mary and the lip service of chivalry had little effect, in practice, to improve what was the rather degraded position of the weaker sex in medieval society. The universities and great schools were certainly only for the male sex; there were no colleges for women, no co-educational universities, no public schools for girls; no feminine counterparts of William of Wykeham. Little girls may sometimes, however, have attended the song schools.

Occasionally an educated woman appears in a convent or in a court: a woman like Hilda, abbess at Hartlepool and Whitby, for whom Bede had high praise; Christine de Pisan, scholar and poetess; or the Lady Margaret Beaufort, mother of Henry VII. The Lady Margaret knew but little Latin, but she could read and write in English, had a sound knowledge of French, and was

[1] A. F. Leach: *Educational Charters and Documents*, p. 434.

a skilful embroideress. A certain Italian lady of whom we hear delivering lectures—with a mask to conceal her beauty—on behalf of her father, a jurist in Bologna, was perhaps unique. A letter addressed to Heloise by Peter of Cluny refers to philosophy as having been dismissed with contumely by the feminine sex. Women of royal birth or of noble family might well have, however, the opportunity of education by a family tutor, priest, or governess—how far such opportunity was taken would depend on the tastes of the particular girl concerned. Chaucer, in *The Doctor's Tale,* mentions the mistress or governess as a moral guardian rather than an ordinary teacher. Much more usual than learning for women, we can safely assume, were simple religious instruction and household tasks: spinning, weaving, cooking, and sometimes fine work like sewing and embroidery; and, among the upper classes, music, dancing, and singing. An Italian proverb probably well expressed the lot of the average girl: 'A girl should be taught to sew and not to read, unless one wishes to make a nun of her.'

But even in the nunnery it was by no means certain that a girl would receive any real education. Learned nuns are occasionally heard of, but the general level of education in the nunnery was low. In the later Middle Ages the nuns seldom knew Latin and were sometimes known to sing the services in church without understanding them; for the nuns the sermons and episcopal injunctions were usually couched in English. Whereas the great monastic houses produced their chronicles, the nuns produced none, nor did they, like the monks, busy themselves with the copying of manuscripts.

It has often been assumed that the nuns and the monks provided the schools of the Middle Ages but there is little evidence, as the medievalists Leach and Coulton have shown, for any such general provision. The bishops' registers do mention the teaching of novices and also, sometimes, the teaching of girls from outside, occasionally together with small boys. But it was not a general practice. Pupils were few, only girls of good birth were taken as the teaching given was made a source of income to the nunnery, and the education was restricted by the educational limitations of the nuns themselves. And, in any case, 'the whole trend of medieval thought was against learned women'.[1]

In fifteenth-century England it had become customary to put girls out at between seven and twelve, according to their station in life, to domestic service under a mistress or apprenticeship to a trade, or sometimes into a nunnery.[2] By learning the domestic tasks[3] they best prepared themselves for marriage, which commonly took place about the age of fourteen or fifteen. The majority of women, then, must have had the most slender of educations, at least in a bookish sense. It was their lack of education which, at the Renaissance, Vives blamed for the failings of their sex. It was, he thought, 'the only cause why all women for the most part are hard to please, studious and most diligent to adorn themselves, marvellers of trifles, in prosperity proud and insolent, in adversity abject and feeble; and for lack of good learning, they love and hate that only the which they learned of their unlearned mothers'. It was the husband's duty, thought Vives, 'to teach the woman'.[4]

[1] Eileen Power: *Medieval English Nunneries*, p. 238. See her chap. vi for the question of education in the nunneries.

[2] G. Gardiner: *English Girlhood at School*, p. 14.

[3] For an account of the domestic economy of medieval times see *Le Ménagier de Paris* (*The Goodman of Paris*, translated by Eileen Power).

[4] From Vives's *De Officio Mariti* (1529), translated by Foster Watson (*Renascence Education of Women*, p. 200).

PART THREE

Modern Education

CHAPTER VIII

RENAISSANCE AND REFORMATION: A NEW WORLD

THERE is nothing new without the loss of the old. 'Renaissance' and 'Reformation' are terms which historians use of two vast, many-sided complexes of events, changes, and movements which appear to mark both an end and a beginning in the affairs of Europe. The Middle Ages were coming to an end; modern times were beginning, somewhere about the end of the fifteenth century—or so it seems to the historian who must, if he is to make intelligible to the human mind the continuous flux of history, seek in that flux some seeming pattern which he can establish by means of recognizable marks. Such marks he uses to divide one period from another; such marks he has found to divide the ancient from the medieval, the medieval from the modern. Many events in many different spheres of human activity appear at the end of the fifteenth and the beginning of the sixteenth century to mark a change. The establishment of strong, centralized monarchies in England, Spain, and France, indicative of the new political phenomenon of the national state; the geographical discoveries in East and West opening up new worlds to exploration, conquest and settlement; the establishment of the Ottoman Turks in south-eastern Europe, and the end of the Eastern Empire; the Reformation which broke the religious unity of Christendom; the Renaissance of literature, art, and the human mind itself—all these announce the advent of a new age. Much that was old was disappearing. When John Leland, perhaps the first English antiquary, travelled the countryside in Henry VIII's reign he observed many 'lofty towers downrazed'; the walls of the recently dissolved monasteries and of the out-dated feudal castles were falling into ruin. At the same time, with the revival of letters, mental walls of ignorance were also falling. But the changes were, of course, gradual; no exact date can be given for the end of the Middle Ages either in England or on the Continent. 'All that we can say is', as Professor Trevelyan reminds us in the case of England, 'that, in the Thirteenth Century, English thought and society were medieval, and in the Nineteenth Century they were not. Yet even now we retain the medieval institutions of the Monarchy, the Peerage, the Commons in Parliament assembled, the English Common Law, the Courts of Justice interpreting the rule of law, the hierarchy of the established Church, the parish system, the Universities, the Public Schools and Grammar schools.'[1]

Perhaps the most important and most characteristic feature of the Renaissance—and, indeed, also of the Reformation so closely linked with it—was a new and powerful assertion of individuality. Man rediscovers himself; the individual puts his name to his own work as against the anonymous present and the anonymous past; he struggles for his own fame, his own position, his own rights as against the shapeless mass; he pits his own judgement against the weight of established authority and tradition; he asserts his own right to enjoy what is enjoyable for its own sake here and now; in the last resort, he stakes his own life against the great impersonal forces both of nature and society. Like Icarus in the Greek legend, retold by Renaissance poets in the vernaculars, Italian and French:

> Here Icarus fell, audacious youth and brave,
> Who dared to mount to heaven on man-made wings.[2]

About the Middle Ages there had been something crabbed and cramping. The human spirit was confined; it was dominated by the Church, and darkened by the belief that the best which this world could offer was evil. A painful probation was man's lot on earth: only in the next world might salvation be found,

---

[1] *English Social History*, p. 96.
[2] Translated from the French sonnet of Philippe Desportes (1546–1606), itself based on the Italian sonnet of Sannazaro (1456–1530).

and that only for the few. Man's path through life was menaced on every hand by devils, their snares lay hidden to trap him, and his end threatened to be but the introduction to an eternity of torment. A Dutch medievalist has remarked on the prevailing sadness in the medieval portraits which survive.[1] As against the other-worldliness of the Middle Ages the Renaissance is a reassertion of worldliness, but of worldliness in the best sense. Reborn is the classical ideal of the goodness of this life with its opportunities and possibilities, and of man himself as a noble creature. Individualism, since its rebirth, has not ceased to influence western Europe; it has been reconciled with Christianity, for the Christian faith has also its doctrine of individualism in the importance which it attaches to each and every soul in the sight of God; and it is in those countries whose cultural life was most affected by the ideals of Renaissance and Reformation that the liberal values, those values characteristic of Western civilization, have been established. In eastern Europe, especially in Russia, almost untouched by the humanizing movement of the Renaissance, the individual has remained the enemy, and the whole of society has been remodelled to safeguard itself against the enemy in its midst, which is nothing other than that same human individual. For communism in practice has proved to be but the reaction of the mass against man himself, and the suppression of all spontaneity and originality by a power stronger and far more ruthless than the medieval Church.

With the assertion of individuality which marked the Renaissance went a release of energy and a wave of optimism. It was as if the waters of human energy dammed up during the Middle Ages had been suddenly released. Talent of the first order appeared in almost every sphere; in painting, sculpture and architecture, works were produced which rivalled the great masterpieces of antiquity. The Italian genius for form and colour had shown itself already in the Middle Ages with Giotto and Fra Angelico; during the Renaissance it reached its highest achievements in the work of Botticelli,

[1] J. Huizinga: *Waning of the Middle Ages.*

129

Michelangelo, Raphael, Leonardo da Vinci, and Titian. The human body was studied once more, as in Greek times, to provide a model for art; beauty became the concern of the artist instead of, or at least as well as, the religious symbolism dominant in the Middle Ages. Italy has not ceased since that time to be a school of art for the civilized world. Scholarship, literature, science, all flourished. Every Italian city had its artists and workshops, its scholars, its writers, its schools, and centres of study. Florence was perhaps pre-eminent, and under the patronage of the governing Medici family established the Platonic Academy in conscious imitation of the ancient Greeks.

It was indeed the revival or rebirth in the West of the Greek language and of the Greek way of life which was most typical of the age and gave it the name of Renaissance. Greek had virtually disappeared from Europe with the collapse of the Roman world and its bilingual system of education. But about the end of the fourteenth century its study was recommencing in Italy. Just why this was is hard to say. At any time during the Middle Ages an Italian city might have imported a dozen Greek scholars from Constantinople and employed them as teachers of Greek. But it was not done. Now in the concluding century of the Middle Ages Greek studies revived. This revival cannot simply be traced to the Ottoman capture of Constantinople in 1453 and the consequent flight of scholars westward; the Greek revival had commenced years before that date. It was, however, not unconnected with growing Turkish pressure on what remained of the Eastern Empire. Manuel Chrysoloras was sent by the emperor in 1393 to seek help in the West. Two or three years later he was made professor of Greek in the University at Florence. From then until his death in 1415 he spent much of his time in Italy; he translated Homer and Plato; he compiled the *Erotemata*, the first Greek grammar to be used in the West. An Italian scholar, Filelfo, who had worked in 1419 in the Venetian consulate at Constantinople, married into the Chrysoloras family, learnt Greek, and became a determined collector of manuscripts. The passion for Greek grew and spread; it was especially strong in Florence, and in Rome among the clerks of the papal curia. Niccolo Niccoli, Poggio Bracciolini, Biondo, Pomponius Leto, Lorenzo Valla were among the many scholars who turned back for their scholarship and their inspiration to the classic past. The study of the Greek language and literature and the new light cast on Roman letters brought a ferment also in thought. Plato was revived and the great humanists like Marsilio Ficino and Pico della Mirandola sought to reconcile Platonism with Christianity. Men of all-round talent appeared, like Leon Battista Alberti, architect, artist, musician, engineer, and the supreme genius, Leonardo da Vinci.

The rediscovery of so much of the classical legacy and the renewed faith in the potentialities of human reason combined to create, what Stefan Zweig has called, 'a moment of intense optimism throughout the Western world'.[1] Human reason had been the means of rediscovering and interpreting the Greek texts, human reason could also be the means of removing the abuses of the time, especially those of the Church which had challenged the reforming zeal of Christendom ever since the councils of Pisa, Constance, and Basel early in the fifteenth century. Discovery, change, reform were in the air—one might almost say progress, though one must beware of putting this nineteenth-century idea back into the period of the Renaissance. But humanism spread from Italy to the other countries of western Europe, and electrified the air. Great things had been achieved, were being achieved, by man: much more, it was confidently felt, would be achieved. Through Germany, the cry of the humanist Ulrich von Hutten, 'It is a joy to be alive', rang like a trumpet call. We have to wait until the epoch of the French Revolution for a comparable optimism.

Just as the French Revolution was followed by reaction and disillusion so, too, was the epoch of the Reformation. And as Goethe pointed out to the age of the Revolution the dangers inherent in the new-fashioned ideas of democracy and nationalism so the greatest humanist of them all, Erasmus, pointed out in the age of the Renaissance the dangers that lurked in the

[1] Zweig: *Erasmus*, p. 120.

enthusiastic reform programme of Luther. For the victories of human reason over man himself are not easy victories; it was easier far to interpret the Greek texts than to understand the nature of man; it was easier far to denounce the wickedness and worldliness of individual popes and clerics than to eradicate the evils and weaknesses in human nature in which individual wrongdoing had its roots. In spite, also, of the genuine scholarship and culture of the Renaissance, and of the more superficial pomp and glitter of the court life of Italian cities, it was, underneath, a crude, cruel and savage age. Two modern French historians, natives of a country itself not unknown for its literary culture and the somewhat less praiseworthy standards of its sanitary hygiene, have given us a glimpse into the material and social standards of the past. Michelet speaks of a Europe unwashed for a thousand years—a period which included that of the Renaissance. Taine has given us an account of Renaissance life which we should describe to-day as an 'off-the record' account—John Morley spoke of it as 'in the literary undress of a private letter'. After reading Cellini, Machiavelli, Vasari, the Frenchman Taine commented: 'This Italian society of the sixteenth century is an assemblage of ferocious brutes with passionate imagination. The footmen of to-day would not endure the company of the Duke and Duchess of Ferrara, of Paul III, Julius II, Borgia, etc. No wit nor grace nor ease nor amiability, no gentleness, no ideas, no philosophy. Pedantry, gross superstition, risk of death at every instant, the necessity of fighting at every street corner for life or purse, harlotry and worse than harlotry—all with a crudity and a brutality beyond belief.'[1] The feuds of Montague and Capulet in Shakespeare's *Romeo and Juliet* are no work of the imagination; they represent the daily life of Italian cities of the period scarcely less barbarous than that of an earlier feudal age to which the fortified towers of rival families still testify in places like Bologna or San Gimignano.

Men of the Italian Renaissance turned back to the pagan past for inspiration and devoted their energy to classical literature;

[1] Quoted by John Morley: *Politics and History*, p. 88.

in northern Europe the men of the new learning turned first rather to the study of biblical texts and to theology. But Northern humanists and reformers also looked back—to a past in which they could find a greater purity of manners and doctrine in the early Church before the domination of Rome. The invention of printing about 1455 divides approximately the period of the revival of letters in Italy from that of the Transalpine movement. At the end of the fifteenth and the beginning of the sixteenth century the new scholarship was most powerful in Germany in preparing the way for the Reformation. That movement was the result partly of a reaction against the abuses in the Church, partly of disagreement as to doctrine, and partly also of the clash of rival nationalisms. Italy looked back to a distant past when Rome had been the mighty mistress of the world and the patron of its civilization; this enhanced a feeling of Italian patriotism, and often made Italians intolerant and condescending towards the people of the North whom they still tended to regard as barbarians. As a result, German students and scholars often returned with a hatred of the Italians. 'The ancient hatred between us can never be dissolved', wrote a German coming home to Ingolstadt in 1492. 'But for the Alps we should be eternally at war.'[1] Germans, on the other hand, were less interested in the greatness of a Roman past and when enlightened by the new learning were more than ever likely to regard the Roman Church in Germany as an alien imposition, to throw off which they were the more ready as their sense of German nationalism developed. Indeed in Germany and England—and also even in France, although Paris through the Middle Ages was the home of scholastic theology—there was already a long tradition of national opposition to the papacy as the head of a foreign power. There was, in especial, a hatred of papal taxation and the fear of national impoverishment by money going 'out of the country' into Italian coffers. There had, too, been a growing volume of criticism of the lives of the clergy and monks. All this went far to prepare men's minds for change which was to come in radical fashion when Luther

[1] Quoted by P. S. Allen: *Age of Erasmus*, p. 265.

challenged the Roman Catholic Church in 1517; it helps to account for the success of the Reformation in the northern countries. And the Reformation when it came shattered the ideological unity of medieval Christendom and strengthened the growth of the different nationalisms of Europe.

'Erasmus laid the eggs and Luther hatched the chickens', cried a Catholic preacher, or, as Bayle put it in the seventeenth century, *Luthérien avant Luther même, Érasme rendit doubteux lequel de lui ou de Luther étoit l'auteur du Lutheranisme.* The greatest of Northern humanists Erasmus had indeed, by the scorn and ridicule with which he attacked the abuses in the Church, encouraged the movement which became the Reformation. But he had at length recoiled from the violence of Luther; and Erasmus never left the old Church. It was in him above all that the two great Renaissance movements had met: he was a scholar of the first order, master of the languages and literatures of both Rome and Greece and their devoted lover, but he gave much of his energy to the study of the Scriptures and to their elucidation. On the one hand his scholarship and his criticism of abuses aided the reformers; on the other his hatred of extremism, his caution, his timidity held him back from any radical break such as that of Luther.

The reputation of Erasmus as scholar and humanist made his influence particularly powerful. Much of his life he spent in study; he travelled, lectured, and taught. He was in England more than once; he was the friend of Linacre, More, and Colet, helping the last-named with the refounding of St. Paul's School; he lectured in Cambridge on Greek and theology. His literary output was immense and various. In the *Enchiridion Militis Christiani*, the handbook of the Christian knight, he argued that, although formal worship is not to be condemned, it is the inward piety that counts; he criticized fasting without true spiritual purpose; he suggested that the customary worship of the saints was scarcely distinguishable from idolatry. Folly was personified in the *Encomium Moriae*. Folly attacks the superstitions and abuses of the Church: the priests are blamed for preying on the people's superstition; and the monks for intemperance; popes, cardinals, and bishops for their wealth and luxury. Theologians are pilloried for the barren character of their disputations—'Can God the Father hate the Son?' 'Can God take the form of a woman, devil, donkey?' and so on. In such of his works Erasmus aided the reformers. At the same time he provided a Greek edition of the New Testament—dedicated to the pope—with Latin translation, notes, and commentary, completed in 1519. This—although the pope accepted the dedication and humanists applauded the work—gave a greatly improved apparatus of theological criticism to the scholars who were attacking the Church. Erasmus's own theological interests led him to edit works of the Fathers; his love of the Greek and Latin classics produced his many editions, including works of Aristotle, Demosthenes, and Euripides, Cicero, Horace, and Livy.

Luther, like Erasmus, had been through the Latin and scholastic education of his day, but had not acquired Erasmus's deep knowledge of Greek. His attitude to the classics was radically different; he did not delight in them as did Erasmus, but read the Latin authors mainly to gain a knowledge of the language. He turned his knowledge to a religious end. Obsessed with a sense of sin Luther became a monk. Later, as a professor of theology in the University of Wittenberg, he took in his lectures an increasingly independent line. His attack on papal indulgences—the selling of pardons—led to a dispute with the Church, and Luther, a man of conviction and courage, did not shrink from the consequences. Allying himself with the German princes who for their own reasons were prepared to break with Rome, Luther found himself leader of a national movement— the German Reformation. His German hymns and his translation of the Bible into German are indications of the national character of the break. Luther's movement was national but it was also one more indication of the assertion of the individual against the mass. The Wittenberg monk challenged the established authority of the Church. The Protestant claimed a right of private judgement based on private study of Scripture.

The Reformation brought not peace but a sword: it was

followed by the Peasants' Revolt in Germany, by civil war, which broke out just after Luther's death, by the Wars of Religion in France, and by the Thirty Years War. Both sides— Catholics and reformers, or Protestants—had appealed to Erasmus. He, though he had so greatly influenced the reformation struggle, feared the results of Luther's movement. 'You have disturbed the whole world', he wrote to Luther. 'My heart is sorely grieved at the widespread suffering and the incurable confusion for which we have no one to thank but yourself, with your unbridled ways.' The attack was perhaps too strong, but Erasmus stands out above all as a man of reason, moderation, common sense, and toleration. 'The battle between Luther and Erasmus', writes an American historian of the period, 'was a real tragedy. The humanist had set himself, as his life task, a peaceful reformation of the Church; abuses he thought would fade away before gentle sarcasm and the cultivation of good letters and the sacred text. The boisterous attack of the Wittenberg monk, said he sadly, destroyed all hope of this. He lived to see his ideal of peace shattered in war, the followers trained to carry on his work reft from him by one side or the other, and his name spat upon by almost all.'[1]

Such wide and far-reaching changes as were those of Renaissance and Reformation might have been expected to bring about a transformation in the character and methods of education. But, although many features of modern education can be traced to these two great movements, their immediate effect upon schools and universities was not as great as might be supposed. Indeed, the first and principal result of the revival of letters was to rivet a classical curriculum even more firmly to the schools. The modern subjects lay still in the future—they had still, in the main, to be created, the vernacular literatures, for example, natural science, and the scientific study of history and geography—and, since in Latin and Greek were contained, as Erasmus argued in stressing their fundamental importance, 'all things which appear to be worth knowing',[2] their educational position was established for many centuries to come. The

[1] Preserved Smith: *Life and Letters of Luther*, p. 212.   [2] *De Ratione Studii.*

greatest single educational result of the Renaissance was, of course, the restoration of Greek to an honoured place in the curriculum, a place it had not held since the days of the old Roman higher schools. Greek found its way, then, into the universities and the better schools: Grocyn, a Wykehamist and Fellow of New College, was perhaps the first man to teach Greek in Oxford, about 1490, after his return from study in Italy; in the new foundation of Harrow, for example, in 1571, Greek was to be taught in the upper forms. It was not, indeed, without a struggle that Greek was introduced; conservatives did not easily modify the scholastic routine of Latin, logic, and theology. At Oxford there was a struggle between 'Greeks' and 'Trojans', as the rival factions were labelled. Eventually Greek established itself and henceforth with Latin it composed what was called a classical education. With the introduction of Greek, too, the conception of a 'liberal' education, if it did not originate, was at least greatly strengthened. Whereas the Latin education of the Middle Ages was a vocational training for the clerical professions, Greek was a subject not directly useful but rather a training of the mind, and more particularly the mind of the gentleman.

Next to the rebirth of Greek studies was the restoration of classical Latin; a new attention was given to Latin style. In this Quintilian and Cicero were the predominant influences as they had once been before, fourteen centuries ago. The discovery of a complete copy of Quintilian's *Institutio Oratoria* was made by Poggio Bracciolini in the Swiss monastery of St. Gall in 1416. Like Manuel Chrysoloras, Poggio was attending the Council of Constance on the question of Church reform; he took the opportunity to search the neighbouring monasteries for manuscripts and struck lucky at St. Gall. 'In the middle of a well-stocked library', wrote Poggio in an excited letter, 'we discovered Quintilian, safe as yet and sound, though covered with dust and filthy with neglect and age.' To which his correspondent replied in ecstatic terms: 'So may you receive the title of the second author of the works you have restored to the world. Through you we now possess Quintilian entire; before

137

we only boasted the half of him, and that defective and corrupt in text. O precious acquisition! O unexpected joy!'[1] As a result of this find the scholars and educators of the Renaissance were able to steep themselves in the work of the greatest of Roman teachers, and the ancient ideal was revived of the 'good man skilled in speaking'. It was a proper ideal for an age of individualism when scholar, statesman, or priest sought to display his skill in well-chosen words and polished sentences. Of Latin style Cicero was the model. As a maxim for budding scholars *A Cicerone nunquam discedendum* was laid down by Vittorino da Feltre. The wheel of academic fashion was soon to come full circle: the old Roman emphasis on a polished style had first degenerated into meaningless debate and empty phrase-making; it had been abandoned in the Middle Ages for a system of training in which Latin grammar was merely a means to dialectic in which the serious theological content was all-important; now form and style had become once more pre-dominant only to lose in turn their own force and spirit when once the fresh springtime of the Renaissance had passed away.

One development, which although not itself a result of the revival of letters was nevertheless most powerful in propagating its products, was the invention of printing. For the printing-press made possible not only a great multiplication of copies of a given book with a consequent reduction in price but also guaranteed a standard text which corresponded closely with what had originally been written by its author. However carefully a medieval writer had written, his work must be copied many times by hand to make it available to those who would read it. In the process of copying, however careful the copyist, mistakes would creep in. Sometimes, too, an author would himself alter a copy, cutting out passages and adding others. Consequently, every *copy* of a work was likely to be different from every other. Printing—provided proofs were carefully revised—made possible the diffusion of a large number of identical copies, and made a much greater accuracy

---

[1] Translated by J. A. Symonds: *Renaissance in Italy* (Revival of Learning), pp. 98–100.

possible in scholarship. Soon reliable editions of the Greek and Latin classics provided by the new presses were available to scholars everywhere.

The renewed study of classical texts was, as we know, only one of the educational results of the Renaissance. The Greek spirit of inquiry, the spirit which was ultimately to produce modern science, revived. Even in the Middle Ages alchemists had sought for a method of transmuting the base metals into gold. Roger Bacon, in the thirteenth century, was an example of a genuine experimental scientist. At the Renaissance a new impetus was given to scientific work: Copernicus, Galileo, Leonardo all engaged in scientific or mathematical investigations. Copernicus showed that the earth revolved on its axis and moved round the sun; this was to upset the teaching which had prevailed since Ptolemy of Alexandria and to revive that of an earlier Greek, Aristarchus. A revolution in man's attitude to the universe was beginning: the earth was not the centre of that universe, but merely one planet in a solar system. The new scientific hypothesis was contrary to the teachings of the Church and was at first opposed by both Catholics and Protestants. Vives and Francis Bacon put forward the collection of facts as a means to proceed to knowledge, induction rather than deduction. Under the influence of the Greek ideal of physical beauty the human body took on a new dignity in place of the brutalizing treatment it received as the seat of original sin at the hands of medieval asceticism. The training of the body by physical exercises—not, of course, unknown in the education of the medieval knight as distinct from that of the clerk—now became an honourable practice for the gentleman, and part of the tradition we can trace in our modern cult of physical training which has become universal in our schools and throughout the armed services under the abbreviation 'P.T.' The growth of national sentiment encouraged the development of vernacular literatures. Although this was hardly the result of a movement which emphasized above all the value of the classics, a remarkable flowering of national literature accompanied the classical Renaissance. This flowering was but another indication of the vast release of human energy which characterized the age. For some of the greatest names in the national literatures as contrasted with the literature of the classical revival appeared just before, during, and just after that revival—Dante, Petrarch, and Boccaccio in Italy, Chaucer, Shakespeare, and the whole galaxy of Elizabethan genius in England, Rabelais in France, Cervantes in Spain.

Indeed from this time on the mere number of personal names attaching to individual contributions to literature and knowledge of all kinds becomes an increasing embarrassment to the student and a new source of delight to the maker of compendiums, dictionaries, and encyclopaedias of all kinds. Just as the ideological unity of medieval Europe was destroyed by the growth of national sentiment and the Reformation with the result that Europe split into distinct national states each with a developed sense of national personality or individuality, so now the contributions of individual scholars to learning became more numerous, more personal in character, and more clearly distinguishable in their manner and style one from another. The individualism of the Renaissance powerfully quickened the human urge to create; the printing-press provided the means of multiplying and perpetuating the fruits of that creation. Thus we find during the Renaissance an embarrassing number of scholars, teachers, schools, and educational theorists.[1] From this time on almost every writer who achieved distinction—and many who did not—may well be found to have written something at least on education or to have made some contribution to its development. The work of the educational historian is dependent more and more upon a severe process of selection.

The Greek ideal of the full man was revived in the theory, and to some extent in the practice, of the Renaissance age. Vergerio (1349–1420), a lecturer in the University of Padua, wrote treatises both on the work of Quintilian and on the manner and education of a gentleman in general. To train and

[1] For a detailed account of the most important see W. H. Woodward: *Studies in Education during the Age of the Renaissance, 1400–1600.*

develop the 'highest gifts of body and mind' was his object, not forgetting that in practice it would be necessary to adapt the subjects taught to the age and disposition of a given pupil. Probably the greatest practising schoolmaster of the time was Vittorino da Feltre (1378–1446). Well taught by scholars of distinction at Padua University, he became a great Ciceronian stylist before he undertook the education of a noble family, that of the ruler of Mantua, Gianfrancesco Gonzaga. Here he taught for more than twenty years, in a special house with some sixty or seventy scholars; some were sons of nobles, others were poor boys whom he introduced because of their ability, and all lived together under the direction of Vittorino and his staff. The curriculum consisted of Greek and Latin, and it also included the study of the content of the classical writings; attention was given to history, music, philosophy, mathematics, and science. Physical exercises and games had their place in Vittorino's school, and in the daily devotions every effort was made to infuse the whole life of the school with a Christian spirit. Thus, at Mantua, for a space, the Greek ideal of balance, Quintilian's ideal of the well-informed orator able and ready to devote himself to the public service, and the Christian faith were united through the personality of Vittorino himself. But such a school was a court school and schools of that kind were not uncommon; there was little idea as yet of opening such an education to a large circle. No provision was made for teaching the vernacular language. Greek and Latin were predominant, and among other teachers and in other schools not fired by the broad, liberal humanism of Vittorino there were very soon signs of that concentration on the classical languages for their own sake which points the way to the emptiness of mere style.

Although humanism was most powerful in the court schools of the Italian cities, it was also influential in northern Europe where the growing city life encouraged a demand for education. In the free cities of the Netherlands there had been town schools in the Middle Ages. Towards the end of the fourteenth century there had originated at Deventer a voluntary brotherhood for undertaking charitable works, the Brethren of the Common

Life. Among their tasks they undertook teaching, and at the end of the fifteenth century they were running numerous grammar schools both in the Netherlands and western Germany. One of their most famous pupils—at Deventer itself—was Erasmus, though he showed little early promise and did not rise high in the school. Later he described it as 'barbarous', that is, still based on the old scholastic Latin. Nevertheless, the headmaster, Hegius, of whom, as he only taught at the top of the school, Erasmus saw little, introduced Greek, and the schools of the Brethren were well organized and some of them large. The school at Deventer, a little later, is said to have had over two thousand boys.[1] Erasmus himself made, among his many literary works, considerable contributions to education. These included several books for schools, one of which was a revision of the Latin grammar of Lily, the first headmaster of the refounded St. Paul's School, and also the treatises *De Ratione Studii*, *De Civilitate Morum puerilium*, and *De Pueris statim ac liberaliter instituendis*. In the last named, with the double end in view, *ad virtutem ac literas*, Erasmus dealt at length with the education of boys, and he urged that their education must start as soon as possible, for the old remember those things which they learnt in their early years. As a man of reason and tolerance, Erasmus was not only an educator but also an internationalist and a pacifist. He regarded the heritage of Greece and Rome as a common European possession which might make the basis of a cultural and cosmopolitan civilization. He wished by his work to make available to northern Europe, from which he sprang, the refined learning which Italy had once more provided for mankind. At the same time, and above all, education was to be a means towards a better life in the moral sense. Erasmus clearly stated his aims: 'The first and principal thing is that the young mind may take in the seeds of piety; next that it may master and love the liberal studies; third, that it may be instructed in the duties of life; fourth, that from the beginning it may be made accustomed to good manners.'[2] As for method Erasmus knew that, although grammar and con-

[1] Allen: *Age of Erasmus*, p. 35.   [2] *De Civilitate Morum puerilium*, I.

tinuous exercises were necessary to the learning of a classical language, they were the means and not the end, and that, unless it leads to knowledge and understanding of the subject matter, language study is barren. He suggested also that the provision of a proper education was a public obligation.

So far as he went, Erasmus was the greatest of humanists, and his ideal of the highest culture of the past as a basis for the civilization of present and future was a noble one. But he was still thinking like the men of his time largely of the training proper to a class of scholars, hardly at all of the mass of ordinary men. Outside his ken were the vernacular languages and cultures which were, in fact, to play an ever-growing part in the civilization of the future. In some ways the Spanish humanist Vives (1492–1540) went further than Erasmus, though his general educational attitude was similar. He spent some time in England while Catherine of Aragon was the queen of Henry VIII and acted as tutor to their daughter, Mary. As a result he wrote treatises on women's education, and was something of a pioneer in that respect, although under the influence of Italian humanism the education of princesses and noble ladies was not uncommon. Vittorino's Mantua school had included ladies of the ruling family among its pupils. Vives, like Erasmus, sought to combine Christianity and humanism. He attacked the old scholastic education for a more profound reason than Erasmus had done; he saw its principal failing in its assumption of general ideas from which it argued. Instead, he maintained, man must first collect facts from his experience and then upon these he might base a general idea or principle. This method —induction instead of deduction, which we observed above— was pregnant for the future when fully developed by the natural scientists. For the teacher of boys Vives regarded the M.A. training as insufficient; he suggested in addition to this academic training a course for intending teachers under the careful eye of a headmaster. Vives was also a psychologist; in his *De Tradendis Disciplinis* and his *De Anima et Vita* he explains, and this was a novelty, the importance of the learner's mind as apart from the subjects of study. With his appreciation of the part played by the mind of the individual learner went his emphasis on the principle that instruction must be suited to that particular mind. He expounded also the idea of sense perception. 'Our first teachers are the senses' and by means of those we learn the first individual facts, and can then proceed to groups of facts, and so to the universal conception.[1] Vives was aware that sense experience was to be gained in all kinds of places where the older and more conventional men of learning would never have looked. 'The student', wrote Vives, 'should not be ashamed to enter shops and factories and to ask the craftsmen questions in order to understand the details of their work.'[2] This is to look forward to the eighteenth century. Such advice was repeated in similar words by Rousseau—Émile was to learn by entering workshop, farm, and forge. And Rousseau was the pioneer of much in our modern education.

[1] *De Anima et Vita*, II, 9 (*De discendi ratione*).
[2] *De Tradendis Disciplinis*, IV, 6 (translation by Foster Watson).

CHAPTER IX

THE STRUGGLE FOR EDUCATION:
PROTESTANTS AND CATHOLICS

IF the Renaissance opened a period of intellectual vitality, the Reformation launched what we should call to-day an ideological conflict, and in that conflict much of the vitality ran to waste in the barren subtleties of theological discussion and, worse still, in the disaster of religious war. Both sides sought to control, or to create, the instruments of education and in so doing both recognized the importance of education as a means of moulding the nature of man. While each side aimed at producing adherents of its own cult, each had necessarily to give special attention to the creation of new schools to serve that end.

The reformers, with their emphasis on private reading of the Bible and private judgement, soon realized the importance of the schools. In them would be decided the future of the Reformation. As one of the French reformers, Pierre Toussaint, wrote in 1537: 'The college will do more for the Gospel than all our sermons. The future is there, *in pueritia recte instituta aut instuenda.*'[1] There indeed, it seemed, was the secret—'in the proper teaching of boys'. To take the spirit when it was like wax and mould it—that was the work of the schools. The schools must produce the *élite*; the *élite* would provide the leadership of the masses. While, with the decay of scholasticism and the advance of humanism, the older church schools were in retreat, a real opportunity offered to those who could first create new schools in keeping with the spirit of the Renaissance. That spirit was

[1] Quoted by F. de Dainville: *La Naissance de l'Humanisme Moderne*, p. 31.

not seldom hostile to the old Church, and with the growing bourgeois class of the towns anxious to advance their sons through the new education, the times were favourable to reformers who could find a footing in the field of education.

Indeed, at first in Germany and France there appears to have been at work a subtle process of infiltration of protestant ways of thought into the schools. Municipalities and parents did not inquire carefully into the religious beliefs of teachers. Teachers in an age of humanist criticism of the old Church tended to be of reformist sympathies; though they might claim to teach only Latin and Greek, these subjects might easily be a cover for religious instruction. A modern Catholic historian describes the process in terms which might easily be used by a conservative of to-day to describe what he supposes to be the spreading of dangerous revolutionary ideas by socialist teachers in schools. 'One could not conceive a more dangerous and more effective proselytism than this underground action. By it, heresy insinuated itself, infiltrated, into all places.'[1]

While humanists turned back to the civilization of Greece and Rome, the reformers looked to what they supposed to be the simplicity and purity of the early Church. This attachment for early Christianity might have resulted in a movement hostile to education. Extremists, like the Anabaptists, could view culture as a dangerous luxury unnecessary to the Christian life, and revived the doubts that had worried the Fathers as to an education based in pagan civilization. Faith could be set against reason and worldly knowledge. Dr. Dell, during the Commonwealth in England, advised the learning of Latin and Greek from Christian authors to avoid 'the lies, fables, follies, vanities, whoredoms, lust, pride, revenge, etc., of the heathens'. 'The Sufficiency of the Spirit's teaching without Humane Learning' was the title of a treatise written by a cobbler. But the leaders of the reformers realized the value of letters, for a knowledge of Greek and Latin was as necessary to the biblical scholar as it was to the humanist. Thus the Latin schools of the Middle Ages

[1] F. de Dainville: *La Naissance de l'Humanisme Moderne*, p. 35.

must be given new life. Something more, however, was required of protestant reformers: they must provide the necessary education for the people to read the Bible and to learn the catechisms which the new system of religion made the duty of all.

Luther, although he considered religion as of supreme importance and everything else as secondary, knew well enough as the result of his own studies that education was the key to the Scriptures. 'Therefore,' he wrote, 'so dear as the Gospel is unto us, even with such diligence let us apply ourselves to languages.' This was in 1524 in his *Letter to the Burgomasters and Councillors of the Cities of Germany on behalf of Christian Schools.* In this and in a later discourse, a *Sermon on the Duty of Sending Children to School*, he urged the duty of parents and of public authority to concern themselves with education. He emphasizes the importance of the teacher's work, and suggests that just as a city may compel men to fight in its defence so may it compel its youth to go to school. Girls also were to be included. His translation of the New Testament into German and his preparation of two catechisms supplied the means of popular instruction in the new Protestant faith. Luther appears to have grasped the idea of education in school as a means of preparing children not only for scholarship—for that in itself was secondary with him—but also for life in the Christian community. It was the city's duty to see to the education of its young because thereby they would provide the next generation of preachers, statesmen, lawyers, physicians, and so on. At the same time in the *Letter to the Burgomasters* he seems to have been thinking, uncertainly perhaps, of some kind of education for all. To the objection 'we cannot bring up all our children to be students for we need them at home to work' he answers: 'I ask only that boys shall attend such schools as I have in view, an hour or two a day, and spend the rest of their time at home, or in learning some trade . . . thus both matters will be cared for together.' In the same way 'little girls may easily find time enough to go to school an hour a day, and yet do all their household duties; for they now devote more than that to overmuch play, dancing and sleep'. He went on to maintain that 'the devil is better pleased with rude blockheads' and therefore it was imperative to attend to education 'not merely for the sake of the young but also for the stability of our institutions, temporal and spiritual'. People had been too long in the darkness of ignorance. 'Too long have we been German beasts—let us act now as reasonable beings.'

Protestantism led, in fact, to a considerable reorganization of education in Germany, and the driving force behind this movement—so far as it depended on the personality of any single figure—was Philip Melanchthon. An indefatigable lecturer on classics and theology at the reformed University of Wittenberg, the centre of Protestant studies from about 1530 onwards, he also provided a number of text-books of Greek and Latin grammar, theology, rhetoric, and logic, and formulated the principles on which the new Protestant educational system developed. He came to be known as *Praeceptor Germaniae,* and this title was no exaggeration for not only did he reorganize the schools and universities but also by his own teaching and writing did much to train a generation of teachers to fill them. His influence was predominant throughout the Protestant territories of Germany. That country—a country only in geographical nomenclature—was, under the shadowy authority of the Holy Roman Empire, divided into several hundred states, territories, and cities of many different sizes and description. The territorial divisions were accentuated by the split in the Church, and each territory, whether its ruler was Catholic or Protestant, tried as far as possible to make itself ideologically watertight by controlling its own spiritual and temporal affairs. As part of this control, in the states newly Protestant, the existing means of education had to be re-formed or reorganized and brought into keeping with the new order in religion. With Melanchthon's active help grammar schools were established between 1521 and 1526 in Magdeburg, Eisleben, and Nuremberg. New universities also were created, or old ones re-formed. The first new Protestant university was that of Marburg in 1527, followed within the next fifty years by Königsberg, Jena, and Helmstedt.

Up and down Germany, in the states which became Protestant, the old ecclesiastical organization and the schools depending on it had to be remodelled on Lutheran lines. *Kirchenordnungen*, or new regulations, were issued to make clear the necessary changes. A set of rules issued in 1529 for the city of Hamburg included among its contents regulations for schools, pastors, matrimony, midwives, and the visitation of the sick and the poor. In 1527 the Elector, or prince, of Saxony sent Melanchthon and others around his country to make a visitation of the churches, and for the guidance of the clergy Melanchthon published certain *Visitation Books* containing a summary of Lutheran teaching. These books included an educational plan. Many of the school codes still exist: Brunswick had its regulations in 1528, Schleswig-Holstein in 1542, Mecklenburg in 1552, while in Württemberg in 1559 and in Saxe-Coburg-Gotha in 1642 very comprehensive state systems of education were organized.[1]

Not unnaturally, in view of the long tradition which made it a matter of course to think of education in terms of a prolonged and arduous bookish training in an ancient language, the reformers' educational codes gave the largest attention to secondary and higher education. The schools created by the city governments in the later Middle Ages and new schools set up in the period of the Reformation by territorial sovereigns were available as an instrument to the reformers. Princes might take pride in the creation of a new school on humanist lines, and sometimes used for this purpose the endowments of the dissolved monasteries. From the established tradition of such schools dates the classical curriculum of the modern German *gymnasium*. Latin remained, for the reformers as for the educationalists of the Middle Ages, the principal subject in schools. It occupied the greatest amount of time and called for the greatest expenditure of energy since the teacher's object was to give a full and easy command of that tongue: Latin was still a

---

[1] These Reformation school regulations were not necessarily the earliest. Brunswick's went back to 1251. See *Braunschweigische Schulordnungen* in *Monumenta Germaniae Paedagogica*, I.

spoken as well as a written language. Grammar had to be assiduously studied for, as Melanchthon stressed in his *Visitation Books*, 'no greater injury can be done to learning than where youth is not well practised in grammar'. Melanchthon thought that children should concentrate on Latin—teachers should not burden them with German, Greek, and Hebrew; practice in Latin conversation should go on at all times, and a teacher who found the routine of grammar too burdensome should be dismissed and replaced by another who would 'keep the children at their grammar'.[1]

Upon the foundation of Latin grammar was built the superstructure of imitation of the best classical authors: in the intermediate stages, Ovid, Aesop, Terence, Caesar, and in the more advanced, Cicero and Virgil. A fine Latin style, closely modelled on that of Cicero, was still the aim and the mark of the cultivated. For the serious scholar Greek was also necessary, though much less important than Latin. Hebrew, too, because of its value in biblical study, found a place in some of the schools. Apart from ancient languages, some time was given to mathematics and to music. Religious instruction took an important place in the curriculum of the Protestant schools, both in the formal teaching of the Creed, the Lord's Prayer, the Commandments, and Luther's catechism and also in the exposition of Scripture in the sermons preached at the church services. One particularly famous school was the gymnasium of Strassburg, under its rector John Sturm (1507–1589), the friend of Melanchthon. It was a large school, sub-divided into classes; its classical training was particularly thorough and it had a wide influence upon the schools of the Protestant countries. As for the universities, their framework remained much the same, though the necessary changes were made in the teaching of theology. For the Protestant pastor preaching and explanation of the Scriptures is of special importance, and it therefore became much more common for the student in the faculty of arts to pass on to the higher faculty of theology and complete a course there.

[1] *Unterricht der Visitatorum*, section *Von Schulen*.

What was particularly characteristic of Protestantism, however, and what is especially interesting in the development of
education, was the attention given to elementary instruction.[1]
Provision of higher education, of some kind or other, there had
always been, but any attempt to supply the elementary
instruction of the common people was something new. This
attempt rested upon the Protestant conviction that the Bible,
not the authority of the Church, was the source of divine truth.
It was necessary, therefore, to open this source to all so that all
might have the opportunity of finding through its truth their
way to salvation. Boys and girls must at least be taught to read
so that they could themselves study Luther's translation of the
Bible into German; to guide them in understanding the Scriptures Luther wrote his two catechisms, one for general use, and
another, longer one for the assistance of teachers and pastors.
The Lutherans were too optimistic in supposing that such
instruction would enable men to understand Scripture correctly and escape the dissensions over conflicting interpretations
which had troubled the old Church for centuries, but from this
new importance attached to the ability to read sprang their
elementary schools. Luther himself, as we have seen, felt his
way somewhat uneasily towards the necessity of general
elementary instruction and Melanchthon's school regulation-
in the *Visitation Books* of 1528 for Saxony made provision for
Latin, and German was excluded though it is possible nevertheless that religious instruction of the youngest boys was in
German, otherwise they could not have understood. But the
school regulations of Württemberg in 1559 made express
reference to 'German Schools', to be set up in the villages and
hamlets, to be free and for the ordinary people, and to give
instruction in reading and writing German, and in religion and
music. Just as education had always been the concern of
the Church and the schoolmaster required the licence of the
bishop, so now the new schools were under the control of the
Lutheran Church and one of its officers was responsible for
licensing the teacher. Saxony, in its later regulations of 1580,

[1] Rein: *Encyk. Handbuch*, II, 55-6 (*Die protestantische Volksschule*).

incorporated the advance made in Württemberg, and in the seventeenth century Saxe-Coburg-Gotha offered an extraordinary example of a comprehensive and closely ordered state system of education. To some extent the Protestant states were continuing the tradition of the German writing and reading schools which cities had created during the later Middle Ages. But the Saxe-Coburg-Gotha regulations, first published in 1642 and several times revised and republished, included also provision for instruction in science, and the state arranged for the supply of text-books, namely, the *German Hornbook and Speller*, and also a German reader, an arithmetic and books covering natural science, religion, and the general behaviour proper to children.[1]

But it was not only in Germany that the Reformation infused a new energy into education. In Switzerland, Zwingli in his *Christian Education of Boys* (1523) had suggested, in addition to the classical languages and instruction in the Scriptures, nature study, music, arithmetic, and physical exercises. Calvin, though born a Frenchman and bred a scholar in the University of Paris, found his life's work in making the city of Geneva a theocratic republic and creating a new, Calvinist form of the Protestant faith. His *Institutes of the Christian Religion* marked him out as a foremost Protestant theologian, and coupled with his work in Geneva puts his name on a level with that of Luther in the history of the Reformation. At the same time his reorganization of the schools in Geneva and its influence on other Protestant countries gives him a place in the history of education. He provided carefully, of course, for religious instruction, but also for the teaching of the French vernacular and arithmetic. At the secondary level the curriculum was, as is to be expected, a classical one. Calvin had taught for a time in Sturm's gymnasium at Strassburg, and the Collège de la Rive he created in Geneva was much influenced by his experience. By 1559 his college was fully organized; it was in two parts. There was a school, *Schola Privata*, divided into seven

[1] See 'Public Instuction in Saxe-Coburg-Gotha', in Barnard's *American Journal of Education*, XX.

classes, and a higher *Schola Publica* giving courses of a university nature. At the time of Calvin's death in 1569 the school itself had 1,200 pupils and the higher school 300.

The curriculum of Calvin's college is worth study for it provides a clear picture of the classical and humanistic training given in the best schools of the day. In Geneva, however, there was rather less attention to Cicero than was generally the case, and also the use of the vernacular was allowed in teaching the youngest boys. Through its seven classes (sub-divided into groups of ten under an older pupil), there was annual promotion, with proper ceremony, starting from the seventh class at the bottom to the first at the top.

The following is the curriculum[1] in outline:

CLASS VII. Pupils learn the letters of the alphabet, and write them to form syllables, using a Latin-French reading book. Reading French and afterwards Latin, from a French-Latin catechism. Practice in writing the letters.

CLASS VI. Declensions and conjugations begun (half-year). Parts of speech learnt in French and Latin. More practice in handwriting. Easy Latin sentences learnt and repeated for practice in conversation.

CLASS V. Parts of speech finished. Elements of syntax. Virgil's *Eclogues* read. First steps in written Latin composition. Latin and French side by side.

CLASS IV. Latin syntax continued. Cicero's *Letters* begun, with composition exercises based on them. Prosody, and reading of Ovid for illustration.
Greek begun: declension and conjugation; elementary construing.

CLASS III. Greek grammar systematically learnt; comparison of the two languages. Cicero's *Letters*, *De Amicitia*, and *De Senectute* to be turned into Greek. Virgil's *Aeneid*, Caesar and Isocrates read.

CLASS II. Emphasis on reading: Livy, Xenophon, Polybius, Herodian, Homer.
Logic begun: propositions, syllogism. To be illustrated from Cicero's speeches.
The Gospels in Greek, once a week.

[1] Translated in W. H. Woodward: *Studies in Education*, pp. 159-60, from Calvin's *Leges Academiae Genevensis*, printed in full in C. Borgeaud: *Hist. de l'Univ. de Genève*.

CLASS I. Logic, systematically from a book such as Melanchthon's; in connection with this the elements of rhetoric, and elocution. Rhetoric as illustrated by Cicero and Demosthenes; Homer and Virgil also analysed for rhetorical purposes. Two original *declamationes* prepared monthly. An Epistle of St. Paul or other apostle in Greek, read once a week.

Calvin's influence in education spread to every place where his religious system penetrated. In France, the Huguenots organized their own elementary schools, secondary colleges, and also several universities. In England, among the Puritans the dominant force was that of Calvin. His was the faith of the Reformed Church in Holland, and later in the New Netherlands in America. At the Synod of Dort, in 1618, the Dutch laid a common responsibility for the Christian instruction of the young on parents, schoolteachers, and ministers. Parents were to instruct children in the faith and strengthen that instruction at family worship, and schools were to be provided not only in cities but also in country places where 'heretofore none have existed'. The combination of religious instruction and elementary education is illuminated by the text-books used, such as the ABC book, the Heidelberg catechism (that of the Reformed Dutch Church), and, for exercises in reading, the Gospels, the Epistles, and the proverbs of Solomon.

When Scotland broke away from Rome in 1560 John Knox, who had spent a period in Geneva with Calvin, produced his *First Book of Discipline* in which he outlined a plan for elementary schools, secondary schools, and universities. Knox favoured compulsion in the matter of school attendance; all must have elementary instruction, and boys of ability, sons of the rich or the poor, must be trained so that their talents could contribute to the public good. Knox's scheme was not carried out entirely but, later, in 1646, legislation was passed by the Scottish parliament 'that there be a Schoole founded, and a Schoole master appointed in every Parish (not already provided)'. The fact that education was closely bound up with their own Presbyterian form of worship, is one reason for the traditional respect in Scotland for education.

The infiltration of Protestantism into Catholic society has already been compared with the similar spread of revolutionary ideas in the modern capitalistic society of the West. If this comparison be admitted, then the Counter-Reformation of Catholicism can be compared with the growth, in the twenties and thirties, of fascism as the violent reaction of the Right against the revolutionary extremism of the Left. The Society of Jesus, the principal weapon of the papacy in its counter-attack on the reformers, was an organized *élite* which struggled for the maintenance of the Catholic order of society; in its creation of a great system of schools it was also a powerful educational influence; and in its origin, it offers an example of one of those struggles within the human soul which transform the individual and alter the course of history. Something happened in the life of one man: as it happened to Paul on the Damascus road, to Francis at Assisi, to Luther gripped by an over-ruling sense of sin. In 1521, only four years after Luther's theses against papal indulgences, a Spanish nobleman, Ignatius of Loyola, was wounded in an obscure war in Navarre. The result of slow recovery and convalescence was that Ignatius abandoned the glory of a soldier's career and became instead a warrior of Christ.

Ignatius first devoted himself to prayer and the austerities of a hermit's life. Gradually he evolved a plan: he would become a priest, gather his followers, and set out for the Holy Land to preach to the Mohammedans. For him the urge of the Crusades still lived. But for the kind of crusade he planned, education was necessary, and Loyola was a knight and no scholar. Back to school he went at the age of thirty-three to learn Latin with the boys of Barcelona; next he studied in the university at Alcala, and finally in Paris, where he took his M.A. in 1534. Meanwhile, living on alms, for he had given his own possessions to the poor, he attracted to him by the force of his personality a group of able men. They included Francis Xavier, afterwards to become an apostle to the Far East, and James Laynez, one of the theologians who was to assist at the Council of Trent which, by its redefinition of Catholic doctrine, after the attacks of the reformers, marked the progress of the Counter-

Reformation. In 1534 at the church of Montmartre in Paris the first Jesuits—eight in number—took their vows of poverty, chastity, and obedience, and in 1540 they received official papal approval. Such were the beginnings of the Jesuit Order.

The Jesuit ideal was the life militant for Christ, its motto *Ad Majorem Dei Gloriam*; its object the salvation of souls—by preaching and works of charity, and by instruction in the Christian religion. The original project of a mission to the Holy Land was dropped, for with the growth of Protestantism there was work in plenty at home awaiting the Jesuits. They provided the pope with just the weapon needed for the struggle against heresy. Organized on military lines and sworn to the strictest obedience, they came under no ecclesiastical power save that of their own officers and of the pope himself. A powerful, organized, international *élite* had been created which was to prove an important factor in the prolonged conflict between Catholics and Protestants.

Just as both Lutherans and Calvinists had soon realized the importance of education, it was not long before Ignatius and the Jesuits made it one of the principal duties of the new order. In an age when the teachings of the Catholic Church were challenged, Ignatius knew that his order must depend for success on enrolling as members priests who had only the best education behind them. Such men were increasingly needed as the conflict with Protestantism developed. Hence the foundation in Catholic territories of schools conducted by the Jesuits, and, as it was thought that a sound education would also be useful to Catholic laymen, boys not destined to the priesthood came to be admitted. Like the Protestants the Catholics used the argument of moulding soft wax: the good of Christian society depended upon the proper education of the young, for they, like soft wax, easily took on the desired form. Because in practice it was difficult to find enough teachers who combined learning with a virtuous example, the Jesuits devoted themselves to the humble but fruitful task of instructing the young.[1]

[1] From a Jesuit letter of 1556 quoted by F. de Dainville: *La Naissance de l'Humanisme Moderne*, p. 37.

The first Jesuit College was opened at Coimbra in Portugal, in 1542; two years later it was opened to lay students. Success was immediate and many other colleges followed, at first in Spain and Italy and later in south Germany; they were established also in France and what is now Belgium, and in the outposts of the Germanic world, in Vienna, Prague, and Posen. These colleges generally offered education of both secondary and university level, and the average college was large. That in Rome had over 2,000 students, Munich had 665. During the seventeenth century Rouen averaged about 2,000; in the same century, La Flèche (near Le Mans) had about 1,700 and the Paris college of Louis-le-Grand between 2,000 and 3,000.[1] It was this great expansion of Jesuit education which helped to make the Order so powerful a Catholic weapon in checking the spread of Protestantism.

The Jesuit plan of education was a systematic one; it was centralized and highly organized and depended also for its success upon the discipline, zeal, and devotion of the highly trained Jesuit Fathers who administered it. The general character of the educational mission of the Jesuits was expressed in the Constitutions of the Order, written by Ignatius himself between 1540 and 1550. The plan was set out fully in the *Ratio Studiorum*, or system of studies, of 1599. It was based upon years of educational experiment: a commission of educational experts had drawn up a provisional scheme, which was tried in practice for some years; it was watched, reported upon, modified, and used again in practice; only then, after this lengthy period of trial and error, was the final scheme set out for universal application throughout the Order. The *Ratio* held the field until its revision in 1832, which admitted an important change. Jesuit Provinces were to be allowed to adapt the school curriculum to the particular needs of the countries in which their schools lay, a change which indicates the influence of nationalism and the growing pressure for the teaching of

---

[1] See the figures for the Paris school in Dupont-Ferrier: *Du Collège de Clermont au Lycée Loius-le-Grand*, III, Appendix F. A figure of 3,000 students is suggested as early as 1570. The majority would be day-boys.

modern subjects. In spite of the fact, however, that the *Ratio* was officially unchanged for over 200 years, which suggests a complete rigidity, modern Jesuit scholars maintain that there was nevertheless a certain development or evolution internally in Jesuit educational methods.[1]

The Jesuit schools were generally founded by some public or private benefactor—a king, noble, bishop, or a city government—who made provision for food and lodging, while the actual conduct of the school was entrusted to the Jesuit Order. The Jesuits gave their services to the school, so that Jesuit education was free education. Colleges might be boarding-schools, day-schools, or a combination of the two. They did not provide elementary instruction, and boys on entering had to be able already to read and write and go into the elementary Latin class. The pupils were boys who were intended for the Jesuit Order and other boys of good family, sometimes sons of the reigning house. The schools provided a curriculum, *studia inferiora*, not very different from that of the great Protestant schools of the day; some of the Jesuit schools provided also higher or university studies, *studia superiora*. Among these higher studies was a course in pedagogy for those members of the Order who were intended for teaching.

Of the subjects taught in the Jesuit schools the most important was, as elsewhere, Latin. That language, since the Jesuits belonged to an international organization, was particularly useful as a means of communication. Greek took a less important place in their curriculum. The study of Latin authors brought in also a certain amount of history and geography. In the teaching of Latin careful attention was given to expression and style as was natural in an educational system which had grown up under the influence of the Renaissance ideal. In addition to the reading of the best Latin prose and poetry, the performance of plays was undertaken as a means both of furthering knowledge and improving eloquence. At the higher, or university, level of studies there was a three-years' course in

---

[1] F. de Dainville: *La Naissance de l'Humanisme Moderne*, p. xvi. See also on this point A. P. Farrell: *Jesuit Code of Liberal Education*, chap. xv.

philosophy followed by four of theology. In these courses the philosophy of Aristotle and the theology of Aquinas were dominant. It was in the higher studies in philosophy that mathematics and science were to be found, and also instruction in medicine and law.

The Jesuits gave attention to hygiene and physical training; they tried to secure good buildings and to make school life cheerful; they lightened the routine of intellectual training by games and sports and by excursions into the countryside. Their school discipline also was lighter than was usual elsewhere, and corporal punishment was made as little use of as possible. In place of fear as an inducement to work the Jesuits used a system of emulation.[1] Special marks, dignities, and privileges were awarded. Class matches were organized in which teams competed against each other for marks. Religious and moral instruction had an important place: both directly by way of lessons and indirectly through the daily mass and the high tone of the school. Each master had to set an example to the boys in his own life and conduct.

The Jesuit was a priest and gave himself entirely to the church: but at the same time he had to be able to hold his own with men of the world and work for the interests of the Church amid the complexities, problems, and intrigues of courts.

The success of the Jesuits was striking. They checked and brought to a halt the advance of Protestantism. As a German Protestant historian has put it: 'By the end of the sixteenth century, little more than fifty years after the beginning of the Order, the training of the Catholic priesthood in Germany was almost entirely in its hands. From the mouth of the Rhine to that of the Vistula the Jesuits held the centre of heresy surrounded with a chain of their colleges, as if by a belt of fortresses.'[2] During the seventeenth and eighteenth centuries, its schools were the best in Europe.

Success, however, made enemies for the Order, and it

[1] For a detailed discussion of this favoured Jesuit method, see Dupont Ferrier, I, 240–52.
[2] F. Paulsen: *Geschichte des gelehrten Unterrichts*, I, 416.

suffered vicissitudes. In 1764 it was expelled from France, in 1773 it was, under Bourbon pressure, suppressed by the pope. The year 1814 saw another pope restore the Order, but having lost its endowments the Jesuits found that they could no longer offer free education. Fees had to be charged, but Jesuit teaching revived. The famous English school of the Jesuits founded at St. Omer in 1592 had a particularly adventurous history: driven thence, as a result of the Order's changes of fortune, to Bruges and then to Liège, it was able in 1794 when penal laws against Catholics were being relaxed in England to find its final home on a Catholic gentleman's estate in Lancashire, and to-day Stonyhurst College—with the modern subjects added to its curriculum—has become one of the great public schools.

Tributes to the influence of Jesuit education have been many, from Protestants as well as Catholics. Among the famous men educated in Jesuit schools were Descartes and Voltaire. Descartes remembered his own schooldays at the Jesuit College of La Flèche and his letters give the credit to his old schoolmasters for 'the little knowledge I have of good letters'.[1] When advising a correspondent who had inquired about sending his son to school, Descartes answered: 'I must do my masters this honour—to say I think there is no place in the world where they teach better than at La Flèche.'[2] And in England a little earlier Francis Bacon had praised the Jesuits for the importance they attached to schools and schoolmasters, for the latter, then as often since, were popularly regarded as pedants and 'scorned upon theatres, as the ape of tyranny'. But the 'excellent part of ancient discipline', wrote Bacon, 'hath been in some sort revived of late times by the colleges of the Jesuits; of whom, although in regard of their superstition I may say "the better, the worse", yet in regard of this, and some other points concerning human learning and moral matters, I may say . . . "they are so good that I wish they were on our side".'[3]

[1] *Œuvres* (Adam and Tannery), I, 383.
[2] *Ibid.*, II, 378.   [3] *Advancement of Learning*, Book I.

CHAPTER X

TUDOR AND STUART SCHOOLBOYS

I N England as elsewhere the period of the Reformation was one of crisis for the schools. Closely bound up as they were with the old Church they were necessarily affected by any change in its position. The chantry priests, in addition to saying prayers for the founder's soul, often kept schools. But now prayers for the dead were held to be superstitious, and the Chantries Acts of Henry VIII and Edward VI suppressed the chantries and placed their endowments in the king's hands. Although the chantry and guild schools were generally compensated, this took the form of fixed payments which fell in value as the currency of the time depreciated. Their landed endowments, often of great potential value, were confiscated. Leach[1] made a careful study of the work of the chantry commissions and of the certificates and continuance warrants which survive. Of just over two hundred schools, 132 still existed when he wrote in 1896, although nineteen of those had fallen to the level of elementary schools. The others had disappeared. In addition, Leach found mention of forty-five elementary schools, that is of schools variously described as ABC, reading, writing, and song schools, and with the disappearance of the chantry priests elementary instruction also suffered. Many of the schools existing at the time of the Reformation were already of old foundation. 'As for poor Edward VI, meaning thereby the ruling councillors of his day, he cannot any longer be called the founder of our national system of secondary education. But he, or they, can at least claim the distinction of having had

[1] A. F. Leach: *English Schools at the Reformation*.

a unique opportunity of reorganizing the whole educational system of a nation from top to bottom, without cost to the nation, and of having thrown it away.'[1]

Such was the opinion of Leach, and in this Professor Trevelyan echoes Leach. 'Another great chance had been missed', wrote the Master of Trinity. 'If all, or even half, the endowments of masses for the dead had been devoted to schools, and if at the same time those schools had been left with their old landed property, England would soon have had the best secondary education in the world, and the whole history of England and of the world might have been changed for the better.'[2] Whether any possible reorganization of English education at this time could have had such great results may, nevertheless, be doubted. The curriculum of the grammar schools was an education in Latin for a narrow range of professions, and it is difficult to believe that the mere multiplication of Latin grammar schools could have been so far-reaching in its results. And in any case, as Professor Trevelyan himself points out, 'Members of the rising class of gentry and individual lawyers, merchants and yeoman did much by private beneficence to retrieve the educational position. In Elizabeth's reign, Camden notices newly founded schools at Uppingham, Oakham and other towns; the yeoman, John Lyon, founded a free grammar school for boys at Harrow. . . . The grammar school at Hawkshead, where the poet Wordsworth was educated, had been founded in the reign of Elizabeth by Archbishop Sandys.'[3] From that reign date also the foundation of Westminster, Merchant Taylors', and Rugby. Repton was founded in 1557, and Shrewsbury and Christ's Hospital originated in 1552, in Edward's reign. Though the name of Edward VI was given to a number of schools they were not new foundations but simply old schools which in the general grab for chantry lands had been allowed to survive. But Christ's Hospital was a foundation of Edward VI. Founded on a monastic site and intended at first as a foundling hospital, it became the 'bluecoat school'. Another school afterwards

[1] *Ibid.*, p. 122.   [2] G. M. Trevelyan: *English Social History*, p. 114.
[3] *English Social History*, p. 115.

famous, Charterhouse, dates from the reign of James I, being founded in 1612. Thus though some of the older schools decayed, new foundations appeared to take their place.

So far as control and character went the Reformation had little effect on the schools. The new Church of England took over the control of education which the old Church had exercised. But whereas in the old days the ultimate power behind the Church was the pope, now it was the secular sovereign. The Act of Supremacy of 1534 had made the king 'the supreme head in earth of the Church of England'. Thus the king's government might prescribe a text-book or exhort the archbishop to a more careful administration of his control over education. In 1540 Henry VIII, and later Edward VI and Elizabeth, ordered the use in schools of Lily's Latin Grammar. The object was to prescribe one system and set of rules in place of the many grammars in use. Lily acquired a position of authority and replaced Donatus, the standard medieval text-book. In 1580 the Queen's council wrote to the archbishop: 'For as much as a great deal of the corruption in religion grown throughout the realm, proceedeth of lewd schoolmasters . . . it is thought meet for redress thereof, that you cause all such schoolmasters as have charge of children, to be by the Bishop of the diocese, or such as he shall appoint, examined touching their religion: and if they shall be found corrupt and unworthy, to be displaced . . . and fit and sound persons placed in their rooms.'[1] Thus the principle was maintained that all schoolmasters must be licensed by the bishop. After the restoration of Charles II schoolmasters were subjected to new restrictions by the Clarendon Code of legislation against nonconformists. The Act of Uniformity of 1662 enjoined on all clergy and schoolmasters a declaration that it was unlawful to bear arms against the king and that they conformed to the Church of England, and fixed terms of imprisonment for anyone teaching before he had obtained the bishop's licence.

Such restrictions were, however, external and the character

[1] Quoted by A. M. Stowe: *English Grammar Schools in the Reign of Queen Elizabeth*, p. 178.

of the schools and their curriculum did not radically change.
The hard grind at Latin grammar continued to be the daily lot
of the schoolboy, in spite of the enthusiasm and enlightenment
of the Renaissance and the serious purpose of the Reformation.
With Shakespeare's

> whining schoolboy, with his satchel
> And shining morning face, creeping like snail
> Unwillingly to school.

we seem to hear for almost the first time a voice from outside
the small, exclusive circle of pedants—the voice of the boy
himself. Perhaps Shakespeare recalled the weary hours spent
in pouring over his Lily in the grammar school at Stratford-
on-Avon. Let us see, so far as it is still possible to do so, how
some of the great figures of the period spent their boyhood.

Sir Thomas More, humanist and lawyer, Lord Chancellor
and friend of Erasmus, author of *Utopia* and defender of the
right of conscience against Henry VIII, was born in 1478 in
Edward IV's time and was probably at school during the
reign of Richard III and certainly during the first years of
Henry VII. His father's will, proved in 1530, provided for
prayers for the soul of Edward IV. More's education, then, took
place in a London which was still medieval. His father was
officer in charge of the servants at Lincoln's Inn and later a
judge, and the boy Thomas was 'brought up in the Latin
tongue at St. Antony's', then an important school in Thread-
needle Street, which had been endowed by Henry VI though
it was destined, after Colet's foundation of St. Paul's, to decay.
More learnt his Latin and to dispute in Latin, it seems, much as
boys had done for centuries, as they had done for example in
Becket's day. The lack of detailed information about the early
life of almost every medieval figure also obscures the education
of Thomas More. But at a somewhat later date Stowe's *Survey
of London*, published in 1603, mentions St. Antony's School as
sending up the best scholars to the schoolboys' public debates.
'The arguing of the schoolboys about the principles of Grammar hath been continued even till our time', wrote Stowe.
'For I myself in my youth have yearly seen, on the eve of St.

Bartholomew the Apostle, the scholars of divers Grammar schools repair unto the churchyard of St. Bartholomew, the Priory, in Smithfield, where, upon a bank boarded about under a tree, some one scholar hath stepped up, and there hath apposed and answered, till he were by some better scholar overcome and put down.' Stowe also noticed that, although the public disputes at St. Bartholomew's were discontinued after the dissolution of the monasteries, boys of rival schools would still, on meeting in the streets, challenge each other to disputation. This would lead 'to questions in grammar, they usually fall from words to blows, with their satchels full of books, many times in great heaps, that they troubled the streets and passengers, so that finally they were restrained with the decay of St. Antony's School'.

More's schooling must have been in one of those bare, crowded schoolrooms where the boys sat around the master while the latter, before the days of printed books, first dictated the Latin passage which he went on to construe and comment upon. It was a slow and laborious process. The 'satchels full of books', which attracted Stowe's attention in the streets of London of a later generation, were indicative of the great change as a result of the invention of printing which More must have seen coming about in his own lifetime. Before there was variety of books and before the confusion of the many subjects in the modern curriculum, the boy had to concentrate on the one, central subject. He might at least achieve the satisfaction of a certain mastery in that. The process of learning, however, involved steady application and patient attention which are but seldom agreeable to the young. The Tudor schoolboy—like schoolboys before him and after—was induced to make the effort by fear of the rod or birch, and kept at the task by its frequent use. A little later than More's time a Winchester schoolboy complained that, after he had risen at five o'clock in the morning and attended prayers at six, he devoted himself to writing Latin verse 'chained as closely to his desk as Prometheus to the crag on Caucasus.' In an age when the 'best schoolmaster' was held to be 'the greatest beater' it is unlikely that More escaped unscathed. As a day-boy at a London school More had the added temptation to lie in bed in the mornings though tormented at the same time by fear of the inevitable beating. More in one passage of his works refers by way of simile to a mother's treatment of her child: 'When the little boy will not rise in time for her, but lie still abed and slugg, and when he is up, weepeth because he hath lien so long, fearing to be beaten at school for his late coming thither, she telleth him then that it is but early days, and he shall come time enough, and biddeth him, "Go, good son, I warrant thee, I have sent to thy master myself, take thy bread and butter with thee, thou shalt not be beaten at all." And thus, so she may send him merry forth at the door that he weep not in her sight at home, she studieth not much upon the matter, though he be taken tardy and beaten when he cometh to school.'

The medieval custom of sending a child to live, as part of its education, in a great household was still common, and More at about the age of twelve was received into the household of John Morton, then Archbishop of Canterbury, Lord Chancellor, and Henry VII's chief adviser. In the house of this shrewd, experienced but kindly ecclesiastic and statesman More learnt his court manners. His modern biographer finds in More no trace of the knight of an earlier age. 'But though without any touch of the "fair mien" of chivalry, More is always well bred and self-possessed.'[1] He represents not the old feudal class, but the new men of brain but humble birth, lawyers, merchants, officials, and the rest. In spite, however, of humble birth More was in fact as well, or better, brought up as men of the old aristocracy, and his natural gifts and education made him pre-eminent among them.

More was sent to Oxford. He was then about the age of fourteen and he spent two years at the university. For us there is a magic charm about medieval Oxford springing from the beauty of college buildings which have survived into so different an age. But the life of the medieval student was hard enough; poverty ever dogged his path. Early rising, long hours

[1] R. W. Chambers: *Thomas More*, p. 63.

of study, and simple fare were his lot. Plain living induced concentration on the work in hand, and in later life More praised
his father's strictness which had made it impossible for the
young student to learn the meaning of extravagance or easy
living. With no money to spend, he had nothing to think about
except his studies. More was probably at Canterbury College—
which has since disappeared, part of Christ Church to-day
occupying its site. Of his actual instruction in Greek and Latin,
in which tongues his early biographers say he was 'sufficiently
instructed', we know nothing. Did, perhaps, the first Oxford
teacher of Greek, Grocyn, teach the youthful More? From
More himself, however, it appears that a serious study of
Greek came later when he had left Oxford.

After Oxford came the law in London—first at New Inn,
now altogether disappeared, then at Lincoln's Inn, where the
great hall of More's day still stands. Indeed for the young man
of ambition London and the law—rather than the scholastic
training of Oxford and Cambridge—was the opening to a
successful career. For such men the English capital had then no
other university than the Inns of Court, which provided the
training suitable for a man of affairs and turned out barrister
and serjeant as the universities turned out bachelor and master.
Now More lived well in comparison with his Oxford standard,
and was able to mix with the best society of his day. When More
was twenty-one, in 1499, Erasmus visited England and a lasting friendship began. Erasmus later described in a letter how
More had taken him, early in that friendship, to visit the future
Henry VIII—then nine years old—in the great hall of Eltham
Palace, standing still and lately used as the Army's School of
Education. More's studies were still to continue, especially in
Greek, but his education had already sufficed to lay the
foundations. More was about ten years younger than Erasmus,
yet More could take his place with the man who was becoming
Europe's foremost scholar. English education in those days must
have been little behind that of the Continental countries, for
Erasmus paid great tribute to its results in the English scholars
whom he knew. In a letter of 1499 Erasmus tells how 'I have met

with such kindness and so much learning, not hackneyed and trivial, but deep, exact, ancient, Latin and Greek, that I am not hankering so much after Italy, except simply to see it. When I listen to Colet, I seem to hear Plato himself. Who does not wonder at Grocyn's grasp of all knowledge? What is more keen and more profound that the judgment of Linacre? Did nature ever produce anything sweeter than the genius of Thomas More? . . . It is marvellous how plentiful and widespread is the harvest of ancient learning which is flourishing in this country.'

Later on when More married and became head of a family, his character and attainments made its spiritual life a thing of great beauty. Of the assembled family Holbein left a pleasing and instructive drawing, and the scholar-statesman's household Erasmus described as Plato's Academy on a Christian footing. The educational influence must indeed have been great both over members of the family and over servants and retainers. Nightly prayer there was and mass each morning and, of course, attendance at church on Sundays and feast days. More himself gave much of the night and early morning hours to study or devotion, and tried as a rule so to spend his Fridays. Study, music, gardening were encouraged in the household. When on missions abroad More wrote to his children in Latin, in prose or verse. And not only his son but also his daughters were carefully educated by tutors at home. They learnt Latin and Greek, and studied also philosophy and theology, mathematics and astronomy. More's success in educating his daughters convinced Erasmus of the value of giving women higher education. Nor were More's daughters blue-stockings: all, in fact, married.

What we know of More's household gives the pleasantest impression of what the educational effect can be of life in the Christian family. Nor, when he died the martyrs' death and royal disfavour set in for those who had been closest to him, was he forgotten. Daughters, son, and sons-in-law suffered for their loyalty to the head of the family, and More's life and death were for them an abiding example.

In the last year of the sixteenth century was born the greatest Englishman of the next. A Welshman on his father's side,
Oliver Cromwell ultimately owed both name and fortune to
Henry VIII's minister, Thomas Cromwell, the enemy of More
and the hammer of the monks. The confiscated wealth of the
monasteries went to the making of many English families, and
of one of these Oliver was a member. 'I was', he said, 'by birth
a gentleman living neither in any considerable height nor yet
in obscurity.' His father, Robert Cromwell, inherited an estate
at Huntingdon, was a member of parliament and a justice of
the peace for the county. The kind of education he gave his
son can be regarded as typical for boys of that class. 'The years
of Cromwell's youth and early manhood, up to his twenty-
ninth year when he first entered public life, have no interest to
general history: they have the highest particular interest in the
question how such a man came to be.' But unfortunately, 'his
worshippers, who have collected every scrap of information and
tradition available, have discovered very little about him'.[1]
Once more the investigator of the early training of a great man
must perforce be content with the merest outline.

Oliver went to the grammar school in Huntingdon, then
housed in a solid stone building which dated from Norman
times. Here the schoolmaster, Dr. Thomas Beard, was a puritan
churchman and much taken up with his thesis that the pope
was antichrist. He had a great influence on Cromwell, already
by his family connected with puritanism, and influence and
friendship endured later in life. Beard was a man of some learning and the curriculum which Oliver followed was doubtless a
study of Latin, the common schooling of his time. But a stronger
educational factor in the life of the young Cromwell must have
been the Bible—the effect of which can be traced in his whole
life. The new English Bible, the Authorized Version, 'would
have reached the household at Huntingdon when he was between thirteen and fourteen; he had it in his ears week by week
and most probably daily, year after year, all through his early
manhood. The influence was so violent that it produced in him

[1] Hilaire Belloc: *Cromwell*, pp. 51-2.

169

(as in thousands of his contemporaries and scores of his social equals) that special vocabulary which seems to us grotesque but which soon became to them native. The strange names of half-savage Orientals, the metaphors drawn from the climate of Syria or the life of the desert, the characters of little highland tribes in Syria—three thousand miles away from England in distance, three thousand years in time—became in that group so thoroughly adopted that to this day men think of them as English. As for Oliver, the thing possessed him and spoke through his lips his whole life long.'[1]

When he was seventeen, Cromwell went to Cambridge, to Sidney Sussex College, where his portrait now hangs in hall. The college had been founded in 1598, the year before Cromwell's birth, and there the young man was once more in an atmosphere of puritanism of which the college was regarded by Laud as a nursery. The master of the college in Cromwell's time was a learned but stern clergyman, who made his scholars produce careful accounts of the sermons and, if they offended, had them whipped in hall.[2] Of Cromwell's life at the university, scarcely anything is known. He left without a degree. Some of his Latin he must have retained, even if he spoke it 'very viciously and scantily' as Burnet reported, for he was said when Protector to have conversed in Latin with a Dutch ambassador. His advice to his son Richard may throw light on his own early training: 'Read a little history; study the Mathematics and cosmography. These are good with subordination to the things of God. These fit for public services for which a man is born.' A special recommendation he gave to the *History of the World* by Sir Walter Raleigh, whose execution, as Carlyle fancied, Cromwell might have witnessed while a law student in London. A tradition also attached to the young Oliver as a lover of games and field sports.

A little after his time at Cambridge Cromwell was at his law studies in London. He is said to have been, like More, at Lincoln's Inn. Here we can picture him acquiring some of the practical knowledge of affairs necessary to a gentleman who

[1] *Ibid.*, pp. 60–1.   [2] Firth: *Oliver Cromwell*, p. 6.

must manage his estates, take a part in local government, and also, perhaps, serve in parliament. Cromwell, however, was not long engaged in these studies for he married in 1620 and settled down at Huntingdon to farm his lands. For the tasks of a country gentleman his education was doubtless adequate; many have done well with less. For the tasks of generalship and statesmanship what education is requisite none can say. Of education in the formal sense of advanced study in school and university, some of the world's dominant figures have had least: Lloyd George and Hitler are, in our own time, outstanding examples.

If the account we can give of Cromwell's education is slender, can we perhaps say more of that of Milton? Like More, Milton was a scholar. Immortal through his English poetry, Milton in his own day was of importance as a Latin writer, puritan pamphleteer, and secretary for foreign tongues to the Commonwealth. His education, clearly, had been long and careful, and an American scholar has recently published a volume entitled *John Milton at St. Paul's School*. Leach said that: 'Almost everything to do with Milton's schooldays depends not on documentary evidence, not even on "oral tradition", but on inference and conjecture.' To a large extent this is true but a lot is known about the English grammar schools in general, and by a careful study of this knowledge (as well as of the much scantier material relating specifically to Milton) Professor Clark has been able to infer the kind of education Milton must, in fact, have had.[1]

Born in 1608, it is not certain in what year he entered St. Paul's, but it was perhaps in 1615 at the age of seven. He was studious from his early boyhood, and not strong physically. He perhaps learnt to read and write at home. He speaks himself of

[1] D. L. Clark: *John Milton at St. Paul's School* (1948). A. F. Leach wrote forty years earlier. See 'Milton as Schoolboy and Schoolmaster' in *Proceedings of the Royal Academy*, III, 296. A storehouse of information on the education of the period is Foster Watson: *The English Grammar Schools to 1660: their Curriculum in Practice* (1908). An American, T. W. Baldwin, has exercised great industry in examining the question of the kind of education Shakespeare must have had. See his two works, *William Shakespeare's Petty School* (1943) and *William Shakespeare's Small Latine and Lesse Greeke* (2 vols., 1944).

having had private masters later on as well as of attending the grammar school. His father, a London scrivener who had made money, intended him for learning and the Church. Humane letters, Milton said himself, 'I seized upon so eagerly that from my twelfth year I hardly ever left my nocturnal studies for bed before midnight, which was the first cause of the ruin of my eyes, to whose natural weakness were added frequent head-aches. Since all this did not retard my ardour for learning, he [my father] caused me to be instructed daily at the grammar school and under other masters at home. When I was thus instructed in various languages and had acquired no small taste for the sweetness of philosophy, he sent me to Cambridge, one of our two colleges. There, remote from all shame, with the approbation of all good men, I followed for seven years the usual course of studies in the arts and sciences, until I obtained, cum laude, the degree of master, as it is called.'[1] There, in a few words, is Milton's own account of his education; it indicates succinctly the framework of formal education common enough at the time, within which the individual genius, when present in the pupil, would develop. His natural love of letters at an early age suggests the presence of that genius which formal education could, and did, further. Milton also suggests a reason for his later blindness which his enemies attributed to divine judgement on his support for the king's execution. His 'nocturnal studies' have caught the fancy of his biographers from John Aubrey in the seventeenth century to E. M. W. Tillyard in the twentieth. And Aubrey, who gained his information from Milton's brother and others close to him, adds in his notes of Milton: 'He went to schoole to old Mr. Gill at Paules schoole' and says of him that, at ten years of age, he was already a poet.[2]

Gil followed the more famous teacher, Mulcaster, as High Master of St. Paul's. Although Milton does not refer to him anywhere by name he may nevertheless have influenced the young poet by the stress he put on the value of native English.

[1] Translated from the Latin of Milton by Clark, p. 23.
[2] In *Early Lives of Milton* (ed. Helen Darbishire), p. 2.

Gil was, of course, like every scholar of the day, primarily a good Latinist, and Milton's studies at school and at home made him a master of languages, both ancient and modern. He thanks his father for the expense undertaken on his account whereby 'there were revealed to me the eloquence of the language of Romulus and the graces of Latin, and also the sonorous vocabulary developed by the oratorical Greeks, a vocabulary that fitted the mouth of Jove'. Of his father, Milton continues, 'you urged me to add the beauties of which the French language is so proud, and the speech that with degenerate lips testifying by his words to the wars of the barbarians the Italian of to-day pours forth, and the mysteries uttered by the prophets of Palestine'.[1] But it was, after all, in English not Latin that Milton was to write his greatest poetry, and Gil, a lover in especial of Spenser's *Faerie Queene*, had urged in Latin (!) the claims of the English tongue. Turned into English, his exhortation runs— 'O you English! You, I say, I implore by that blood of your fathers which beats in your veins, retain, retain what still remains of your native speech. . . . Or will you make your own language a province of Rome, whose Roman arms your ancestors disdained!'[2] And Milton himself, at the age of nineteen, broke out in English:

> Hail native Language, that by sinews weak
> Didst move my first endeavouring tongue to speak.

Milton was speaking at a university function in Cambridge. After first using Latin, he had turned to English verse. He went on to express what he already felt—his own destiny as poet in the English tongue:

> Yet I had rather, if I were to chuse,
> Thy service in some graver subject use.[3]

[1] From the Latin poem *Ad Patrem* (translation in *The Latin Poems of John Milton*, ed. W. MacKellar).

[2] Translated by Clark, p. 72, from A. Gil's *Logonomia Anglica*, a book written for foreigners understanding Latin and wishing to learn English.

[3] 'Lines at a Vacation Exercise' in *Milton—Private Correspondence and Academic Exercises* (translated by Phyllis Tillyard), pp. 101-2.

To picture the boy Milton at St. Paul's School we must first rid ourselves of any impression we may have of the prosaic, modern pile of red brick in Hammersmith. The school which Colet founded, or refounded, and which Milton attended, occupied a stone house built by Colet at the east end of St. Paul's Cathedral. This, of course, was the old St. Paul's: cathedral, school building, and the Milton family dwelling in Bread Street, everything which Milton knew as he walked daily to school for seven in the morning and again for one in the afternoon, vanished for ever in the Great Fire of 1666. Perhaps there lingers in *Il Penseroso* a boyhood memory of—

> the high embowéd roof,
> With antique pillars massy proof,
> And storied windows richly dight,
> Casting a dim religious light.

Eight hours a day—from seven to eleven and from one to five—were spent at school. Of the schoolroom a picture can be made with the help of an account written by Erasmus nearly a hundred years before Milton's time and the 1720 edition of Stowe's *London* edited by John Strype, who was himself at St. Paul's between 1657 and 1661. It was a large room to house 153 boys, in eight classes, arranged in benches along the walls; there were in addition to the high master, two assistant masters. Erasmus spoke of the occasional use of a curtain to divide the schoolroom into sections, one for religious instruction, another for those taught by the under-master, a third for those taught by the high master, and the fourth a chapel. It was common usage in the past to have one great room or hall for the teaching of a school, difficult as it must have been, and the young Milton spent the six or so years of his schooling in such a room. To this school Milton and his fellow Londoners went daily for it was a day-school, and their schooling was free. Colet's endowment which he had placed in the care of the Mercers' Company covered the salaries of the teachers.

Good religion and morals were, in addition to good letters, essential aims of Colet's school, and Lily, the first high master, set down a code of manners, *Carmen de Moribus*, afterwards

always printed in copies of the Lily Latin Grammar and therefore an exhortation to schoolboys everywhere.

In the edition of 1638 construed by William Haine English
follows Latin as a means to the pupils' instruction:

'Monita Pedagogica *Scoolmasters precepts*, seu *or* carmen *a
treatise in verse*, Guilielmi Lilli *of William Lilly*, ad discipulos
suos *to his schollers* de moribus *concerning manners*.

Puer *little youth* qui *which* es mihi discipulus *art my scholler*
. . . concipe *conceive well* haec dicta *these sayings* animo tuo
in thy mind' and so on throughout.

'Betime in the morning leave thy bed, shake off sweet sleep.
Humbly go into the church, and worship God. But first of all
let thy face be washed and thy hands: let thy garments be clean,
and thy hair combed. Be thou there avoiding idleness when my
school shall call thee. . . . Let a penknife, quills, ink, paper,
books be implements always ready for thy studies. If I shall
propose to thee anything, thou shalt write it. . . . But thou shalt
not commit thy Latins or verses to loose papers which it is meet
to have written in books. Oftentimes repeat to thyself things
read, and meditate . . . he who asketh many questions, shall
observe my precepts. He that doubteth of nothing getteth
thereby no good. . . . And be thou attentive. . . . Take pains
and the glory of thy labour is obtained. . . . Also there is an order
always to be kept in speech, lest too much babbling offend me
. . . to speak very eloquently in thy speech, see that thou learn-
est the most famous writings of ancient men . . . sometimes
Virgil . . . sometimes Terence . . . sometimes Cicero. Whom
he that hath not learned hath seen nothing but dreams and
striveth to live in great ignorance.' Then Lily warns his pupils
against idlers, triflers, boys who with hands or feet disturb
others, and boys who boast or use unsavoury language. 'Thou
shalt give or sell nothing: thou shalt change or buy nothing
. . . leave money, the enticement to evil, to others. . . . Let noise,
battling, scoffing, lies, thefts, scornful laughter be far from you,
and fighting far off. Thou shalt speak nothing at all which is
filthy or not honest. . . . Account it horrible wickedness to give
evil words to anyone, or to swear by the sacred titles of Almighty

God. To conclude thou shalt keep all thy things and books and thou shalt bear them with thee as often as both thou goest and returnest.'[1]

By reason of his serious nature the young Milton, we may suppose, observed these precepts carefully. But the schooling of his day was fortified by a theory of rewards and punishments which had its rigorous ways of dealing with the lazy or mischievous youngster. The good were to be encouraged 'first with words of praising them for their well doing', then 'with rewards'. But those who did amiss were to be 'reformed and corrected by admonition, rebuking and punishing, according to the quality of the fault'. If possible the conscience was to be touched: 'if this will not serve . . . add also punishment, sometimes with the rod, which according to Solomon's saying, driveth away foolishness, that is tied to the child's heart, and maketh him wise and learned: sometimes punishment, by restraining that liberty of recreation, which otherwise should have been granted, and sometimes by service of drudgery, as may be the sweeping of the School, and etc. . . . But if any be so incorrigible, that neither the sweet rewards of virtue can lead him, nor the bitter correction of vice draw him to amend, let him be cut off from the School.'[2] So his evil example could be prevented from infecting his fellows.

What was the actual course of study Milton followed at St. Paul's? It is possible, as Professor Clark shows, to make a very reasonable reconstruction. The earliest St. Paul's curriculum dates from about fifty years after Milton's time. The curricula of other schools can be drawn upon, and Charles Hoole wrote, about 1637, a full account of the system at the grammar school in Rotherham which, he said, 'is the same that most schoolmasters yet use'. At St. Paul's, as at many of the other grammar schools, the first four classes or 'lower school' covered Latin grammar, conversation, the easier authors, and written exercises in Latin; the 'upper school', taught by the headmaster,

---

[1] *Lily's Rules Construed* (edition of 1638—*Carmen de Moribus* at the end of the book).

[2] William Kempe: *Education of Children in Learning* (1588).

went on to Greek, Latin poetry, and a certain amount of Hebrew. Before lessons started, there was each morning at seven o'clock a chapter read from the Bible and set prayers in Latin. Written exercises and themes were done throughout the course and the boys made use of certain text-books, of which in Latin Lily's Grammar had been prescribed by the king.

Milton's course of study[1] must have been broadly as follows:

CLASS I. Latin Grammar (Lily)—boys memorized rules. Read *Sententiae Pueriles* (simple moral maxims in Latin and English) and Lily's *Carmen de Moribus* (code of school behaviour).

CLASS II. Latin Grammar. Read Cato's *Disticha Moralia* (sometimes called *Disticha de Moribus*). Easy Latin, but the moral maxims were really more suited for adults. A very generally used text-book for centuries; was published by Caxton in 1483. The work was put together about the third or fourth century, and was wrongly attributed to Cato the elder. Aesop's *Fables* (in Latin).

CLASS III. Latin Grammar. Read Erasmus's *Colloquies* (amusing dialogues) and Terence's *Comedies*, for colloquial Latin, and Ovid's *De Tristibus*, to begin poetry.

CLASS IV. Latin Grammar. Read Ovid's *Epistles* and *Metamorphoses*; perhaps other elegiac poets; Caesar; perhaps Justin (a summary of ancient Macedonian history).

CLASS V. Begin Greek Grammar. Continue Latin Grammar. Read Sallust (for history) and begin Virgil's *Bucolics*.

CLASS VI. Greek Grammar. Greek Testament. Begin Cicero (possibly *Letters* and *Offices*). Continue Virgil. Perhaps begin Martial.

CLASS VII. Greek Grammar. Read minor Greek poets (perhaps selection from Hesiod, Theognis, Pindar, and Theocritus) and Cicero's *Speeches*, and Horace.

CLASS VIII. Hebrew Grammar. Psalms. Read Homer, Euripides, Isocrates, (perhaps Demosthenes), Persius, Juvenal. (Perhaps Dionysius for history, and Aratus).

[1] This is based on the 'Conjectured Curriculum of St. Paul's School' in Clark, p. 121. Whether Milton worked through all eight classes or not is unknown as his date of entry to school is uncertain. F. Clark, pp. 26–8, and Tillyard: *Milton*, p. 7.

Such then was Milton's course of study. He learnt to imitate the best classical authors and, with the help of rhetorical rules, to express himself in writing and speech. He was one of the choice examples of what the humanistic school could do, and he much preferred its training to the surviving scholasticism he found at Cambridge when a student at Christ's College. His education was not different in any important respect from that to be obtained at the great Protestant or Jesuit schools on the Continent or at the good grammar schools in England. The classical languages were dominant in the curriculum; the centuries-old position of Latin was still unshaken. Milton indeed, in his *Tractate of Education*, suggests that boys should read widely, in ancient authors, on mathematics, natural philosophy, and practical subjects like agriculture, fortification, and navigation, but the overpowering emphasis in the schools was still upon language. For signs of coming change we must look elsewhere.

Milton himself, while at the university, had criticized the system of barren disputation which still went on under the name of philosophy. To gain his degree the student had to perform certain oratorical exercises both in college and in the public examination schools—he had to defend or attack certain theses often of an abstract and unreal nature. Thus we find Milton beginning one such thesis, in Latin, that 'In the destruction of any substance there can be no resolution into first matter', with the words 'This is not the place in which to enquire too nicely whether Error escaped from Pandora's box or from the depths of the Styx. . . . This much, however, is clear . . . he has grown to such portentous size that I believe Truth itself to be menaced by him.' Against such futilities Milton delivered a spirited 'Attack on the Scholastic Philosophy'. He condemned 'the crabbed arguments of wiseacres', the 'petty disputations of sour old men'. 'These studies', he declared, 'are as fruitless as they are joyless, and can add nothing whatever to true knowledge. . . . Between them all the student hesitates, as at a cross-roads, in doubt whether to turn or what direction to choose, and unable to make any decision . . . at last he reaches such a pitch

178

of madness as to believe himself utterly blind when in fact there is nothing for him to see . . . all these problems at which you have been working in such torment and anxiety have no existence in reality at all, but like unreal ghosts and phantoms without substance obsess minds already disordered and empty of all true wisdom.'

He went on to suggest an alternative: 'How much better were it, gentlemen, . . . to let your eyes wander as it were over all the lands depicted on the map . . . then to spy out the customs of mankind and those states which are well-ordered; next to seek out and explore the nature of all living creatures, and after that to turn your attention to the secret virtues of stones and herbs.'[1] Fancy, perhaps, but a fancy which would eventually materialize in a new education. Milton was, in effect, suggesting history and geography and natural science; he went on to press the study of astronomy and of time, and also to hint at the study of the mind itself. Although he suggests new subjects at the university, he still doubtless thought, like Erasmus, that all knowledge worth knowing was to be found in the ancient writers. As instructor he named Aristotle, 'who is already your delight'. Was Milton looking backwards or forwards? Whatever the answer, he was certainly influenced to some extent by the novel ideas of Francis Bacon, whom somewhere he described as among 'the greatest and sublimest wits in sundry ages'. And Bacon was feeling his way to a new conception of education.

[1] *Milton—Private Correspondence and Academic Exercises* (translated by Phyllis Tillyard), pp. 67–73.

CHAPTER XI

THE BEGINNINGS OF EDUCATIONAL REFORM: THE ACADEMIES

FRANCIS BACON understood, perhaps better than any man, both the weakness of humanistic education and the vanity of the scholasticism which had preceded it. He said clearly and distinctly, three and a half centuries ago, what writers on education by the score have repeated after him *ad nauseam.* He points out two 'distempers of learning': the emptiness of mere words and style, and the folly of mere theory unrelated to material reality. He finds with unerring aim the Achilles' heel of Renaissance and Reformation scholarship. In his *Advancement of Learning* he writes:

'These four causes concurring, the admiration of ancient authors, the hate of the schoolmen, the exact study of languages, and the efficacy of preaching, did bring in an affectionate study of eloquence and copy of speech, which then began to flourish. This grew speedily to an excess; for men began to hunt more after words than matter; and more after the choiceness of the phrase, and the round and clean composition of the sentence, and the sweet falling of the clauses, and the varying and illustration of their works with tropes and figures, than after the weight of the matter, worth of subject, soundness of argument, life of invention, or depth of judgment. . . . Then did Sturm spend such infinite and curious pains upon Cicero the orator and Hermogenes the rhetorician, besides his own books of periods and imitation and the like. Then did Car of Cambridge, and Ascham, with their lectures and writings, almost deify Cicero and Demosthenes, and allure all young men that

were studious unto that delicate and polished kind of learning.
. . . Then grew the learning of the schoolmen to be utterly
despised as barbarous. In sum, the whole inclination and bent
of these times was rather towards copy [i.e., imitation] than
weight.

'Here therefore the first distemper of learning, when men
study words and not matter; whereof though I have represented an example of late time, yet it hath been and will be
secundum majus et minus in all time. . . .

'But yet notwithstanding it is a thing not hastily to be
condemned, to clothe and adorn the obscurity even of philosophy itself with sensible and plausible elocution. . . . But the
excess of this is so justly contemptible . . . And thus much of the
first disease or distemper of learning.

'The second, which followeth, is in nature worse than the
former; for as substance of matter is better than beauty of
words, so contrarywise vain matter is worse than vain words.
. . . This kind of degenerate learning did chiefly reign amongst
the schoolmen; who having sharp and strong wits, and abun-
dance of leisure, and small variety of reading; but their wits
being shut up in the cells of a few authors (chiefly Aristotle their
dictator) as their persons were shut up in the cells of monasteries and colleges; and knowing little history, either of nature
or time; did out of no great quantity of matter, and infinite
agitation of wit, spin out unto us those laborious webs of learning which are extant in their books. For the wit and mind of
man, if it work upon matter, which is the contemplation of the
creatures of God, worketh according to the stuff, and is limited
thereby; but if it work upon itself, as the spider worketh its
web, then it is endless, and brings forth indeed cobwebs of
learning, admirable for the fineness of thread and work, but of
no substance or profit.

'This same unprofitable subtilty or curiosity is of two sorts;
either in the subject itself that they handle, when it is a fruitless speculation or controversy (whereof there are no small
number both in divinity and philosophy), or in the manner or
method of handling of a knowledge; which amongst them was

this; upon every particular position or assertion to frame objections . . . breeding for the most part one question as fast as it solveth another.

'Notwithstanding certain it is, that if those schoolmen to their great thirst of truth and unwearied travail of wit had joined variety and universality of reading and contemplation, they had proved excellent lights, to the great advancement of all learning and knowledge. But as they are, they are great undertakers indeed, and they are fierce from being kept in the dark . . . in the inquisition of nature they ever left the oracle of God's works and adored the deceiving and deformed images which the unequal mirror of their own minds or a few received authors or principles did represent unto them. And thus much for the second disease of learning.'[1]

Thus Bacon clearly and ruthlessly exposed the weaknesses of education in his and preceding times. As to the future, which none can clearly foretell, he could at least suggest his inductive method, with the use of apparatus and experiment—'other helps are required besides books'[2]—and the study of nature in its many phenomena. James Harrington, an admirer of Bacon, republican writer and friend of Charles I, who could discuss commonwealths with the doomed monarch, also indicates the need for changes in the character of education. Education, he wrote, is 'the formation of a Citizen in the Womb of the Commonwealth'. It is of six kinds: at school, in the mechanics (i.e. in agriculture, in manufacture, or in commerce), at the university, at the inns of court, in travel, and in military discipline.[3] Harrington felt the need for something wider than school and university ordinarily supplied: even a knowledge of Greek and Hebrew is not sufficient to enable one to understand the Scriptures; to interpret them correctly a knowledge of past times and conditions is also necessary. Harrington is one of the first writers to appreciate economic factors in history and to make full use of the historical method. He was himself a traveller—and we must not forget travel as an educational

---

[1] *Advancement of Learning* (1605), Book I.
[2] *Ibid.*, Book II.   [3] *Oceana*, (1656) (edited Liljegren), p. 168.

influence in the intellectual development of the great men of the day. Since the Renaissance Italy had proved a magnet; in the seventeenth century, Pym, Hampden, Penn, Locke, Marvell, and Milton were all in varying degree influenced by their experience abroad. 'No man', wrote Harrington, 'can be a Politician, except he be first an Historian or a Traveller; for except he can see what Must be, or what May be, he is no politician: Now if he had no knowledge in story, he cannot tell what hath been; and if he hath not been a Traveller, he cannot tell what is: but he that neither knoweth what hath been, nor what is; can never tell what must be, or what may be.'[1]

Both Bacon and Harrington give voice to the growing feeling that a new and wider education was becoming necessary, at least for certain classes of people. For the politician, the courtier, the man of affairs, the bookish learning of grammar school and university was insufficient and much of it unnecessary. Whereas the Middle Ages had separated the education of clerk and knight, it was becoming necessary for the modern man of affairs to combine them. The Greek ideal of a balanced education of mind and body had been revived by the Renaissance. There was, as Ascham put it in *The Scholemaster* (1570), a new inclination 'to joyne learning with cumlie exercises'. The nobility itself was becoming more civilized than in feudal days: already in 1428 Vittorino da Feltre with the help of his princely patrons had made a court school a real centre of Renaissance culture. Above all, perhaps, a utilitarian urge was powerful: new subjects were becoming not only desirable but essential to the man of action himself. Mathematics and science were making a science of the art of war. For those who stood behind the soldiers and made war and peace, for diplomats, politicians, statesmen, subjects such as modern languages, history, and geography were becoming of increasing importance. Philosophers who were moving ahead of their times, like Bacon and, rather earlier, the Frenchman, Peter Ramus, and rather later, the Czech educationist, Comenius (1592–1670), were urging the claims of the 'New Philosophy' of experimental science.

[2] *Ibid.*, p. 175.

Comenius pressed the importance of the study of science in schools and universities, although he did not foresee the modern problem of overloading in the school curriculum. Optimistically he called his book *The Great Didactic, setting forth a universal system of teaching everybody everything*. Those in England interested in the new experimental science were meeting privately in Oxford and London, and formed in 1662 the Royal Society. All this it is true did not yet affect the grammar schools. But outside them there was growing up a polite conception of education—the Doctrine of Courtesy—and a new type of educational institution, the Academy, to meet the demand for an education more suited to the conditions of the time.

The ideal of the scholar-gentleman was best set out in *Il Cortegiano* (*The Courtier*) of the Italian count, Baldassare Castiglione. 'The best book that was ever written upon good breeding', Dr. Johnson called it more than two hundred years later, but it was much more than that. Castiglione was, not unfittingly, a Mantuan—where the tradition of Vittorino da Feltre lingered—and when he transferred his services to Urbino he was at a˙ducal court which owed its intellectual greatness to an earlier duke, a pupil of Vittorino. Castiglione was born and bred in the midst of the Italian Renaissance. His book appeared in 1528 but it had been written by 1516, the year in which were published More's *Utopia* and the *Orlando Furioso* of Ariosto. Machiavelli had completed *The Prince* three years earlier, though the first edition was not published until 1532. But it was in the campaigns and diplomacy of the Italian wars that Castiglione spent his active life in the service of princes. 'For it is very convenient for the philosopher to recount what he hath read, but the knight or gentleman, it becomes him not well, but to speak of things that he hath done.'[1] This contemporary opinion still savours of the medieval dichotomy: it was the work of Castiglione to reunite, as the Greeks had first united, the ideals of action and learning.

---

[1] From *The Familiar Epistles of Sir Antony of Guevara, Preacher, Chronicler, and Counsellor to the Emperor Charles the Fifth* (translated from the Spanish by Edward Hellowes, 1574).

In the days before cinema and radio conversation was a form of entertainment, and in the sophisticated society of an Italian court, love and the relation of the sexes were popular subjects. In writing an account of such intimate discussions in the court circle at Urbino Castiglione delineated the character and qualities of the ideal courtier. By the courtier Castiglione means the man of action, the man engaged in the service of a prince, on the field and in the council chamber, the man completely at home in the society of gentlemen and ladies. It is for him that the new education or training is designed. He must be most carefully exercised in arms and horsemanship—'the principal and true profession of a courtier ought to be in feats of arms'—and must have the highest quality of courage although he must be at the same time no bully or braggart. His mind also must be trained. He must know Latin and Greek, the poets, orators, and writers of history, but be also able to express himself well in his mother-tongue. Sports, games, and recreations must be cultivated; at least a moderate skill should be acquired in swimming, hunting and hawking, tennis, music and dancing, drawing, painting, and chess, and he is 'to play for his pastime at dice and cards, not wholly for money's sake, nor fume and chafe in his loss'. He must seek to do well what he does—to excel—and here we observe again the characteristic individualism of the Renaissance when men looked at life as a glorious competition of the brave, the strong, and the fair. But what he did and said must be done as though to the manner born. A polished carelessness must conceal the effort he makes, as though whatever he achieved were the outcome of inbred ability.

The girls and ladies of the palace were to share in this courtly education. Castiglione makes the Duchess of Urbino the central figure around whom the entertaining conversation of her circle goes on, and the noble ladies of the group engage the gentlemen on equal terms and are eager to defend their sex. Such topics—as old as the hills of Urbino—as that love is blind and sees only perfection in the loved one, that the 'natural' woman is to be preferred to the woman with make-

185

13

up, and that there are rightly two standards of sex-behaviour, one for men and one for women, such topics called for lively exchanges. The final discussion kept its participants, all unwitting, out of their beds until morning, and they went to their rooms, without a need for torches, in the pale, clear light of an Italian dawn. At the end of his book Castiglione gave 'A brief rehearsal of the chief conditions and qualities in a courtier' and a similar summary of the qualities needed in a lady.[1] Each list is a demand for perfection; only a paragon could meet its requirements. But such was the demand of the Doctrine of Courtesy—the best.

Castiglione's book became a classic of its kind; it was written not in Latin but in Italian, and was widely translated into other modern languages. Its spirit was that of the Renaissance in its liveliest and most human form; it appeared to offer an alternative to the medieval scholasticism which the humanists had attacked and also to the narrow linguistic education into which humanism had all too easily slipped. At the same time (1531) there appeared in England *The Boke named the Governour* by Sir Thomas Elyot, scholar, friend of More, and holder of several public offices under Henry VIII. Elyot wrote his work in English, and it may, perhaps, be described as the first book in our language on education.[2] Yet it is not a treatise narrowly confined to education. As he says in his dedication to Henry VIII, 'I have now enterprised to describe in our vulgar tongue the form of a just public weal'. But if the state is to flourish it must have good and wise governors, and therefore his book 'treateth of the education of them that hereafter may be deemed worthy to be governors of the public weal under your highness (which Plato affirmeth to be the first and chief part of a public weal)'. As a Platonist, then, Elyot appeals to the *Republic* as giving pre-eminent importance to the education of the guardians or governing class.

As a humanist, Elyot gives pride of place in his educational

[1] *The Courtier* (done into English by Sir Thomas Hoby, 1561), p. 368.
[2] The claim is made by Foster Watson in his introduction to the Everyman edition of the *Governour*.

scheme to Latin and Greek. But he knows that one who 'hath nothing but language only may be no more praised than a popinjay, a pye, or a stare, when they speak. . . . There be many nowadays in famous schools and universities which be so much given to the study of tongues only that, when they write epistles, they seem to the reader that, like to a trumpet, they make a sound without any purpose, whereunto men do harken more for the noise than for any delectation.'[1] Elyot therefore appeals to the educational ideal of Cicero and Quintilian, the ideal of the orator, the man well informed and also eloquent. In addition to Latin and Greek Elyot urges the value of music, painting, and carving, and the importance of a knowledge of history and geography. He urged also the essential place in education of exercise by which 'the health of man is preserved, and his strength increased', and recommended wrestling, running, swimming, hunting and riding, dancing, and—like Ascham in *Toxophilus* and Mulcaster in the *Positions*—archery.

The idea of all-round education for the young man of birth became a popular and influential one as the number of publications on the subject testifies. All variations on the same theme are James Cleland's *The Institution of a Young Nobleman* (1607), Richard Braithwait's *The English Gentleman* (1630), and Henry Peacham's *The Compleat Gentleman, fashioning him absolute in the most necessary and commendable Qualities concerning Minde or Bodie* (1622).

At the same time the great schoolmasters of the period, Mulcaster and Brinsley, were pressing the value of English as a medium of expression 'not any whit behind either the subtle Greek for crouching close, or the stately Latin for spreading fair', and suggesting specific schoolteaching of the use of the native language. Nor was the concept of education absent from the minds of some of the greatest literary geniuses of the day. Milton's views on university education were noticed in the last chapter. At an earlier date Spenser's *Faerie Queene* had been said by the poet to have as an object 'to fashion a gentleman or noble person in vertuous and gentle discipline'. In France, the

---

[1] *Governour* (Everyman edition), p. 55.

two most famous sixteenth-century figures, Rabelais, the creator of *Pantagruel* and *Gargantua*, and the essayist, Montaigne,[1] were both dissatisfied with the surviving medieval character of the older education, and they wrote of a wider curriculum related to life rather than to books alone.

An interesting proposal for a practical course of education suited to a gentleman was the so-called Queen Elizabeth's Academy put forward by Sir Humphrey Gilbert, the half-brother of Raleigh. The scheme came to nothing, but Gilbert had clearly in mind for the Queen's wards and other young gentlemen an institution with, in addition to Latin and Greek, a modern curriculum, and conducted by teachers who were to undertake experiment 'by the fire and otherwise, to search and try out the secrets of nature, as many ways as they possibly may'. The curriculum was to include besides modern languages, history and what we should call civics and economics, a training in arms, gunnery, physical exercises and the application of mathematics and science in the art of war. There was also to be a library into which 'all Printers in England shall for ever be charged to deliver' one copy of each book they published. He suggested the creation of such an institution because he could find no existing means of providing the right training for young men of birth and position. 'At this present', as he put it, 'the estate of gentlemen cannot well train up their children within this realm but either in Oxford or Cambridge, whereof this ensueth: first, being there, they utterly lose their time, if they do not follow learning only. For there is no other gentleman-like quality to be attained. Also by the evil example of such, those which would apply their studies are drawn to licentiousness and idleness; and, therefore, it were every way better that they were in any other place than there. And whereas in the universities men study only school learning, in this Academy they shall study matters of action meet for present practice, both of peace and war.'[2]

Academies, with such an end in view, sprang up on the

---

[1] See, for example, his essay *Du Pédantisme*.
[2] *Queen Elizabeth's Academy* (ed. F. J. Furnivall), p. 10.

Continent. In France, the Académie Royale originated in a seminary for priests set up by the Oratory of Jesus, a religious order founded in 1611 to promote the education of young men for the priesthood. Louis XIII gave a new character to this particular school by persuading the Oratorians to take as pupils boys of noble birth along with novices for the priesthood. Latin and Greek still held their place, but the study of the French language, of mathematics and physics and of subjects like geography, French history, and heraldry was introduced, as well as accomplishments such as music, drawing, dancing, and riding. Another school of similar type was the Academy of Richelieu, founded by the famous cardinal in 1640, and following closely its royal model. In Germany after the chaos of the Thirty Years War, certain new schools similar to the French academies were founded. Such schools for the young nobility, known as *Ritterakademien*, existed at, for example, Colberg and Vienna. Rather than Greek or Hebrew, they taught modern languages such as French, Italian, English, and Spanish. In addition to languages, mathematics, and physics, geography, law, heraldry, and genealogy found place among the subjects of study, and the accomplishments of the gentleman—fencing and riding, courtly manners and dancing—were given special attention. The academy type of education influenced some of the modern German universities, as, for example, Halle and Göttingen, and the Bavarian university of Erlangen which dates from 1743 traced its origin to an academy founded rather more than forty years earlier. But as time went on the academies began to approximate to the grammar schools, and were eventually absorbed into the system of secondary education.

The movement for a new kind of education reached also beyond the ocean. In New England the classical education which led to Harvard College and the ministry was found to be too narrow except for the scholar, and in 1743 Benjamin Franklin was suggesting an education which would prepare the student not simply for college but for life. Once more modern studies were advocated. Franklin himself would even have excluded Latin and foreign languages, but he was prepared to make language study a matter of choice in order not to break too violently with the established linguistic tradition. An academy was opened at Philadelphia in 1749, and others followed—among them the two famous Phillips' Academies, one in 1778, the other in 1781. The academies had an important influence on the development of American secondary education, and in time they simply became secondary schools preparing boys for entry to college (i.e., university).

In England, in spite of Sir Humphrey Gilbert's proposals, no courtly academies as such were created. The young nobleman or gentleman, if he were not sent to one of the great schools, would have his tutor at home. At Oxford and Cambridge, by 1700, it seems that instruction could be obtained in the modern subjects from private and unofficial teachers. Riding, hunting, and manly exercises the young man might learn on the family estate, and, if he wished to add something of Continental culture and polish, then there was the 'grand tour'. Since the later Middle Ages the Inns of Courts in London had supplied an education for lawyers and others—both More and Cromwell had studied there. For the man of birth this was an appropriate education—much more so than the scholar's toil in the Latin disputations of the university. A knowledge of the law was of direct interest and service to the young man of wealth who would, in time, inherit the responsibility of landed estates.

But if England did not have courtly academies she did have another and very interesting educational development, that of the Nonconformist or Dissenting Academies. Legislation passed after the restoration of Charles II practically excluded Nonconformists from teaching in the established schools and universities, and this led to some of the Nonconformist teachers setting up their own institutions for the teaching of their fellow Nonconformists. As they were outside the pale of the older tradition and system, the Nonconformists were more open to new ideas and the modern subjects found a welcome in their schools. Indeed, during the seventeenth and eighteenth centuries their schools were, in England, the most progressive. As they have been described by their historian: 'During a period when the grammar schools slept and when universities were sterile the Dissenting Academies were not merely in existence, but were thoroughly alive and active, doing remarkably good work.'[1] They built on a foundation of ideals and idealism which had marked the Commonwealth period and the preceding years. To this the growth of the interest in natural science contributed, and Puritans such as Samuel Hartlib, Dury, and Milton were all keenly interested in education. The visit to England of Comenius in 1641 and his close contacts with this circle strengthened the feeling for educational reform, but the outbreak of the Civil War turned men's energies to less fruitful endeavour. Under the Commonwealth grants were actually made to the universities and to Scottish education and also to certain small schools which were faced with financial difficulties, and a scheme for a new university in the north of England was considered. But the Restoration brought, not unnaturally, a conservative reaction, and this gave a new lease of life to the traditional education of the grammar schools and universities.

By 1670 the severe measures against Nonconformists were slackening. The judgement of that year in the Bates case declared that a schoolmaster who was nominated by a founder or lay patron of a school could not be ejected for teaching without the bishop's licence. This and later judgements—in spite of a temporary setback with the Schism Act of 1714 against Dissenting schoolmasters which was repealed three years later—eased the position of Nonconformist teachers and led to the endowment by dissenters of many schools, especially elementary schools. The Academies, on the other hand, were schools at a higher secondary or university level. Just why they came to be known by that name is not certain, though the term was in common use and was often applied to universities. It may be that the Nonconformists wished to distinguish their institutions, different as they were in character and curriculum, from the ordinary grammar schools.

The earliest academies, from 1663 to 1690, were private

[1] I. Parker: *Dissenting Academies in England*, p. 45.

small and conducted, generally, by one tutor. The tutors were men who had, earlier, qualified at the universities and had sometimes also taught there. At this stage Latin was still dominant, and the curriculum was not always very different from that of the grammar schools. But at Newington Green, where Daniel Defoe was educated, there were Greek and Hebrew in addition to Latin; some logic, mathematics, and science and modern subjects like history, geography, French, and Italian were also taken. Samuel Wesley (father of John) was also a pupil at the Academy and reported, later, 'a laboratory and some not inconsiderable rarities with air pump, thermometer, and all sorts of mathematical instruments'. There were other academies in London, including a second at Newington Green. Mill Hill School to-day attempts to trace its origin to one of the academies. There were at least twenty-three academies[1] up and down the country, although they were harassed by persecution and obliged frequently to move their location because of the Five Mile Act. Three were especially noteworthy—Rathmell (in Yorkshire), Sheriffhales (Shropshire), and Shrewsbury. Rathmell is said to have had, at one time, about eighty young men as students.

Later, from about 1690 to 1750, the academies were more often controlled by some group or organization, such as the London Congregational Fund Board (established in 1695). There are about thirty-four academies known to have been at work during this period, in addition to some of the older ones which still survived. Latin has a rather less important place in the curriculum, and English a more important place; more time was given to modern subjects. There was evidently a growing demand from the middle classes for a realistic education, for in addition to training boys for the Nonconformist ministry the academies also educated many boys who were going into commerce. The academies provided an education often better—certainly better in the latter case—than could be obtained elsewhere, and much cheaper. Anglicans might, and sometimes did, send their sons to the academies, for they might

[1] See the lists given by I. Parker: *Dissenting Academies*, Appendix I.

prefer an education under virtuous and learned Nonconformists rather than the exposure of youth to the temptations and idleness of the old universities. From the academies came occasionally a man destined to position in the Church of England: Archbishop Secker was a product of the academy at Tewkesbury.

In the second half of the eighteenth century even more attention was given to modern subjects, and students specialized on certain courses. At the important Warrington academy, between 1757 and 1783, students could be classified as taking the following courses suited to their intended careers:

Law	22
Medicine	24
Divinity	52
Commerce	98
Course unspecified	197[1]

It was here that one of the pioneers of science teaching, Joseph Priestley, was engaged from 1761 to 1767. But in addition to various branches of science, he lectured on languages, history and geography. Priestley worked out a syllabus of lectures on history, including a systematic survey of English history. With him the teaching of this subject was beginning to take its modern pattern.[2] He had himself had a most thorough education: Latin and Greek at a grammar school; French, Italian, and High Dutch he acquired himself; other subjects, including mathematics and science, he learnt through private lessons with a minister and at the academy in Daventry. The Warrington academy fell into debt, and in 1783 a new academy was opened in Manchester and to it was transferred the Warrington library. There were a number of changes of place in the history of the new establishment, Manchester New College, but it finally came to rest at Oxford as Manchester College—now a theological college under mainly Unitarian control.

Priestley in his *Essay on a Course of Liberal Education for Civil*

---

[1] I. Parker: *Dissenting Academies in England*, p. 107.
[2] *Ibid.*, Appendix VI, gives the syllabus in full.

and Active Life clearly pointed the way to a new school curriculum. 'Formerly', he wrote, 'none but the clergy were
thought to have any occasion for learning. It was natural
therefore that the whole plan of education, from the grammar
school to the finishing at the university should be calculated
for their use.' But since times had changed a 'different and
better furniture of mind is requisite to be brought into the
business of life'. When we remember the set classical curriculum of the old grammar schools and when we ask how
mathematics, science, modern languages, history, and geography found their way into our schools we must recall the
example of both the courtly and the nonconformist academies.

CHAPTER XII

THE VOICE OF FREEDOM: ROUSSEAU

THOUGH the spirit of the Renaissance and the activities of the academies suggested the existence of a new conception of education, it was long enough before the grammar-school curriculum changed its character. Its tradition was established and powerful; Latin was still its principal subject. When the optimism of the Renaissance had been dissipated by the long religious wars which followed the Reformation and the serious religious purpose in the education of Calvinists and Jesuits alike had lost some of its meaning in the indecisive outcome of the devastating conflict, there was for a period no driving force strong enough to create any new movement in the schools and universities. A calm followed the storm, a calm which all too easily became stagnation. Educational institutions and methods retained their outward form but had lost the inner fire which once had given them life. And economic and social conditions—still largely those of the hierarchical class structure of the Middle Ages—were not yet sufficiently changed to make possible any great development of the existing education. Individuals might theorise to their hearts' content and organizations practise on a small scale but it would be a long time yet before education could advance on a broad front.

Comenius with his *Great Didactic* and his many text-books—among them the *Orbis Pictus*, published in 1658 at Nuremberg, the first schoolbook with pictures and popular for years to come—had grasped the conception of the value of a broad general education. This was inherent in his method of teaching Latin—in his text-book the *Janua Linguarum*—by arranging

Latin words and sentences in groups, each group giving information on a particular subject, and, taken together, giving a conspectus of human knowledge. He urged also that education should be provided for all by means of a mother school in every home, a vernacular school in every village, a Latin grammar school in every city, and a university in each country or in every province. Thus Comenius clearly put forward the suggestion of universal elementary education—in line with Luther and the Protestant tradition—for his suggested vernacular schools were 'to teach all young people, between the ages of six and twelve, such things as will be of use to them throughout their whole lives', reading, writing, arithmetic, religion. Comenius added instruction in economics and politics.[1]

In England among those in contact with and influenced by Comenius, Dury had suggested universal education in which children between eight and thirteen should observe 'all things natural and artificial extant in the world', and Sir William Petty had argued for trade schools to teach handicrafts to children of all classes. But the hard fact was in the seventeenth century that the average man—the peasant or the domestic craftsman—did not require a book education for his livelihood, and that the economic system could scarcely have borne the expense of providing adequate buildings and teachers for the education of all. Little was in fact done for the people, though De La Salle, who founded the Brothers of the Christian Schools in 1682, did something in France, and the charity-school movement which began at the end of the century in England did more.

In France the teaching order, the Oratorians, and the religious group known as the Port Royalists were influenced by the rationalizing philosophy of Descartes and favoured a broader curriculum in the grammar schools, but the schools of the latter order—the Little Schools of Port Royal—were forced to close between 1656 and 1660 because they had incurred the jealousy of the Jesuits. In the work of these teaching congrega-

[1] *Great Didactic* (Keatinge), chaps. xxvii–xxxi.

tions—both rivals of the Jesuits, much of whose work was taken over by the Oratorians when the Jesuits were expelled from France in 1764—there was a general tendency to give attention to the teaching of the French language and rather less to Latin, and to introduce modern subjects.

There was, in fact, a fairly large measure of sporadic discontent with existing education. It showed itself in the repeated attempts to broaden or simplify the curriculum, to find short cuts or improved methods in the learning of Latin and Greek, and in the tendency to stress as important in education not words but things: 'I know not', wrote John Locke in 1693, 'why anyone should waste his time and beat his head about the Latin grammar, who does not intend to be a critic, or make speeches and write dispatches in it.'[1] A gentleman must acquire a good knowledge of Latin, but he need not concern himself with the finer points of grammatical rules. 'A great part of the learning now in fashion in the schools of Europe, and that goes ordinarily into the round of education, a gentleman may in good measure be unfurnished with, without any great disparagement to himself, or prejudice to his affairs.'[2] The kind of education which Locke prescribed—except that he preferred the private tutor to any school—was very much that of the academies. Modern studies were introduced (and Locke actually dropped Greek), and attention was given to physical training and exercises such as riding, fencing, and dancing. There was also in Locke a renewed appeal to sense-experience characteristic of the discontent with the older methods of education. In his *Essay Concerning Human Understanding* (1690) Locke explained how he regarded the mind as at first a blank, and then what came to be written on it he thought of as the result of experience. 'These two are the fountains of knowledge,' he said, 'from whence all the ideas we have, or can naturally have, do spring. First . . . sensation . . . secondly . . . reflection.'

It is interesting to observe that in the case of Locke and Rousseau there is once more a close connexion between

[1] *Some Thoughts concerning Education*, section 168.   [2] *Ibid.*, section 94.

education and politics. Just as for Plato and Aristotle their educational theory was a part of their wider political theory and of their philosophy as a whole, so the educational ideas of Locke and Rousseau are of particular significance not only because they are important educationally but also because Locke and Rousseau were outstanding political thinkers who virtually created the democratic liberalism of modern times. Any complete political philosophy must necessarily embrace a theory of education; Plato and Aristotle had conceived of the statesman as using education to shape the citizen. The medieval Church and the Protestant reformer had each appreciated the use of education to influence the young for religious ends. In the eighteenth century the state was showing an inclination to create systems of education for its own ends. Theorists and reformers were for reforming the state itself. It is always easier to criticize than to construct; the eighteenth century was an age of rationalism, and it was not difficult to pick out the failings of the existing order. It was much more difficult to suggest the lines on which a future order could be established. Men had forgotten the desperate warning of Hobbes in the preceding century who, appalled by the collapse of civil order in the English Civil War, had implied that even bad government was better than no government at all. The eighteenth century was an age of prose, reason, and political optimism: reform was in the air. The theorists were for sweeping away at a stroke the old abuses apparent in the established monarchies and allowing the natural goodness of man to replace them with an ideal state, but even some of the rulers—the so-called Benevolent Despots—toyed with the idea of reform. And the new idea of the overriding importance of sense-experience made education appear the means of giving the right experiences, the right training and environment, to produce the right kind of citizen for the state. Rousseau himself advocated a national system of education,[1] and that education would be an ideal one only if

[1] *Économie politique*, originally published in the *Encyclopédie* (1755): '*L'Éducation publique . . . est donc une des maximes fondamentales du Gouvernement populaire ou légitime.*' Also in *Considérations sur le Gouvernement de Pologne*.

it took place in the ideal state. His ideal was the free citizen in the free state, and man must be prepared for that full realization of his nature which Rousseau came to see could only take place in an ordered society.

The German Protestants, as we said in an earlier chapter, had made a beginning with popular education in the systems of one or two of the German states, of which the most noteworthy example was that of Saxe-Coburg-Gotha. In the eighteenth century a state system of elementary education began to take shape in Prussia. In 1716–17 Frederick William I, under the influence of German educational reformers, made attendance compulsory at the village schools which were maintained by the Protestant clergy. The work was continued by his son, Frederick the Great. He gave support to the village schools and in 1763 reinforced the previous measures by regulations making attendance compulsory for all children between the ages of five and thirteen or fourteen. Control of the schools was in the hands of the Lutheran Church, the parish maintaining the school building and the dwelling of the teacher, whose payment depended on the small fees paid by the pupils. Those pupils who were in need might gain help from parish funds. In Austria also after 1760, under Maria Theresia and Joseph II, educational reconstruction was undertaken by the government. With the suppression of the Jesuits in 1773 their funds and buildings were taken over by the state, a system of elementary schools established, and a beginning made with the introduction of modern subjects into secondary schools. But the French Revolution made new ideas suspect and caused a reaction in which education languished once more.

In England, during the first part of the eighteenth century, there was something like a system of elementary education—but it was a voluntary, not a state system. The Society for Promoting Christian Knowledge, founded in 1698, set up its charity schools up and down the country and in thirty or forty years had two thousand schools with forty thousand pupils. Some of the schools were for girls. The main aim of the S.P.C.K. was religious teaching in the doctrines of the Church of England, but the schools provided instruction in reading, writing, and arithmetic. This system of charity schools belonged to the Established Church, and as many of the country clergy were Jacobite in sympathy, the movement did not get the whole-hearted official support it might have expected. The Nonconformists also had their schools but far fewer in number. When Robert Raikes of Gloucester formed, in 1785, his Society for the Support and Encouragement of Sunday Schools in the Different Counties of England, another voluntary organization added its efforts to those already being made towards the supply of elementary instruction, for the Sunday-schools did not confine themselves to religious teaching and some of them taught adults as well as children. Apart from these voluntary organizations which were pioneering in the elementary field, there was a marked sterility in English education. Great individual scholars, of course, appeared. Though Gibbon was a bitter critic of the Oxford of his day, his own scholarship was sufficient to produce the *Decline and Fall of the Roman Empire*. But serious courses and examinations were few at Oxford and Cambridge. More characteristic was Lord Eldon's description of his graduation at Oxford in 1770. He was asked two questions, 'What is the Hebrew for place of a skull?' was one. The answer 'Golgotha' satisfied the examiners in Hebrew. 'Who founded University College?' was the other question. The answer 'King Alfred' satisfied the examiners in history.[1]

The great contribution of the eighteenth century to the development of modern education was in the field of theory and came from the erratic and fascinating genius of Jean Jacques Rousseau. Born in Geneva in 1712, his own education, in any formal sense, was scanty. He was deprived of his mother by her death at his birth, and his upbringing by his father was rather casual. As a boy he read a miscellaneous collection of books at home and Plutarch's *Lives* made a lasting impression. When he was ten years old he was sent along with a cousin to a tutor for two years. The young Rousseau could not escape something of the conventional education of the day for he says the tutor

---

[1] G. M. Trevelyan: *History of England*, p. 521, note 2.

taught them 'Latin and all the useless stuff that goes with it'. Afterwards he was apprenticed to an engraver but did not enjoy his occupation. Returning late from a day's excursion, he found the city gates closed for the night. Shut out for the hours of darkness he was too impatient to wait, decided to break with his native place and made his way to France. Then began a life of wandering and various occupations, none of which lasted long. But in his wanderings and various experiences is to be found his real education for a life which seemed to be based on the paradox: Do the contrary of what is usual and you will then do what is necessary and right.

With the aid of his *Confessions* one can still follow his footsteps in southern France, around Grenoble, Annecy, and Chambéry, and in Provence, where he found the Roman aqueduct of the Pont du Gard the only famous monument with which he was not disappointed. He managed to live at the expense of those willing to befriend him and his sentimental adventures were of the most extraordinary kind. At Les Charmettes (near Chambéry) he lived for a time with Madame de Warens, who was to him both mother and mistress. His life passed in thought and fantasy, in passionate love affairs, in travelling, in writing— and writing brilliantly. New ideas are seldom original, and the idea of a social contract as the basis of government was to be found in the work of John Locke; the education of *Émile* was clearly influenced by Rousseau's reading of Montaigne and Fénelon. But it was the supreme art of Rousseau to be able to set out his ideas in a style so striking as to catch and hold the imagination of men. Even a brilliant writer, however, had to live and sometimes, for a while, Rousseau would be tutor, or copyist, or secretary. As a secretary he worked for the French ambassador in Venice. It was there, he tells us, that he missed his opportunity of supreme happiness with Zulietta, a lady who suddenly changed her mind and bade the disappointed Rousseau: 'Give up the ladies and study mathematics.' As for a wife—though not formally married—Rousseau lived with Theresa le Vasseur, an illiterate woman. At the same time he was in touch with the great men of his age—Frederick the

Great, Gibbon, Hume, Boswell. His *Contrat Social* proclaimed the principles of human society; as an individual his life was of a kind to make organized social life impossible. His own five children he abandoned on the steps of the foundling hospital. Yet this was the man who succeeded in writing one of the most famous books on education.

'Everything is good as it comes from the hands of the Author of Nature; but everything degenerates in the hands of man', declared Rousseau in *Émile* which appeared in 1762 and in which he set out his thoughts on education. By nature, Rousseau generally means inborn faculty or habit. To allow this to develop naturally, without human restraint, must be the method of education. The main thing is not to do anything; in the early years at least, education must be negative; instruction must only come later when its need is felt by the pupil.

'Civilized man', says Rousseau, 'is born, lives and dies in a state of slavery. At his birth he is stitched in swaddling-clothes; at his death he is nailed in his coffin; and as long as he preserves the human form he is fettered by our institutions.' Let him alone.

Émile, the boy to be educated, is to be provided with a tutor, who should be a young man and should take charge from birth onwards for about twenty-five years. Rousseau says the father would really be best but that he would have no time. Yet how impracticable for *each* boy to have a tutor, and how *unnatural* for a child to have an adult solely devoted to him! Émile, it is assumed, is naturally healthy—you cannot teach anyone to live whose only care is not to die. What would Rousseau do for the delicate, the infirm, the crippled, the backward? Émile must be hardened, even if it involves risk. He must be gradually accustomed to ugly or frightening things—noise, the dark, fire-arms—so that by familiarity they lose their power to alarm. He must not be encouraged to complain or to order people about; he must be left to shift for himself. The child must learn to limit his desires according to his powers of satisfying them; we must only answer to his real needs, and pay no heed when he cries needlessly or capriciously. The tutor must be unmoved by minor hurts—Émile must learn to suffer.

Rousseau attacks what he regards as the pedantic mania for instruction. Do not teach a child to walk: let him play freely out of doors. Let him learn by experience; let natural obstacles and circumstances themselves check him rather than human commands. Do not tell him to obey, but let him act from force of circumstances. Let well-regulated liberty replace the old educational instrument of emulation, vanity, and fear. Morality, a sense of right and wrong, Émile will learn by experience for Rousseau assumes there is no innate sense of right and wrong. If the child breaks something, he must do without it; if he lies, he will not be believed. 'Nature would have children be children before being men.' 'Treat your pupil according to his age.' This is, perhaps, Rousseau's most practical suggestion.

Rousseau thinks the most important rule of education is not to gain time, but to lose it, for the mind should develop naturally and without being forced. The tutor must exercise the pupil's body, senses, and powers, but keep the soul lying fallow as long as possible. 'You are alarmed at seeing him consume his early years in doing nothing! Really! Is it nothing to be happy?—to jump, play, run, all day long?' The village offers a better environment than the town for the upbringing of Émile, because the village will offer fewer attractive forms of vice.

Rousseau attacks verbalism in education—'*words*, words, nothing but words'. Speaking of the education of the children of his day, Rousseau says: 'All the premature studies of these unfortunates relate to objects entirely foreign to their minds.' Rousseau would have praised the modern kindergarten, and anticipates Froebel. Like Locke, he puts forward the fundamental principle that wherever possible sense experience should precede reason. He attacks languages, especially the dead languages. Children may learn five or six vocabularies, but have only one language. Words are learnt, but are not understood. History and geography are taught before they are intelligible. How true! 'Reading', says Rousseau, 'is the scourge of infancy.' This was, indeed, almost true at that time— books suited to children hardly existed. 'Émile, at the age of twelve, will hardly know what a book is.' But he will learn to read and write before the age of ten—because he will have found these arts of present use in dealing with notes and invitations from friends.

Rousseau slips a certain amount of 'instruction' (or learning by the pupil) into his play of jumping, climbing, balancing: making a swing will involve measuring a length of rope; running races will involve judging and measuring distances. All children take to drawing because they are great imitators: this will make the eye accurate and the hand flexible—but 'he shall have no master but Nature, and no models but objects'. Rousseau's treatment of geometry was revolutionary. Figures would be drawn by the children in play, measured and superimposed. The pupil would then make his own deductions instead of learning the demonstration as offered to him by a teacher. Music the child would learn by ear and sing to the harpsichord, and he would compose simple phrases of his own.

Thus has Émile been educated between the ages of five and twelve; he has grown slowly and naturally. But now a period of labour, instruction, and study begins—a very important period. During adolescence he has a surplus of powers; he will now make up for the time spent in play during his earlier years, and his real studies begin. Geography commences with observation of the rising and setting of the sun; he maps his local district, and he learns the use of the compass by getting lost in the forest. He develops the habit of giving continuous attention to the same subject. He asks questions about everything; he is led (by seeing the tricks of a juggler at a village fair) to investigate electricity and magnetism. He reads only one book, *Robinson Crusoe*, because it shows so well the simple life and how one natural need after another is satisfied by ingenuity. He enters workshops; he takes part in the work of the farm, the forge, and the carpenter's shop; he learns the trade of cabinet maker. He discovers the simple use of money and exchange. Thus, he learns. It may be little but it is well understood, and is really his own.

Now, at fifteen, comes the time for Émile's moral and

religious education. His reason must now be developed; his rising passions are not fed needlessly but his questions are answered simply and truly. He beholds the simple life of the country; he learns that man is naturally good but is depraved by society. As yet he knows nothing of religion, but at length the moment comes when he rises from the study of Nature to the search for its Author. Now he must be informed of the existence of God. This is also the period for Émile to read good books and to find a new companion.

This companion is Sophie, but her education is directed *not* to developing her own nature for its own sake, but simply to developing it for her husband. 'Woman is made specially to please man'..... She has to be constrained and taught docility, because 'docility is necessary to her all her life for she never ceases to be subject to man or to the judgement of man'. In order to please a being as imperfect as man 'she must at an early age learn to suffer and to bear the wrongs of her husband without complaint. It is not for him, but for her own sake that she must be soft and sweet.' By these indirect methods Rousseau suggests that a woman gets her way in the end, and *not* by a frontal attack.

The significance of Rousseau in the growth of modern education is immense. He is a revolutionary, a critic of the society of his day. In his first essays, on *Whether Progress in the Arts and Sciences has tended to Improvement in Morals and Manners* and *On the Origin of Inequality Among Men* he attacked society as he knew it and appealed to the simplicity of nature; in the *Contrat Social* he attacked the basis of monarchical authority by showing (as he thought) the origin of the state in consent, i.e., in contract. However, he came, in the end, to justify the state. He was a revolutionary because he was a romantic and sentimentalist, thin-skinned, over-sensitive to injustice, shy, nervous, and a hater of imposed authority.

He appeals always to nature as against civilization and society. Firstly, because he is himself a lover of nature—of mountain and stream, of sunrise and sunset, of solitude and the country life. But he forgets that nature is also cruel and brutish.

Human society, learning, civilization *are* the assertion of human nature (the nature of man's soul) as against brute nature.

In asserting the value of nature in education he was attacking the bookishness of the Jesuit education of the day, and nature comes before religious instruction. Rousseau was, therefore, in turn attacked for his dangerous doctrines. *Émile* was condemned by the Parlément of Paris in 1762 and Rousseau fled from France to Switzerland. A long period of exile followed. The Archbishop of Paris forbade the reading of *Émile*. 'We condemn the said book as containing an abominable doctrine, ready to subvert natural law and to destroy the foundations of the Christian religion, setting up maxims contrary to the morality of the Gospels; tending to trouble the peace of states, to cause subjects to revolt against their sovereign; as containing a large number of propositions false, scandalous, full of hate against the Church and its ministers, derogatory to the respect due to holy scripture and the tradition of the Church, erroneous, impious, blasphemous and heretical. In consequence, we expressly forbid anyone in our diocese to read or to have a copy of the said book. . . .'

But in vain! Rousseau's influence on education has been very great. Pestalozzi and Froebel on the Continent, Herbert Spencer in England caught much of their inspiration from *Émile*. Rousseau influenced also the thinking of Kant and the educational experiments of Tolstoy with the peasant children on his estates.

Of the most influential and the best remembered in the field of education of those inspired by Rousseau, Pestalozzi (1746–1827) was also a Swiss, though while Rousseau came from French Geneva Heinrich Pestalozzi was born in German Zürich; Froebel (1782–1852) was a German. Powerfully affected by his reading of *Émile* and also of the *Contrat Social*, Pestalozzi arranged a kind of school for the destitute children engaged to work on his farm: reading, writing, and arithmetic filled their time in the intervals between their farm and household duties. Next he turned to writing, and *Leonard and Gertrude* made him a reputation among all who were interested in education. His method was the homely one which Gertrude employed in her peasant household: children learnt arithmetic by counting objects in their home, general knowledge by observation of the things around them, and a simple craft by using the spinning-wheel. Later Pestalozzi was employed by the Government both as an infant teacher and as head of a training college, and added to his literary output *How Gertrude Teaches her Children*. Then he set up his own institute at Yverdon. The fame of his work brought him visits from Talleyrand and Madame de Staël, and praise from von Humboldt and Fichte.

Like Rousseau Pestalozzi thought that all true education was the fruit of personal experience, but he saw the means of education not in Émile's tutor but in the environment of the peasant home. On the child's personal experience of facts— his *Anschauung*—Pestalozzi could base his method of the 'object lesson' which established itself in elementary education. To count objects would provide lessons in arithmetic, drawing them would give lessons in form and would make a link with writing, instruction in their names would develop a knowledge of language. The teacher, however, would be most successful when he most developed the self-activity of his pupils, and that activity would be best directed when it followed the psychological order of learning—from the simple to the more difficult, from the known to the unknown.

Friedrich Froebel came early in life under Pestalozzian influence, first in Frankfort where he taught in a school inspired by such principles and later when, during his stay at the famous institution at Yverdon, he came under the personal guidance of the master himself. It was later in life, about 1840, that he opened his first *Kindergarten*, and it is upon these that his fame largely rests.[1] He provided for very young children, from birth to about six years of age, who, on the metaphor of the plant, were to develop in a 'garden of children'. Such development, in the Froebel system, takes place by means of various educational activities organized as play but increasing in

[1] In addition to his foundation of Kindergartens Froebel wrote *Über die Menschenerziehung* and other works.

difficulty as the child grows older. Games and songs, gardening and the keeping of pets are all employed. Most characteristic was the series of 'gifts' which Froebel introduced—gifts given to the children in an ordered sequence: a ball; a sphere, cube, and cylinder; a cube sub-divided into smaller cubes; and so on. By feeling, observing, and playing with such toys the child gets its early impressions of size, form, space, movement, time. By introducing educational play into the schools for young children Froebel made himself a lasting name in the history of education.

Further experiments in using the self-activity of children to the fullest possible extent have been made in the twentieth century, by the Italian Madame Montessori with her graded educational apparatus, and by the teachers in the United States and elsewhere who, influenced by Professor John Dewey, have used with older pupils the Project Method, or the Dalton Plan. Dalton, Massachusetts, gave its name to the system of Miss Helen Parkhurst in which responsibility was thrown on to the pupils by the fixing of an 'assignment' of work to be carried out with the necessary books and apparatus in the 'subject room'.

Such detailed application of new principles lay in the future, but the dominant trends in modern education, sense experience or sense perception (and practical work and observation), self-instruction based on curiosity and interest, mild discipline, the sacredness of childhood and the importance of studying the child as a child and not regarding him as a little adult, the care of health—all this is to be traced to Rousseau. To comprehend the revolutionary nature of Rousseau's *Émile* one must recall to mind the children of the times, embroidered, gilded, dressed-up, powdered little gentlemen, decked with sword and sash, and alongside them, little ladies of six years, still more artificial, so many veritable dolls to which rouge is applied, and with which a mother amuses herself for an hour and then consigns to her maids for the rest of the day.[1] Into the artificiality of these child-lives and into the barbarities of the schoolroom Rousseau blew a strong draught of fresh air.

[1] As described by Taine: *Les Origines de la France Contemporaine* (*Ancien Régime*, II).

CHAPTER XIII

THE INDUSTRIAL REVOLUTION AND NATIONAL SYSTEMS OF EDUCATION

EDUCATION for the common man—dreamed of before, advocated before—was first made possible and necessary by changes in the methods of economic production which altered the character and structure of society. What was lacking to make popular education a practical policy in earlier ages was any close connexion between the education of the schools and the working life of the common man. The idea of popular education was not new: it was inherent in protestantism with its emphasis on individual reading of the Bible; it had even been glimpsed in the Middle Ages in the obligation on the priest to give instruction to the children of his parishioners. By the eighteenth century the idea was gaining ground that the state must establish a system of education. A beginning had been made, as we have already observed, in Prussia and in Austria, and schemes had been made and discussed in France even before the Revolution. La Chalotais, a French lawyer, wrote in 1763 his *Essai d'éducation nationale* in which he made a strong and closely reasoned case for state control of education. His book was influential. With Rousseau's *Émile* it had a great effect on Basedow, who was working in Germany both for the method of education through play and also for the careful state control of the whole upbringing of the young. The French produced a spate of proposals and the years of the Revolution saw the discussion of many educational plans although their result was small.[1] Adam Smith, the Scotch economist and

---

[1] Before the Revolution, in addition to Rousseau and La Chalotais, Rolland, Helvetius, Turgot, and Diderot all put forward educational

creator of the economic theory of the coming industrial epoch, was much influenced during his travels in France by the philosophers' ideas of Nature and freedom. But his strong advocacy of freedom of trade as against the prevailing Mercantilism or state regulation of trade did not prevent him from suggesting the need for public provision of elementary instruction for the common people. But most comprehensive of all was the plan the Marquis de Condorcet placed before the French Legislative Assembly in 1792. He conceived of a complete national system of education, covering all stages, including the adult, *pendant toute la durée de la vie*. He understood, too, the importance of the sciences and practical subjects. As Condorcet put the aim of education: 'To offer to all individuals of the human race the means to satisfy their needs . . . to develop the talents that each has received from nature . . . to cultivate in each generation the physical, intellectual, and moral faculties, and, thereby, to contribute to the general and gradual perfection of the human race, the supreme object towards which all social institutions should be directed: such should be the object of education, and this is for the public authorities a duty imposed by the common interest of society, and by that of all humanity.'[1]

This was a noble statement of a noble aim. But the enthusiasm of revolutionary governments alone could not achieve it. It was to be many years before France had a comprehensive national system. A study of the building during the nineteenth century of a national system of education in England suggests that practical utility was a more potent factor than idealism. 'Upon the speedy provision of elementary education depends our industrial prosperity', said W. E. Forster when introducing the Elementary Education Act of 1870.[2] As it became more and

---

schemes. Diderot provided a complete scheme for Catherine II of Russia, one of the Benevolent Despots also toying with educational reform. It was not carried out. During the Revolution, Mirabeau, Talleyrand, Lepelletier, Lakanal, Robespierre were among those active in proposing educational plans.

[1] *Rapport et Projet de Décret* (1792), pp. 1–2.
[2] Hansard, vol. 199, col. 465 (17 February 1870).

more apparent that elementary education would be useful—or even essential—to the common man in the everyday task of earning his living, so it became increasingly clear that the state must step in to make certain that an effective system was provided.

With the growth of industry a new phase in human existence was beginning, a phase without its like in history. There had in every previous age been an educated few; never an educated mass. Comprehensive educational systems are new in history. Never, before the age of industrialism, was it necessary to organize a system of education to provide all the young with a measure of book learning. Education for all in primitive societies was unnecessary; it was as unnecessary in the Middle Ages of Europe as it was once for the peasant millions of India and the Far East. It might be very nice from a sentimental point of view to be able to think of these masses as literate; it may be desirable for religious objects; it may be an end for the politician. But the fact remains that the vast illiterate masses used to live—or to exist—without what we know as education. For them what we call education was not essential. They acquire the training they need in ways which are different, or less complex, than ours: they learn the operations of a primitive agriculture by working with, and imitating, fathers and elder brothers in the field or workshop; they learn a trade or craft by a form of apprenticeship. For them book education, school education, was not essential.

Nor were the peasants and domestic workers of the past necessarily lacking a certain culture of their own. They lacked the Latin of the educated class. 'And yet', as the Director-General of Unesco points out, 'the mass of unlearned artisans, manual workers, and peasants were not on that account without culture. Fine traditions, a living folklore, a common faith and popular arts still full of vital impulse held the place of the book learning dispensed by our schools. For better or for worse, times have changed: the industrial revolution, better communications, over-urbanization, even the spread of shallow teaching have very often and very quickly sterilized that peasant culture, discredited its traditions, destroyed its beliefs, and dried up the sources of its inspiration.'[1]

For western Europe the economic changes, known collectively as the Industrial Revolution, which began powerfully to affect society during the eighteenth century, wrought a radical change. Primitive methods of agriculture and domestic craftsmanship were replaced by scientific farming and by mass production of goods with the aid of machinery, driven first by water and then by steam power. This fundamental transformation in human economy came first in England—between about 1760 and 1850—but spread to the west European countries and North America. It resulted in a parallel transformation in Western education. An increasing demand developed for technicians, engineers, chemists, foremen, clerks, accountants, and trained men of every kind. All these needed at least an elementary education: in reading, writing, and arithmetic. 'The new schools were as necessary as the new machine tools and the new railways.'[2]

As time went on, secondary or technical education had to be added, and this meant the introduction of modern subjects into the curriculum. Mathematics and science, modern languages, history, and geography, pushed Latin and Greek further and further into the background. A good general education became increasingly important to provide not 'hands' but trained men for a multitude of posts.

In our own time we can draw a parallel from Soviet Russia. There the sudden creation by the Five Year Plans of an industrial system, in a country previously predominantly agricultural, made it essential to widen vastly the educational system, to make it comprehensive, and to bend it almost entirely to the shape of the technical needs of an industrial society. No longer in an industrial community is education a luxury or a training merely for a small clerical or governmental class. Modern industry has made it essential. It is true that in the minds of

[1] Dr. J. Torres Bodet in ' The Right to Education ' in *The Times Educational Supplement*, April 30, 1949.
[2] E. L. Woodward: *The Age of Reform, 1815–1870*, p. 454.

those who contributed to the creation or rather the gradual evolution of national systems of education motives were various and mixed. There was a religious motive or simply a moral or ethical one in trying to raise the general level of social conduct; a political motive in educating the people to whom the extension of the franchise was giving political power; a national motive in the use of education to strengthen patriotic feeling and to provide the sinews of war, both military and industrial. It is true also that England, the first country to become industrialized, was one of the last to use the machinery of the state to create a national system of education. There might even be resistance to education. Practical business men might fail to see any value in book learning, and might take alarm at something which threatened 'the cheap labour of early youth'. This objection an educational pamphleteer of 1856 answered by pointing out that education would provide employers with 'a much better and more trustworthy article than has hitherto been furnished'.[1] With growing industrialization the need for general and specialized training increased; it was industrialization which made comprehensive systems of state education practicable as well as desirable. It is the outstanding fact of modern educational history that such systems have been created in every Western state. Broadly speaking, the development of such systems coincides with the growth of industrialism.

Prussia was the first modern nation to use the machinery of state to create a comprehensive national system of education. Prussia, surpassing Austria during the nineteenth century, became the most powerful of the German states and her example was highly influential on the others. The history of German education during the nineteenth century is the history of the transformation of educational institutions founded upon classical humanism and the Protestant tradition of popular instruction into a national system for the purpose of training the citizens of one of the most powerful industrial nations of

[1] *The Education of the Masses, Can it be Accomplished?*—an anonymous pamphlet of 1856.

modern times. So great a development did not, of course, take place all at once. During the earlier part of the century the classical tradition was strongest; but the demands of industry and commerce increased in strength as time went on. Throughout the period the patriotic urge towards national greatness was an impelling force, first most clearly in the state of Prussia, later on a nation-wide scale after the formation in 1871 of the German Empire with the king of Prussia as its emperor.

Considerable educational progress had been made during the eighteenth century in Germany. Under the influence of the courtly humanism of the academies a new spirit had found its way into modern universities like Halle and Göttingen. Mathematics and the sciences came to take a more important place, and the principles of academic freedom—*Lehrfreiheit und Lernfreiheit*—established within the university circle an atmosphere in which the search for truth could be undertaken. At the same time the kings of Prussia had used their great organizing and administrative ability not only for political and military purposes but also to prescribe regulations for general popular instruction.[1] As early as 1717 children were ordered to attend where schools existed. Under Frederick the Great the outlines of a state system were created, for the Government issued detailed directions for the running of the Church schools and also for Catholic schools in the province of Silesia. But opposition was encountered. The plans involved heavy expense, and parents objected both to taxation and to holding their children from work in order to send them to school. The prescription of elementary instruction for all children still outran, it seems, what was practicable or what seemed desirable to the people themselves, and it was extremely difficult to find suitable teachers. Although other German states followed the example of Prussia in issuing codes, it proved in practice no easy task to create a national system. Frederick had, however, at least established the principle of compulsory elementary education, a foundation on which a complete state system could be built later on.

[1] See p. 199.

Napoleon's mastery of Europe involved the temporary eclipse of Prussia. Defeat at Jena in 1806 followed in the next year by the treaty of Tilsit reduced her territories and made her political existence dependent upon the policy of the ruler of France. But national humiliation stimulated a speedy and striking national regeneration. In the hands of able ministers, Stein, Hardenberg, Scharnhorst and Wilhelm von Humboldt, the administration of Prussia was modernized by putting an end to serfdom, reforming the civil service and the army, and introducing into the towns self-government by elected councils. To make the country great once more, said Stein, 'we must rely chiefly on the education and instruction of the young'. At the same time the philosopher Fichte, in his *Addresses to the German Nation* which he gave as lectures during the winter of 1807–8 in Berlin, appealed to education as a means of preparing a brighter national future. 'To reshape reality by means of ideas' was, he thought, something which education would make possible. Prussia was soon able to take her share in the final overthrow of Napoleon and the educational system which was created was one of the factors which made for Germany's subsequent rise to power.

In 1808 a Department of Public Instruction was set up as part of the state machinery of Prussia. A genuine idealism inspired the Prussian educators, and seventeen teachers were sent to Switzerland at government expense to study Pestalozzi's methods. A very considerable development of elementary education took place in the next decades; by 1840 Prussia had thirty-eight seminaries or training centres for elementary teachers and about 30,000 elementary schools. At the same time expansion was taking place in the other German states—though not in Austria where reaction had set in as a result of the fear of revolutionary ideas—and also in Sweden and Holland. Though Pestalozzi had aimed at the development of a child's faculties through the senses and natural interests and had believed deeply in the power of education to improve society as a whole, his teachings were given by the Prussians a more narrowly nationalist character. At a time when, to every patriot, the essential object of all policy must be the strengthening of the Prussian state it is not surprising that education also was used for that end. The German language and the history and geography of Germany could all serve a patriotic purpose, and music could lead the young to participate in festivals for the singing of national songs. Reading, writing, arithmetic, drawing, all could have a practical value; and physical exercises served not only to make healthier citizens but also tougher soldiers, while the training in school stressed the virtues of self-sacrifice, obedience, and respect for authority. Such virtues, and patriotism itself, can be turned to good or to evil. If the German liberals had succeeded in the revolutionary year of 1848 in persuading the king of Prussia to become head of a German federation, founded upon a system of representative government, it is possible that German political evolution might have been democratic and peaceful. But the liberals failed. Froebel himself, though an ardent patriot who had enlisted as a volunteer against Napoleon, ran into trouble with a reactionary ministry of education in Prussia. There was a prohibition of kindergartens in 1851, and Froebel died a disappointed man in the following year. It was left to Bismarck to unify Germany by war, by the policy of blood and iron. Its triumph meant the end of German liberalism and the elevation of the state as the supreme political object of popular veneration.

Where the belief in education was so strong as to produce this new, carefully prepared elementary system, it was natural that attention should be given also to the other branches of education. Von Humboldt, himself a scholar, was appointed in 1809 to be head of the Department of Public Instruction and he reorganized the secondary and higher stages of education. Whereas the elementary schools were directed to educating the people, the secondary schools were to prepare a class of leaders and administrators. Von Humboldt's successors carried on his work. In the next twenty years strict regulations were made for intending teachers in the secondary schools, with a state-prescribed examination and a year of teaching on trial before appointment. At the same time the universities began to give some special attention to preparing students for teaching by means of seminars in pedagogy, of which Herbart's seminar at Königsberg was one.[1]

By 1834 the *Abiturientenexamen* or school-leaving examination was completely established, as a means of entrance both to the civil service and the universities. This official, state-prescribed examination standardized the course of training in the secondary schools, and a school which took the full nine-years' course was known as a *Gymnasium*. In such schools the curriculum was still based on the classics: both Greek and Latin were required, although some attention was also given to modern subjects. While Humboldt was directing Prussian education, in 1809, Fichte's plan for a new university, in Berlin, was realized. To its staff were brought some of Germany's leading scholars, and from the first the new university placed special emphasis on research and the advancement thereby of knowledge. Specialization in some limited field, with what has come to be generally recognized as characteristically German thoroughness, produced work of the first order in many different directions. Niebuhr's *Roman History* and the work of Leopold von Ranke put the Germans into a leading role in historical scholarship. Liebig did much to create the modern study of chemistry. Subjects both old and new flourished: philosophy, theology, and law, but also mathematics, physics, zoology, and the study of medicine along modern lines. Other universities followed the example of Berlin in its painstaking search for truth with the help of new critical methods in history and literature and laboratory experiment in natural science. German universities came to be widely recognized as leaders in the learned world, and drew to their courses students from foreign countries. In particular, the German universities influenced the system of studies which was evolved at the new universities of the United States.

Early in the nineteenth century, then, Prussia had created a

---

[1] Herbart (1776–1841) had an important influence on educational psychology. He analysed the process of teaching and his followers drew from his analysis the 'Five Steps' to be followed by the teacher.

comprehensive national system of education, of a two-class type. For the common people there was the elementary school, the *Volksschule*, where ordinary boys and girls were given a basic education. Attendance was compulsory and, before the end of the century, was made free. For these schools teachers were trained in state training colleges. Quite distinct from the elementary system was the system of secondary and higher education—almost confined to men—which prepared the ruling classes of Germany. Special preparatory classes sent their boys to the *Gymnasium* where the exacting classical curriculum was an appropriate testing ground for the strongest intellects. A further severe process of selection took place at the universities. Bismarck spoke of two-thirds of German university students dying prematurely or failing to make their mark by reason of poverty and under-nourishment or drink and bad habits, but, he said, 'the remaining third rule Europe'. The Prussian educational system was a model for the other German states, and the creation of the German Empire in 1871 led to even closer approximation. The main lines remained unchanged until the First World War. Prussia showed during the nineteenth century what the modern state, with a highly organized administrative system and a rapidly growing industry, could achieve. In this achievement full, and increasing, use had been made of education. It was employed to prepare the minds of Germans for the national unity which Prussian intrigue and military might were to bring; it helped also to mould the obedient and industrious citizens of a new and all-powerful state. Prussia has provided not only the most awful examples in modern history of rampant nationalism and militarism but also produced in Karl Marx the prophet of communism, which in Russia has subordinated the individual to the most complete state tyranny which the world has ever known. Prussia, the first country to be educated, and best educated when others were half-educated, was instrumental in creating a united Germany which became the dominant industrial and military nation in Europe. If the Prussians had never been educated, mankind might have been spared two world wars, and Marx, perhaps, might not have prepared for Lenin the catastrophic doctrine of the dictatorship of the proletariat.

Prussian education—like the German soul—was pulled in two directions. It originated in the liberalism and genuine patriotism of the resistance to Napoleon; it was fostered in the progressive and practical idealism of Pestalozzi. But the downfall of Napoleon left the czar of Russia and the Austrian emperor—both autocrats—the dominant figures in continental Europe. The king of Prussia, nurtured in a conservative tradition, was not unnaturally no special friend to liberal ideas. The excesses of the French Revolution and the aggression of Napoleon produced a European reaction. The powerful Austrian minister Metternich set his face against all liberal movements and, since Austria was then still the leader among the German states, Prussia was at first much influenced by her. A spirit, increasingly nationalist in a narrow sense and militarist, began to permeate Prussian education. What had been so bright and hopeful in liberal hands began to be turned to less worthy ends. Frederick William IV, after the revolution of 1848, when the Germans in many of the states demanded representative government, soundly blamed the elementary teachers: 'You and you alone are to blame for all the misery which the last year has brought upon Prussia. The irreligious pseudo-education of the masses is to be blamed for it, which you have been spreading under the name of true wisdom, and by which you have eradicated religious belief and loyalty from the hearts of my subjects and alienated their affections from my person. This sham education, strutting about like a peacock, has always been odious to me.'[1] The king and his ministers felt that elementary education, if it was to serve their purpose, must be curtailed and controlled. Its content must be reduced to what was of immediate and practical value: reading, writing, arithmetic, religion. Teachers must be taught not to go beyond these, and above all, must make of the schools places where obedient citizenship was instilled. Even in secondary schools

[1] Paulsen: *German Education, Past and Present*, p. 246.

the elements of discipline and formal training were stressed more than before.

But if idealism and then the national motive were at first strongest in contributing to the development of German education, as the nineteenth century went on the demands of industry and commerce became ever greater. The different motives were of course mixed and were not mutually exlusive: industry was itself the most powerful means to State power: what encouraged industry strengthened the State and what the State did to stimulate careful training, discipline, and scientific research in turn encouraged industry. During the second half of the century continuation schools were developed. The manual workers educated in the elementary schools were further prepared for their work by courses of part-time continued education along vocational lines. In the secondary schools a new and increased emphasis was placed on the sciences and also on modern languages. Trade and technical schools were encouraged—a series of them sprang up between 1822 and 1835—and developed later in the century into technical universities. Agriculture was advanced by the work of research stations controlled by the State but generally attached to universities. The chemical and electrical industries were developed, both industries highly dependent on scientific and technical knowledge. The victory of Prussia over France in the war of 1870–1 made Germany the pre-eminent power in Europe. This political pre-eminence was founded upon a solid, and a growing, economic strength. The growth of German industry was the necessary backing for Prussian military power and political ambition. As Lord Keynes put it, nearly fifty years later, 'The German Empire has been built more truly on coal and iron than on blood and iron.'

Great Britain was in 1870 by far the greatest industrial nation in the world but Germany had already surpassed France. French industrial development had indeed been great in the preceding years, but German had been greater still. Germany surpassed France in her railway mileage and in her production of coal, iron, and steel. During the decades following the creation of the German Empire in 1871 its industrial development went on at an increasing pace, assisted by national unity and increased concentration of State power. By 1905 German production of steel was greater than that of Great Britain and Germany had become a commercial rival, as well as a good customer. All western and northern Europe were, to a greater or less extent, industrialized, and in the resulting competition there was a steady stimulus to make use of education and particularly of technical education.

The influence of changing economic and social conditions was plainly marked in the growth of new types of secondary school alongside the classical *Gymnasium*. New secondary schools—without the classics, or with Latin only, and giving more time to modern languages and science—were springing up in the first half of the nineteenth century. They met a real need of the new middle class of industry and commerce. Later the kaiser, William II, supported them. At a conference of educationists in 1890 he declared: 'We ought to educate national young Germans and not young Greeks and Romans. We must depart entirely from the basis that has existed for centuries—from the old monastic education of the Middle Ages, where the standard was Latin with a little Greek added.'[1] Though his picture of medieval education might be inaccurate, his ideas were those of the new age. Eventually, in 1901, new types of secondary school were officially advanced in status. The *Realgymnasium* (Latin but not Greek) and the *Oberrealschule* (neither Greek nor Latin) were given the same status, including power of admittance to the universities, as the *Gymnasium*. German education had indeed long surpassed British— 'Secondary instruction of a superior and systematic kind is placed within the reach of the children of parents of limited means, to an extent of which we can form no conception in this country'.[2]

France went through so many political revolutions between

---

[1] *Reports of Commissioners* (U.S.A. Bureau of Education), (1890), I, 360.
[2] *Second Report* of Samuelson Commission on Technical Instruction (1884), p. 23.

1789 and 1870 that changes in her way of life were kaleido-scopic in frequency and effect. The Revolution destroyed the Church foundations and expelled the teaching orders; idealists and planners discussed the idea of a comprehensive national system of education. Practical results were slight. Napoleon brought back the Brothers of the Christian Schools and the Church became once more the principal agency for elementary education. But Napoleon's organizing genius did create a national system. Although he gave little attention to elementary education—which was left to the Church, or to the communes which were supposed to maintain schools, though there was no compulsion on children to attend them—Napoleon made it a function of the state to provide secondary and higher educa-tion in order to produce an educated *élite* from which the civil service and army officers could be recruited. State *lycées* and municipal *collèges* were organized, either new or making use of some former church establishment; the curriculum was classi-cal, but contained modern subjects also. A number of higher schools or faculties were founded for law, medicine, the sciences, and technical subjects. These higher schools took the place of the old universities, which had been abolished during the Revolution and were not re-established until the period of the Third Republic. Napoleon's system was highly centralized, and in 1806–8 he evolved the University of France, not a university in the usual sense but a governmental organization responsible for all branches of education throughout the country. The high degree of centralization which Napoleon maintained has never ceased to influence French education, which is still to-day marked by uniformity imposed and controlled by the central government.

Later, under King Louis-Philippe and with the support of the statesmen and historians, Thiers and Guizot, steps were taken to improve elementary education. In 1831 Victor Cousin, a leading scholar, was sent to study education in the German states, particularly in Prussia, and reported that it was far in advance of that of France. The French were not above learning from the Germans, and the result was the law of 1833 which provided for a state system of elementary instruction. Every commune—the smallest administrative division—was to maintain an elementary school, towns were to provide higher elementary schools, and provision was made for adding to the existing normal schools for the training of teachers. But there was no compulsory attendance and fees were charged. A big development in French education followed during the next fifteen years. The communes shouldered their task, and parents showed themselves eager to send their children to the schools, although if they could afford it they preferred the *lycée* to the higher elementary school. During the second empire, there was, as in Prussia and for the same reason, fear engendered by the revolutions of 1848, a certain suspicion of the elementary teachers as fomenters of unrest.

The Church enjoyed once more a position of honour and influence. The liberty of teaching was restored by the *Loi Falloux* of 1850, which gave free scope to the Church to run its own schools. The expansion of industry and trade, however, encouraged the practical training which the elementary schools could give. As stated by the law of 1850 elementary instruction, in addition to the usual subjects, might include arithmetic as applied to practical operations, science and natural history as related to ordinary life, and simple instruction in agriculture, trade, surveying, levelling, and linear drawing.

Under the Third Republic, which followed the downfall of Napoleon III when his armies suffered catastrophe at the hands of the Prussians, French education was finally cast into a comprehensive national system. Manhood suffrage could not function with illiterate voters. The country had to be revitalized after defeat, and education was a means of recreating the national spirit. The state strengthened its hold on education at the expense of the Church, until in 1904 the teaching congregations were suppressed in France. The revolutionary ideal of an education, free, compulsory, and secular, was achieved by the education minister, Jules Ferry: elementary education was made free in 1881, compulsory in the following year. *Lycées* were also set up by Ferry, and he provided for the secondary education of girls previously almost a monopoly of the Church. Scientific and technical education was greatly expanded, and between 1885 and 1896 fifteen universities were re-established as state universities.

The main formative influences in modern French education can be briefly summarized as four in number—the Catholic Church, the Revolution, Napoleon, and, in France as in Germany and elsewhere, the development of industry. The Revolution destroyed the old control of the Church and threatened the Church itself. Napoleon imposed a highly centralized system of state control, but the Church was re-admitted in France. The nineteenth century was marked by a long struggle between Church and state. The republican tradition in modern France was strongly anti-clerical. The outcome was the establishment of a state—and secular—national system, although the Church has been permitted to run its own private schools and colleges. The struggle between the classical curriculum of the secondary schools and the modern subjects pressing for admittance has been as keen in France as anywhere. 'Classical culture', declared the vice-rector of the University of Paris in 1880, 'is the basis of our literature, of our arts, of our history, and of all our traditions. It has been the leaven of the genius of France.' The classicists were reported in 1898 to 'see in the abandonment of Latin the beginning of the decline of the French spirit' and they still held that 'to form a directive *élite*, such is the role of secondary education'. But in 1902 the modernists brought about a great modification: in the *lycées* classical and modern courses were established side by side leading to a single *baccalauréat* which crowned the school career and admitted to universities and higher professional schools. That the issue was not, however, finally settled was shown by the fact that as late as 1923 Latin and Greek were almost made compulsory once more. Only a change of government in 1924 thwarted the policy of the education ministry. But in France, as in Germany and generally in western Europe and America, the development of what we know as the modern state founded upon science and industry had brought with it the establishment of a comprehensive national state system of education with curricula adapted to the needs of modern life.

Q

CHAPTER XIV

THE REVIVAL OF THE ENGLISH PUBLIC SCHOOLS

THE development of a comprehensive provision for education to meet the new demands of an industrial society was marked in England by two fairly distinct movements. There was in the first part of the nineteenth century a reformation of the old public schools which led to a great expansion in the number of such schools and gave them an invincible position in national sentiment. These schools were the result of private initiative and voluntary endeavour, and their reformation and revival came first in point of time. Then came the movement, slow at first—though its exponents were vociferous and persistent—but gaining in momentum as the century went on, for a national system of education provided by the state.

In building such a system England was behind the Continent. In England there was an ingrained suspicion, far stronger than elsewhere, of the interference of the state and this suspicion went back to the period of the Civil War. The propertied classes having once won their struggle with the monarchy in the seventeenth century a determination remained never again to risk a submission to an arbitrary government. On the Continent, however, both monarchs and revolutionary governments used the power of the state when they could possess it, and the French Revolution followed by the centralized autocracy of Napoleon with its administrative efficiency strengthened the influence of the state itself. On the continent, then, revolution destroyed the old educational foundations and their control by the Church, and substituted for them a more far-reaching state system of schools. But in England fear of the state was at first too strong among the governing classes, and the demand for educational reform brought reform in the old-established schools themselves. Although they had fallen into decadence during the eighteenth century and in the new reforming age invited interference and might, had events fallen out differently, have even been swept away as on the Continent, the public schools in England produced their own reform when events pressed the necessity upon them. As for the provision of elementary instruction, the churches stepped in to make it before the state was ready to act; the building of a national system came slowly and will be described in a later chapter. As late as 1870, when Gladstone's government passed its important Education Act which introduced the provision of board schools out of local rates, the prime minister notwithstanding expressed privately his own preference for voluntary action—'in all things, including education, I prefer voluntary to legal machinery, when the thing can be well done either way'.[1]

The public school is something very English in its character and development. It is difficult to define; it is the despair of those who attempt to explain it to foreigners; and it is the result of a long, evolutionary development. This development, remarkable in itself, is in keeping with English history which is characterized by a remarkable continuity. Institutions have been gradually modified through the centuries and adapted to meet changing needs and conditions. Thus the public schools, which originated in the Middle Ages, have continued, changed, added greatly to their number, and grown into another age. To-day they exist alongside an important and powerful state system of education; they maintain their position of independence because they are good and distinctive schools. A school is said to be a public school when its headmaster is a member of the Headmasters' Conference—itself a private organization of public school headmasters. The public schools are independent and charge, for the most part, high fees: they are thus exclusive and selective. They have an old and respected tradition of

[1] In a letter to Bright. See John Morley: *Life of Gladstone*, II, Appendix.

leadership and distinction behind them. As educational institutions their history is closely interwoven with the history of England itself.

Two books which appeared within a year of each other and which were both best-sellers have helped to popularize and fix the concept of the public school: one, appearing in 1857, was the famous *Tom Brown's Schooldays*, 'by an Old Boy', and the other, published in 1858, was *Eric, or Little by Little*, by Dean F. W. Farrar. A glance at the biographies of the two authors will show how close is the connexion of the public school with the very essence of English history.

'The Old Boy' was Thomas Hughes, himself educated at Rugby under the great headmaster, Dr. Arnold, who can almost be said to have created the modern public school. Thomas Hughes was afterwards at Oriel College, Oxford, and was called to the Bar at Lincoln's Inn. Later, with F. D. Maurice and Charles Kingsley, he was prominent as a Christian Socialist and helped to promote (afterwards becoming principal of) the Working Men's College, London, a pioneer of adult education.

Dean Farrar was grandfather of Field-Marshal Viscount Montgomery. Farrar was born in Bombay (where his father was chaplain of the Church Missionary Society); he was sent to school at King William's College, Isle of Man, and he became head boy. He was scholar, writer, and preacher; a keen churchman of the evangelical type, a strict teetotaller; a typical head of a typical Victorian family. He was himself assistant master at Marlborough and Harrow. At Marlborough the headmaster was G. E. L. Cotton, afterwards Bishop of Calcutta. Cotton had been a master under Arnold at Rugby. He was the keen, progressive 'young master' of *Tom Brown's Schooldays*. Later, Farrar was himself headmaster of Marlborough. Dean Farrar's daughter, Maud Farrar, married in 1881 the Right Reverend H. H. Montgomery, the Field-Marshal's father. The Montgomerys come of an ancient family, from Normandy. A Montgomery, cousin to William the Conqueror, took a leading part in the Battle of Hastings, and was later Earl of Shrewsbury. In the seventeenth century the family had settled in Donegal, Ireland. H. H. Montgomery was born at Cawnpore, his father being in the Indian Civil Service and playing a prominent part during the Mutiny. The Field-Marshal's father was at Harrow, where he was captain of football and cricket. Afterwards he became Bishop of Tasmania. He was a lovable man, but a strict churchman, brought up, as he said himself, on 'undiluted hell fire' which 'did me immense good'. He passed on this strict religious teaching to his family. Field-Marshal Montgomery himself, after an early childhood in Tasmania, was at St. Paul's School, where he was captain of the first eleven and the first fifteen.

Thus we see how intimate is the connexion of the public school with the political and social development of England; we see in these life stories the links between the public school and so many of the dominant institutions and characteristic aspects of English life. We notice, in particular, the connexion with the older universities, the bar, the Church, the army, and the public services, with India and the Empire, with Evangelicalism, that strict religious attitude to life so characteristic of Victorian times which has left an indelible impress on modern English life, and also, through Thomas Hughes and the Christian Socialists, with the wider democratic and social movements of the coming age. As a result of their established position, the public schools have exercised a great influence on British secondary education in the nineteenth and twentieth centuries. This influence they strengthened by a great increase in their own number during the nineteenth century. They set a certain standard and pattern for the new secondary schools of the 1902 Act; and they educated the men who have made our modern system of education, e.g., Sir Robert Morant (Winchester), H. A. L. Fisher (Winchester), the last permanent secretary of the old Board and the first of the new Ministry of Education, Sir M. G. Holmes (Wellington) and Sir John Maud (Eton), and R. A. Butler (Marlborough), the architect of the 1944 Act.

The public schools exist to-day because of a revival during the early nineteenth century. Before that they had fallen into a state of decadence; they had called forth public criticism—they might even have been swept away. Like parliament, municipal government, the legal system, they called loudly for reform. We must first examine the condition of the public schools at the end of the eighteenth century and the beginning of the nineteenth century; then we must see how and why they were reformed, and how they came to take their modern form and influential position in the new industrial society of the nineteenth and twentieth centuries.

The distinction between the public schools and the rest of the grammar schools (from which, originally, the public schools had not been clearly divided) was, by the eighteenth century, well established. The public schools had increased in prestige and numbers, and in the numbers of their staff. Most of them had become boarding-schools—this is the most important single feature. The public schools were held to be—in 1867 for the purpose of the Public Schools Commission—Eton, Winchester, Westminster, Shrewsbury, Harrow, Charterhouse, Rugby, St. Paul's, and Merchant Taylors'. The last two only were day-schools.

Conditions in the past were bad: criticism could be directed at two sides of the public school life—at the curriculum and at the social conditions in the schools. The curriculum was almost entirely classical, Latin and Greek. It was essentially linguistic and stylistic, and did not reveal ancient life and thought. The classical curriculum was mercilessly attacked in the *Edinburgh Review* of 1830 on these two grounds. To-day, however, we can observe that the schools were bound by their statutes to confine their teaching to the classics. In any case, the great weight of inertia was behind the classics; people do not change easily. It took time before the importance of new subjects was realized; then it was necessary to make them suitable for teaching in school, i.e., to prepare courses, write text-books, and work out teaching methods. The boys did at least learn Latin well— much of Virgil and Horace by heart—and could write sound Latin prose.

Social conditions in the schools were often highly unsatisfactory. Boarding arrangements were bad; accommodation was poor and sanitary arrangements were primitive; food was often insufficient; boys had no private studies to work in; they had nowhere to wash save at the pump. Discipline could not be enforced and was thus severe—flogging was the method. Dr. Keate of Eton was busy at it on one occasion from lock-up on Saturday night until the early hours of Sunday morning. On another occasion—according to a famous but perhaps apocryphal story—he mixed up two lists of names and beat all the candidates for confirmation. Bullying was rife. Boys were locked up at night and left to their own devices. One account of Eton says: 'Cruel at times the suffering and wrong; wild the profligacy. For after eight o'clock at night no prying eye came near till the following morning; no one lived in the same building; cries of joy and pain were equally unheard; and, excepting a code of laws of their own, there was no help or redress for anyone.'

The modern checks on bad behaviour were undeveloped. No confidence existed between master and boys (Keate expected that all boys would lie to him). The older boys, on whom the modern headmaster relies, were ringleaders in misdoing. The moral atmosphere was never very good. Boys saw little of the masters save in class hours and there was thus no influence to check evil and encourage good. School games had not yet developed sufficiently to be an aid in discipline and tone; headmasters had not come to rely on them for the training of character. Yet it was possible for the normal boy to pass unharmed through the great schools. Gladstone and his friends, even under the redoubtable Keate, passed a happy boyhood at Eton, and in after-life retained a real affection for their headmaster. Gladstone described how at the dinner to celebrate the Eton fourth centenary, the applause which greeted the toast to Keate was the loudest of the evening, and that the stern headmaster was so moved by emotion as to be unable to find words to reply.[1]

But the great feature of the unreformed schools was the fre-

[1] Morley: *Life of Gladstone*, I, 45-6.

quent occurrence of mutinies or rebellions. King George III's standing question when he met boys from Eton was 'Have you had a rebellion lately, eh, eh?' At Winchester between 1775 and 1793 there were several mutinies. On the most serious occasion, the boys held the college buildings for two days and hoisted the red flag. The episode was terminated by numerous expulsions. In 1818 a rising had to be put down by two companies of soldiers with fixed bayonets. At Rugby in 1797 the boys, finding a grievance against the headmaster, blew up the door of his study and made a bonfire of his books and the school desks. The boys withdrew to the Island, a moated mound, but soldiers were called in and the island taken by assault. The last serious rebellion was at Marlborough (one of the new schools founded in 1842) in 1851.

But not all the great schools were marked by these disorders. Both Charles Lamb and Leigh Hunt described with pleasure their own schooldays at Christ's Hospital, and there they were able, along with many others, to obtain an education largely classical but sound enough for their time. The Rev. James Boyer, headmaster from 1776–99, was indeed a classical master of the old style famous for his floggings. 'Poor J.B.!' wrote Coleridge when he heard of his old master's death, 'may all his faults be forgiven; and may he be wafted to bliss by little cherub boys, all head and wings, with no bottoms to reproach his sublunary infirmities.' But both Lamb and Coleridge bore testimony to his merits as an educator. And, as Lamb's most recent editor has said: 'To have had charge of the schooling of Lamb, Coleridge, Leigh Hunt, Thomas Barnes, Bishop Middleton of Calcutta, Henry Meyer (who painted the best-known portraits of his three greatest schoolfellows) and John Colborne (who led the cavalry at Waterloo) is glory enough for a schoolmaster.'[1] Thomas Barnes was editor of *The Times*— journalists, scholars, great figures in English literature, all these were turned out by such a school. Leigh Hunt maintained that at the end of the eighteenth and the beginning of the nineteenth century Christ's Hospital 'sent out more living writers,

[1] *Charles Lamb and Elia* (ed. J. E. Morpurgo, 1949), p. 27.

in its proportion, than any other school'.[1] Certainly, the classical education of a school which, like Christ's Hospital, had maintained its intellectual standards was no mean forcing ground for boys who had already native talent in them. For the fathers of Lamb, Coleridge, and Leigh Hunt were all men of education and a certain distinction, and the genius and character of their sons owe much to the family stock as well as to education at a public school. The classics suited them well enough; nor did a classical education hamper the development of the future leader of cavalry.

Christ's Hospital admitted boys whose parents' incomes fell below a certain limit, and thus drew from a different class of boys from that which ordinarily filled the famous schools. This gave the school a middle position among the educational institutions of the day. 'The Christ's Hospital or Blue-coat boy', wrote Lamb, 'has a distinctive character of his own, as far removed from the abject qualities of a common charity boy as it is from the disgusting forwardness of a lad brought up at some other of the public schools.'[2] At the school a few years later than Lamb, Leigh Hunt wrote of it: 'Perhaps there is not a foundation in the country so truly English, taking that word to mean what Englishmen wish it to mean—something solid, unpretending, of good character, and free to all. More boys are to be found in it, who issue from a greater variety of ranks, than in any school in the kingdom. . . . Nobility do not go there, except as boarders . . . but the sons of poor gentry and London citizens abound; and with them an equal share is given to the sons of tradesmen of the very humblest description, not omitting servants.' This mixing of ranks had produced the best effect. 'The cleverest boy was the noblest, let his father be who he might. Christ's Hospital is a nursery of tradesmen, of merchants, of naval officers, of scholars . . . the feeling among the boys themselves is, that it is a medium between the patrician pretension of such schools as Eton and Westminster, and the plebeian submission of the charity schools.' Since those long-ago

[1] *Autobiography of Leigh Hunt* (ed. J. E. Morpurgo, 1949), p. 56.
[2] *Charles Lamb and Elia*, p. 32.

233

16

days the school has moved to the country near Horsham, but originally it was a London school. 'Thousands of the inhabitants of the metropolis', wrote Hunt, 'have gone from west-end to east-end, and . . . never suspected that in the heart of it lies an old cloistered foundation, where a boy may grow up as I did, among six hundred others.'[1]

For the best boys the classical training was probably as good, or better, than any other. 'I am grateful', wrote Leigh Hunt, ' to Christ's Hospital for having bred me up in old cloisters, for its making me acquainted with the languages of Homer and Ovid, and for its having secured to me, on the whole, a well-trained and cheerful boyhood. . . . It did not hinder my growing mind from making what excursions it pleased into the wide and healthy regions of general literature. I might buy as much Collins and Gray as I pleased, and get novels to my heart's content from the circulating libraries.'[2] And, indeed, the school was not confined to the classics; it was sub-divided: the grammar school proper was for those boys intended for the universities and the Church. There were, in addition, a mathematical or navigation school for boys who were to enter the navy, a writing school for those going into trade and business, and a reading school for boys who could not read when they were first admitted to the school foundation. But in the three-quarters of a century of Leigh Hunt's life much was changing or was on the point of changing for he was born in 1784, the year that Dr. Johnson died, and died himself in 1859, when Bernard Shaw was already three years old. A multiplicity of school subjects were breaking, or were soon to break, into the old classical curriculum, and to transform it. But perhaps the completeness of the transition from one age to another is made most striking for us in reading another old pupil's description of the headmaster, James Boyer: 'He was a short, stout, round little man, wearing a white wig, a cocked or three-cornered hat, and having short thick legs covered with worsted stockings, and his shoes adorned with great broad silver buckles.'[3]

---

[1] *Autobiography*, pp. 55–6. [2] *Ibid.*, p. 82.
[3] *Ibid.* quoted from W. P. Scargill: *Recollections of a Blue-Coat Boy* (1829).

The reform of the public schools was brought about partly by the work of great headmasters and partly by the interference of the state. The most notable headmaster was Dr. Arnold, of Rugby, headmaster 1827–42, and a product himself of Winchester, our oldest public school. There has been some attempt at a 'debunking' of Arnold, notably by Lytton Strachey in his *Eminent Victorians*. But we do not go far wrong if we regard Arnold as the principal reforming influence. There were other great headmasters (like Butler of Shrewsbury, 1798–1836) at the time and immediately afterwards, but Arnold's influence was particularly strong and was carried into the other public schools when Arnold's assistant masters and old pupils obtained headships elsewhere.

What, then, were the principal reforms and what was Arnold's part? The curriculum was widened; French and mathematics became regular subjects instead of 'extras'. Some history, even modern history, was taught at Rugby, and Arnold gave an historical bias to the teaching of the classics. In these changes we see the beginning of the expansion of the school curriculum to include modern subjects. Teaching was made more efficient, and greater industry enforced on teachers and pupils alike. School games were perhaps encouraged, although Arnold's part in their development was small; games were developed by Cotton at Marlborough. We cannot blame Arnold for the evils of an exaggerated modern athleticism; games are at least a substitute for the evils of bullying, fighting, drinking, and poaching.

The moral tone of the public schools was greatly raised; strict churchmen and nonconformists came to approve of them. Religion and character training were dominant features; Arnold put religious principles above intellectual ability. Improvements took place also in diet and housing. A new discipline was created by prefects and by closer relations between boys and master, and Arnold's personal influence was powerfully exercised through two means, the school chapel and the prefects. He made the school chapel an essential feature of the boarding-school; through it as an assembly of the whole school he could appeal to all and make his influence felt throughout the school. His success as preacher was a personal triumph of his strong character. In using the authority of his sixth form, Arnold showed how the co-operation of the older boys could be gained, and the headmaster's reliance on them has become a feature of the public schools.

The result of the reform of the public schools was a considerable expansion in their number and also a great increase in their influence. Old grammar schools became first-class public schools like Repton, Sherborne, Tonbridge. J. P. Collis, a pupil of Arnold, built up the reputation of Bromsgrove. Thring turned the small country grammar school at Uppingham into a famous public school and founded, in 1869, the Headmasters' Conference which the older schools soon joined. New public schools were founded, like Cheltenham (1841), Marlborough (1842), Rossall (1844), Wellington (1859), and Clifton (1860). As important contributory factors in this expansion we observe a new middle class, as a result of the Industrial Revolution, able to pay well for the old type of education; railways which made access to boarding-schools possible to a larger class; and the growth of the Empire which made parents on service abroad look to boarding-schools at home for the education of their children.

In the mid-nineteenth century the government set up certain commissions of inquiry into the universities, the public schools, and the other endowed schools. As a result, certain acts of parliament were passed. Two were important in their effect on the development of the public schools. These were the Public Schools Act of 1868 covering the seven great public schools and the Endowed Schools Act of 1869 covering other endowed schools and also Merchant Taylors' and St. Paul's. The result of these acts was that the schools were obliged to modernize their foundation statutes and to make better use of their endowments. In effect, the way was opened for further changes in curriculum and for making more sure the position of the public schools in popular opinion. Some public-school endowments were extended to assist the education of girls.

To-day we can say that, despite all criticism, as, for example, that of Alec Waugh in *The Loom of Youth*, or of T. C. Worsley in *Barbarians and Philistines*, the public schools are still firmly based and are recognized as a leading institution in our secondary education. The main features of the public schools of to-day may now, perhaps, be summarized. The classics have a surer position there than in the ordinary secondary schools; otherwise the curriculum is much the same—general education aiming at the General Certificate of Education. The sixth form is especially important and specialization takes place there because, in the public schools, more boys stay on until eighteen or nineteen. The sixth form will be divided into, for example, four divisions —Classics, History, Modern Languages, Mathematics and Science—each with a specialist master and partly working for university scholarships.[1] Then there are the prefect system, school games (whereby each boy gets a daily change and exercise), and the J.T.C., which provides a nucleus of potential young officers in time of need. The corporate life becomes a reality through the house system, for the school is divided into houses in which senior boys have great responsibility. The smallness of the house intensifies the housemaster's influence over his boys, but throughout the public schools great importance is attached to the impact of boy on boy. Boys learn while at school both to obey and to command and lead. Finally, the school chapel is the tangible symbol of the importance given to character training on a religious foundation.

With these outstanding characteristics the public schools continue to exercise a great influence not only on education but on the whole of English life; the public schools are good schools and the question of the future is whether, and how far, their opportunities can be made available to a wider class of the British community.

[1] Specialization of this kind has come about gradually. G. M. Trevelyan in *An Autobiography* (1949) says 'I suppose I was the earliest "history specialist" at Harrow'. This was in 1892–3; Trevelyan was in the Classical Upper Sixth, but was allowed to give some of the classics time to history.

CHAPTER XV

THE DEMAND FOR POPULAR EDUCATION
IN ENGLAND

PARLIAMENTARY reform and Chartism have received more attention than education at the hands of the historian, but the problem of popular education occupied an important place both in the lives of working-class pioneers like Francis Place and also in the thought and activity of the period. Out of the Industrial Revolution and the movement for parliamentary reform there arose other movements, for the successful development of which the better education of the working classes was necessary. 'Of the three great democratic movements in England during the first half of the nineteenth century, Co-operation, Chartism, and Trade Unionism each paid a tribute to liberal education as a social ideal, however imperfectly they may have contributed to realizing that ideal in practice.'[1]

The years of the Industrial Revolution saw the disintegration of a long-established social order; the old order was forced to give place to a new. At the middle of the eighteenth century the conditions in England were still those of a surviving feudalism. Political and social power rested with the owners of the big estates: with the great families, whether Whig or Tory. The degeneration of the boroughs had put parliament into their hands. Economically, the holders of land were equally power-

[1] Ministry of Reconstruction. Adult Education Committee *Final Report* (1919), p. 17. Modern adult education has followed the liberal ideal in making its work non-vocational and cultural. The technical schools and commercial schools on the other hand devote themselves to education for immediate practical use.

ful. England was still mainly agricultural and self-supporting. What industry there was, was chiefly domestic. The landed squire as justice of the peace was the virtual ruler of the little world—the microcosm—of the eighteenth-century English countryside. The Church was the social counterpart of the landed aristocracy. It absorbed their younger members and offered them a livelihood at the expiration of their years at Oxford or Cambridge.

These conditions had certain advantages. Squire and parson might be humane and easy-going. They, like their tenants, were products of the same countryside and the same economic relation, hallowed by custom and tradition. Goldsmith's *Deserted Village* may give an exaggerated idealization of the happiness and simplicity of country life, but it does give us one aspect at least of a picture which was to be destroyed by the economic changes. For the Industrial Revolution altered the social life of the people, or perhaps more correctly it brought into existence a new class of people—an industrial class. Along with industrialization came a great growth in population as well as a shifting in its density. The enclosures of land and the increasing competition of machinery drove men from the country into the towns; the centres of population were altered from the old agricultural south to what was becoming the industrial north. The increase in the population during the early years of the nineteenth century was striking.[1] In the new class that emerged we see the advent of the proletariat. Long before Marx, Sismondi pointed out that 'The fundamental change which has taken place in society, amid this universal struggle created by competition, is the introduction of the "proletary" '.[2]

The advent of this new class, involving a great increase in

[1] Census figures show the population of Great Britain and Ireland as 16,345,646 in 1801 and as 24,392,485 in 1831. For the causes of the growth see J. H. Clapham: *Economic History of Modern Britain (The Early Railway Age)*, p. 54. The decline in the death-rate due to medical and sanitary improvements is stressed.

[2] J. C. L. de Sismondi: *New Principles of Political Economy, 1819*. See Dr. Shadwell on the origins of Socialism in his *Socialist Movement*, I.

the numbers of those with whom any social policy had to deal, brought with it many social problems, problèms which, if they existed at all before this time, had existed only on an altogether smaller scale. The nature of the economic changes which have been epitomized in the term 'Industrial Revolution' was not clear at the time. Old theories had to be abandoned or modified to meet the new conditions. In due course every variety of problem appeared—the problem of wages and hours, of factory conditions, of sanitation and medical aid, of housing and town life, of education and religion. Above all, what was to be the place and function of the working class in social theory, in the *Weltanschauung* which the philosophers of every age attempt to build? Clearly, whatever the answer to this question might be, it must profoundly influence the attitude adopted towards the question of making provision for the education of this new class.

The 'fury of avaricious commerce' against which Ruskin protested marked the period of unbridled competition and *laissez-faire*. The prevailing view as to the conditions of the working class was that, bad as those conditions might be, they were the necessary outcome of economic laws. Thus as late as 1860 a reviewer of Ruskin's *Unto this Last* writes, 'the masters have the upper hand of the men', and then conveniently states that 'political economy adds the information that to deprive them of this advantage by legislation would diminish the power of producing wealth'.[1]

This popular view of economics was largely the result of the union effected by the economists of two streams of thought which had flowed down from the past. In the eighteenth century the divine right of monarchs had given place to the rights of the subjects. The theory of the Social Contract was used as a vindication of these rights. Here, then, was a theory of the right of the individual as against the monarch, the impersonation of government. To this stream of thought contributed Locke, Hume, and Burke. But to the Social Contract theory Rousseau

[1] *Saturday Review*, 4 August, 1860. Cf. Mrs. Marcet's *Conversations on Political Economy* of 1817.

added the conception of the General Will, and attempted to balance the rights of the individual with those of the community as a whole.[1] Bentham, though an individualist, gives expression to a belief in the common rights of society in his theory of the 'Greatest Happiness of the Greatest Number'. In these theories which emphasize the social side of life we have the second stream of thought. It was left to the economists to perform the divine miracle and to unite the two opposites into one.[2]

Thus arose the conviction of a harmony between private advantage and the public good. Given conditions of freedom—and this it was the duty of government to provide—the political philosopher could retire and leave the accumulation of wealth to the infallible working of natural laws. Here we see the eighteenth-century idea of 'Nature' appearing once more. Later, too, the theory of free competition was strengthened by the work of Darwin. 'The principle of the Survival of the Fittest could be regarded as a vast generalization of the Ricardian economics.'[3] Any governmental control or socialistic interference with the free working of natural forces would therefore be not only inexpedient but also calculated to retard the mighty process of evolution.

But there was an inevitable reaction against the crudities of *laissez-faire*. Human nature revolted at the horrors of industrialism. Thinkers criticized the economic theories. The 'nest of singing birds' at the Lakes sought escape in a return to nature. Robert Owen marks the first phase of British socialism. But

[1] It can be argued that Rousseau effects a nice compromise between Individualism and Collectivism. His ideal is the free citizen in the free state. See Vaughan's edition of Rousseau's *Political Works*, I, Introduction. But Rousseau writes before the complications of Industrialism.

[2] Keynes: *End of Laissez Faire*, p. 10 *et seq*. It should be pointed out that the doctrines of the economist were often distorted by popularizers. Marshall shows that the general belief in Ricardo's adherence to the 'iron law of wages' is due to his unguarded language and that actually he was aware that wages depend upon local customs and conditions and that he was sensitive to the importance of a higher standard of life. See Marshall: *Principles of Economics*, p. 508.

[3] Keynes: *End of Laissez Faire*, p. 14.

there is a lacuna between Owen and the foundation in 1882 of the Social Democratic Federation with its Marxian inspiration. The work of social protest, in the meantime, was left to lone voices. Carlyle characterized economics as the 'dismal science'. Newman pointed out in 1852 that its tenets were but part of knowledge and not absolute in themselves.[1] Ruskin condemned political economy as 'a lie—wholly and to the very root (as hitherto taught)'.[2] Actually, however, during a long period the *laissez-faire* theory of economics held almost complete sway over men's minds. In the popular *Conversations on Political Economy*, for example, published in 1817, the author, Mrs. Marcet, makes Caroline stand out as long as she can for controlling the expenditure of the rich, but at last the girl is compelled to admit: 'The more I learn upon this subject, the more I feel convinced that the interests of nations, as well as those of individuals, so far from being opposed to each other, are in the most perfect unison.'

By 1850 the tone of popular writing on economic topics had scarcely changed. At that time the Society for Promoting Christian Knowledge was distributing widely Archbishop Whately's *Easy Lessons for the Use of Young People*. True liberty, the young are told, is 'that every man should be left free to dispose of his own property, his own time, and strength, and skill, in whatever way he himself may think fit, provided he does no wrong to his neighbours'.

This domination of *laissez-faire* economics was scarcely favourable to education, but the competitive theory was modified in this respect by the idea of progress and by utilitarianism. Adam Smith's *Wealth of Nations*, the foundation of *laissez-faire* theory in England, contributed indirectly to the doctrine of the progress of mankind.[3] For Smith's economic principles were calculated to lead to the production of greater wealth and hence to offer the material conditions of greater human welfare. The

[1] Newman: *Idea of a University*, p. 86.
[2] Letter to Dr. John Brown, August 1862, quoted in Cook and Wedderburn, *Works of Ruskin*, XVII, lxxxii.
[3] See J. B. Bury: *The Idea of Progress*, p. 220.

idea of progress must also be associated with the views of Godwin on education. Godwin adopted the philosophy of the Frenchman, Helvetius, and through Godwin it passed to Robert Owen. According to this view, man's character is the result of his intellectual and moral environment; it can be improved by training. Social difficulties, therefore, are not due to the innate evil of man but to ignorance. This enabled agitators to go a step further and to declare that man's ignorance was accounted for by a wicked government's desiring to keep him ignorant. The prospect of social improvement through enlightenment was important for education. It was at the back of Owen's educational policy. Briefly put it was : 'The character of Man is formed for him, and not by him.'[1]

Utilitarianism—the doctrines of the little group of thinkers who based their philosophy on the teachings of Bentham—is also important in its educational aspects. Malthus's *Essay on the Principle of Population*, which first appeared anonymously in 1798, at first offered a check to the optimism of eighteenth-century believers in progress and the perfectibility of man.[2] But, in effect, Malthus does not deny but corrects the idea of progress. Adam Smith had advocated a system of parish schools giving elementary education to the children of the poor. Malthus went further, demanding that there should be popular teaching of political economy. His object was to spread a knowledge of the principle he had put forward that population tended to increase faster than the means of subsistence and to urge the necessity of self-control. Similarly, Bentham's scheme for reform of the Poor Laws meant a programme of popular education. 'Popular education had already developed in England, through the efforts of the Nonconformists and especially of the Methodists. But Malthus brought a utilitarian formula to the already existing movement. It is *just*, said the Protestants, that all men, since they are equal before God, should share as equally as possible in the knowledge of the sacred books, of the divine law and of the moral law. It is

---

[1] The motto of Robert Owen's *Millennial Gazette* (1857).
[2] Bury: *The Idea of Progress*, p. 230.

useful, said Malthus, that all men should know the physical laws which determine the development and the increase of the species, so that they will understand how to regulate the increase of their needs in accordance with the increase in the amount of pleasures which Nature puts at their disposal.'[1]

Through the utilitarians the influence of Helvetius further affected educational ideas in England.[2] Bentham had been a disciple of Helvetius. James Mill made his son, John Stuart, the subject of an experimental verification of Helvetius's theory. And the education of John Stuart Mill was a common subject of conversation among the friends of Bentham, men who like him were friends of education. The subject was discussed in Francis Place's shop, and Place showed the prevailing Helvetian idea—'The position I take . . . is that the generality of children are organized so nearly alike that they may by proper management be made pretty nearly equally wise and virtuous.'[3] But Mill was not content to confine his efforts to individual experiment. He became interested in the educational activities of Lancaster and his system of teaching children in large numbers by means of monitors. With James Mill, Place, the economist Wakefield, and Lord Brougham were engaged in sketching a plan for secondary as well as primary education in London. Bentham wrote his *Chrestomathia* advocating a day-school for the middle class. These efforts did not effect much result immediately though University College (London) and the London Mechanics' Institute may be regarded as forms of chrestomathic institutions. More important was the general utilitarian attitude towards education. By its means the growth of numbers and of poverty was to be checked. As M. Halévy, the French historian of modern England put it: 'All must therefore receive the rudiments of instruction, and must learn the elements of social science: hence

[1] E. Halévy: *Growth of Philosophic Radicalism,* p. 242.
[2] *Ibid.,* p. 282 *et seq.* There was a connexion between Bentham and Owen. Bentham in 1813 became a shareholder in Owen's establishment in New Lanark. At the same time Bentham and Place were revising Owen's *Essays on the Principle of the Formation of the Human Character.* See Halévy, p. 285.
[3] Graham Wallas: *Francis Place,* p. 7.

the political economy of the utilitarians demanded the intervention of the state as a universal educator.'[1]

The divergent attitudes to popular education can perhaps be summarized:

(1) The reactionary view of the Tories and many of the Whigs that education was dangerous. They were afraid of raising the working man above his station, and therefore attacked all proposals for popular education.

(2) The view that enough education should be given as was required for religious purposes, notably for the reading of the Scriptures.

(3) The utilitarian view that education was necessary for social and political ends. This view might be extended to cover any forms of training which would make for social progress and the advance of science,[2] and could be fitted into the individualistic economics. Though the utilitarians proper wished to keep education free of religious teaching, it was possible to combine a utilitarian view of education with a belief in religious teaching, as in the case of Charles Knight.

(4) The working class view, which is more difficult to define. In many respects it is closely associated with the utilitarian view. Men like Place accepted the orthodox economics. Education was viewed partly as a means of 'getting on'. Those who held such views co-operated with upper- and middle-class advocates of popular education. There were also signs of a more independent working-class attitude. Thomas Hodgskin, one of the moving spirits in the London Mechanics' Institute, held anti-capitalist views. The Chartists, too, advocated education.

These views will appear behind the various movements for the education of adults which are presently to be noted. The conception that education was valuable as a means to an end,

[1] Halévy: *Growth of Philosophic Radicalism*, p. 490.
[2] See a letter of 7 July 1827 from James Hay, Secretary of the Leith Mechanics' Institute, to Brougham, describing a drawing class: ' . . . some of them are shortly to commence copying drawings of the steam engine and other machines varying the scale, a mode of applying their drawing particularly useful to mechanics in their daily occupations.'

rather than as an end in itself, seems to have been general. This is characteristic perhaps of an industrial age, but it might seem to require a modification in the view that it was a 'liberal education' to which the democratic movements of the first half of the nineteenth century paid a tribute.[1] This is not necessarily so. Men like Place, Lovett, and Cooper did appreciate education as a source of intellectual pleasures, which, without education, would be unenjoyed because unknown. The working-class pioneers had their ideal of social improvement in mind, and they regarded education as a means to that end; but they did not regard it as solely a means to a social end. Education was also in itself the way to refined enjoyment.

Dicey in his *Law and Opinion in England* distinguishes three periods—(1) The period of old Toryism or Legislative Quiescence (1800–30); (2) The period of Benthamism or Individualism (1825–70); and (3) The period of Collectivism (1865–1900). But it would be a mistake to suppose that during the period of Individualism there was no form of collective activity. This activity indeed took many forms but it was confined rather to voluntary action than to state interference; though the government itself was in time to be affected by this voluntary association for social ends. As Professor Fay puts it: 'Individualism may suffice to define the dominant legal trend, but it conceals the influence exerted on the legislature from without and from below by the action of voluntary associations. The period of voluntary association coincides with the period of individualism, and bridges the transition to the period of collectivism.'[2]

The number and variety of societies illustrate just how much social activity there was and that, in fact, people were realizing that 'something must be done', that the free play of the forces of individualism required at least the aid of voluntary organizations. 'This is the age of Societies', Macaulay wrote in the year 1823. 'There is scarcely an Englishman in ten who has not belonged to some Association for distributing books, or for

[1] See p. 238. Cf. Newman in the *Idea of a University*.
[2] Fay: *Life and Labour in the Nineteenth Century*, p. 49.

prosecuting them; for sending invalids to the hospital, or beggars to the treadmill; for giving plate to the rich, or blankets to the poor.'[1] In elementary education, the Sunday School Union Society, the National Society (1811), and the British and Foreign School Society (1814) were outstanding examples of voluntary organizations. Perhaps it should be pointed out that attempts were made to go further than mere voluntary action. In 1807 Whitbread introduced the first Education Bill into the Commons but it was thrown out by the Lords. Brougham's Bill of 1820 met with the same fate. In 1818, William Allen, representing the British and Foreign School Society, stated that 'it is indeed gratifying to find, that the vast importance of educating the children of the poor is so increasingly felt by the public'.[2] But he makes clear the prevailing belief in voluntary effort. 'Do you apprehend', he was asked, 'that there would be any danger of weakening the zeal of private subscribers in large towns, by interposing parliamentary assistance to bear part of the annual expenses?' He replied: 'Certainly I do; for we universally find that those things which the public enter into with spirit, from a consciousness of their value and importance to the community, are best supported by that zeal, when left to itself.'[3]

In the first attempts to provide for the education of adults the

---

[1] Macaulay, under the name of Tristam Merton, in Knight's *Quarterly Magazine*, 1823. Among other societies we may mention the following: The Society for Superseding the Necessity of Climbing Boys (i.e., boys who climbed inside chimneys to sweep them). This society promoted bills in parliament. There was an Education Clothing Society (formerly called the Juvenile Benevolent Society) 'for the purpose of giving clothes to those wretched children and sending them to schools, chiefly Sunday Schools' (*Second Report*, p. 11, of the Select Committee of House of Commons, 1818, *The Education of the Lower Orders*). There were other societies, like the Society for Bettering the Conditions and Increasing the Comforts of the Poor, and the Society for Educating the Poor of Newfoundland. An American tract of 1884, *The Elements of Social Disorder by a Mechanic*, declares that 'Religious, benevolent, moral and charitable institutions, as they now exist, however good and praiseworthy in themselves . . . can never succeed in the attempt to moralize society at large' and advocates universal education.

[2] *Third Report*, Select Committee of House of Commons, 1818, *The Education of the Lower Orders*.

[3] *Ibid.*

religious influence was very strong. There was, in the early days' no clear differentiation between the ages of those who attended Sunday schools. Both young and old attended. They might be in different classes, but scholars of all ages were beginning to learn.[1] The Society for the Promotion of Christian Knowledge had already, in 1711, recommended the establishment of evening schools for adults. In Wales the Rev. Griffith Jones, rector of Llanddowror, and a corresponding member of the S.P.C.K., was responsible for establishing a system of schools with itinerant teachers to instruct both young and old. A main object was to teach people to read the Bible in Welsh. From 1785 to 1814 this work was carried on in Wales by Thomas Charles of Bala.[2]

In England, there was opened at Nottingham in 1798 an adult school for Bible-reading and instruction in writing and arithmetic. This was the result of the efforts of a Methodist, William Singleton, and of Samuel Fox, a member of the Society of Friends.[3] At the same time, Hannah and Martha More were at work among the Somerset miners, giving them instruction in the Scriptures.[4] Adult schools, for men and women, were founded at Bristol in 1812.[5] The movement spread rapidly. As a result of a meeting of clergymen at Maidenhead in 1814 there was established 'An Institution for Teaching Adults to Read' in the adjoining parts of Buckingham and Berkshire. The object was clear. 'We content ourselves', the clergy declared, 'with recommending as much as possible the simplifying the mode of instruction, as most conformable to the single object we have in view—the teaching the poor to read, in order to gain an acquaintance with the Scriptures.'[6]

Religious zeal and political apprehension were united in their

---

[1] See Dobbs: *Education and Social Movements*, p. 155.
[2] See Ministry of Reconstruction, *Adult Education Report*, 1919, p. 11, and David Evans: *The Sunday Schools of Wales*.
[3] Rowntree and Binns: *History of the Adult School Movement*.
[4] Hannah More: *The Mendip Annals*.
[5] Ministry of Reconstruction, *op. cit.*, p. 11.
[6] Charles Goddard: *Account of the Origins . . . of an Institution for Teaching Adults to Read*, pp. 4–5.

influence on these experiments. 'Where are the lower classes to hear the Word of God? Where are they to learn the doctrine of that truly excellent religion which exhorts to content and submission to the higher powers?' asked Arthur Young in 1798.[1] The utilitarian motive was also present. It might well prove to the interest of society to educate the poor. 'Give liberally', wrote Dr. Pole, in appealing to the rich to support adult education in Bristol, 'because adult education will put an end to existing crimes and encourage the principles upon which society depends for its security. The lower classes will not then be so dependent on the more provident members of society as they are now. . . . Industry, frugality and economy will be their possession. They will also have learned better to practice meekness, Christian fortitude and resignation. Our poor rate will then be lightened and men exalted by piety and blessed with affluence will yield springs of benevolence and charity to refresh, to console, and to instruct those who are placed in the vale of human life.'[2]

The work of the Mechanics' Institutes had behind it a motive other than that of the adult schools. Education had already been advocated by Adam Smith to counter the evil effects of the monotony of work introduced by machinery.[3] But the very machinery that made work monotonous also introduced to the mechanic the problems of science. Here then was the cause of a new demand for information. Closely allied to scientific curiosity of this character was the utilitarian view that increased knowledge would lead to increased command over natural forces and hence to greater human welfare.

The Mechanics' Institutes date from 1799 when Dr. George Birkbeck was Professor of Natural Philosophy and Chemistry

[1] Young: *An Inquiry into the State of Mind among the Lower Orders*. The doctrine referred to is stated by St. Paul in Romans xiii, 1: 'Let every soul be subject unto higher powers. For there is no power but of God: the powers that be are ordained of God.' In the Anti-Religious Museum in St. Isaac's, Leningrad, this passage was posted in a prominent position as a proof of the alliance between state and Church against the lower orders.

[2] Pole: *History of the Origin and Progress of Adult Schools*.

[3] Adam Smith: *Wealth of Nations*, Book V, chap. i, Part III, Article II.

in 'Anderson's University' at Glasgow, and threw open his lectures to workmen. The years after 1815 saw a rapid expansion of the movement to found Mechanics' Institutes. Between 1821 and 1825 institutes were established in Edinburgh, Glasgow, London, Manchester, Huddersfield, Leeds, and many other industrial towns. The institutes aimed at providing lectures, generally on scientific subjects, for the benefit of their members and also at providing a library. Somewhat later associations, or unions, of Mechanics' Institutes were formed in certain parts of the country in order to take advantages of the services of the same lecturers.[1]

But by the middle of the nineteenth century the movement was in decline. From the beginning there had been difficulties. There was sometimes friction between members of different social class. There was difficulty over the lack of early schooling, and over the raising of funds. Complaints were made that lectures were desultory and that political controversy was excluded. The mechanics tended to be pushed out by men from the higher branches of handicraft and by clerks. As the early enthusiasm wore off some of the institutes became transformed into technical schools: others transferred their premises to the local authorities under the Public Library Acts; others lingered on as billiard saloons or middle-class clubs.[2]

With the Mechanics' Institutes should be mentioned *The Mechanics' Magazine*, which first appeared in 1823 at the price of 3d. Its very motto—'Knowledge is Power'—indicates the popular belief in education. Its object was clearly stated in a preface written later when the *Magazine* was bound into volumes. 'A numerous and valuable portion of the community,' it states, 'including all who are manually employed in our different trades and manufactures, had begun for the first time, to feel the want of a periodical work, which at a price suited to their humble means, would diffuse among them a

[1] See, on the Mechanics' Institutes, Dobbs, *op. cit.*, chapter v, and Ministry of Reconstruction, *Adult Education Report*, 1919, p. 13 *et seq.*

[2] Dobbs, *op. cit.*, p. 181. See also Knight: *Passages of a Working Life*, III, 74–86, and James Hole: *History and Management of Literary, Scientific and Mechanics' Institutes*, p. 21.

better acquaintance with the history and principles of the arts they practise, convey to them earlier information than they had hitherto been able to procure of new discoveries, inventions and improvements and attend generally to their earlier interests, as affected by passing events.'[1]

In the very first number the moral aim of the paper is apparent. James Watt is selected as the subject for an article, which states : 'His good fortune may encourage, and his perseverance instruct the present and all future generations of mechanics. . . . Mr. Watt was also a kind good-hearted man—giving lustre to his art, not only by the prodigious power he created, but by the life he led. He acquired wealth and honour by his own exertions, and was praised for his wisdom as well as for his skill.'[2]

Here was the ideal of the industrial age. To the movement for scientific education all who held utilitarian or orthodox economic beliefs could give support. Both Lord John Russell and Cobden made their contribution, the latter pointing out, among other things, that education would lead to an appreciation of the value of good sanitation.[3]

In addition to the adult schools and the Mechanics' Institutes, there was an educational movement less organized but more independent in spirit. The motive behind this was partly political, partly a demand for a liberal education. 'Nothing can persuade us', some mechanics declared in 1824, 'but that all systems of education are false which do not teach a man his political duties and rights.'[4] The French Revolution, and later the agitation for parliamentary reform, both encouraged a demand for knowledge. The London Corresponding Society (founded in 1792), of which Place was a member in 1794, was a sign of the growing interest in political questions. All the working-class movements—Chartism, Trade Unionism, and Co-operation—paid their tribute to education, and not

[1] *The Mechanics' Magazine*, Preface to vol. I.
[2] *Ibid.*, No. 1, 30 August 1823.
[3] Address by Cobden at Barnsley Mechanics' Institution, 1853, in *British Eloquence* (1855).
[4] *Mechanics' Magazine*, 11 September 1824.

merely to such education as was likely to prove directly useful in an economic or political way.

When out of work in 1793 the radical, Place, studied a variety of subjects including mathematics and law as well as history and economics. He read widely—translations from Greek and Roman authors as well as the literature of England. The same may be said of the Chartists, William Lovett and Thomas Cooper. These men had a genuine interest in intellectual things. As a boy, Cooper 'read voraciously whatever books he could borrow—novels, poetry, history, theology, anything, in fact, that came his way'.[1] Early in the morning he read history or worked at grammar or translation, he read at mealtimes, and then, when he finished his work as a shoemaker at eight or nine at night, he paced up and down his room committing *Hamlet* or some modern poetry to memory.[2] These men acquired their education in face of the greatest difficulty; they worked at it because they really believed in its value. Of Lovett it has been said: 'The pre-eminent importance which he ascribed to education was a triumph of idealism in an age of economic misery, and he deserves a place in history, not only as the parent of Chartism, but as the first and greatest of working-class educational reformers.'[3]

But the desire for intellectual advancement was mixed with a political motive, the motive of social improvement. 'How can a corrupt government stand against an enlightened people?' asks Lovett. Education should be provided free at the public cost. A people who provided education both for children and adults would be occupied in 'accumulating means of instruction and amusement and in devising sources of refined enjoyment to which millions are strangers. It would be industriously employed in politically, intellectually and morally training fathers, mothers and children to know their rights and perform their duties. And with a people so trained exclusive power,

[1] R. Peers: 'Thomas Cooper—The Leicester Chartist', in the *Journal of Adult Education*, October 1931.
[2] Cooper: *Autobiography*, p. 59 *et seq.*
[3] Ministry of Reconstruction, Adult Education Committee *Report*, p. 18.

corruption and injustice would soon cease to have an existence.'[1] With such a statement as this educational idealism finds full expression in a social motive. There is a link here between the working-class advocates of education and the utilitarians.

The Chartists took some steps to provide the means of education. Lectures and classes were organized in connexion with local associations. Both Lovett and Cooper taught for a time. At Leicester, Cooper founded the Shakesperian Association of Leicester Chartists, and lectured on literature and history. Established at Birmingham, Bath, and in parts of Scotland, were Chartist churches, and these conducted classes.[2] Among the early trade unions and co-operative societies mutual improvement classes began to be formed, one of which was that established in 1842 by the Journeymen Steam Engine and Machine Makers' Friendly Society. Here again one of the outstanding motives in the formation of classes for education was the idea that knowledge meant power and power would lead to social improvement. The early co-operative societies, formed under the influence of the propaganda carried on by Robert Owen, advocated education. The society at Birmingham in 1828 maintained a library and debating club. Similar efforts were made elsewhere, and when the Rochdale Pioneers in 1844 laid the foundations of modern co-operation, education was a part of their scheme, and has remained so. There was, besides the philanthropic and utilitarian motives for education, a spontaneous demand for it on the part of the more enlightened sections of working-class opinion.

To satisfy the demand for popular instruction and to supply it with the means there was founded in 1826 the Society for the Diffusion of Useful Knowledge. With its eminent membership which included Lord John Russell, James Mill, and Jeremy Bentham, the Society's object was to make knowledge available to the working classes in the form of cheap books. During the next twenty years the Society's publications were numerous, and appealed to a great variety of needs and tastes.

[1] Quoted in the Ministry of Reconstruction, Adult Education *Report*, p. 19.
[2] Hovell: *The Chartist Movement.*

The Library of Useful Knowledge consisted of treatises, at 6d. each, appearing twice monthly, and covering most branches of mathematics, science, and history in a popular form. *The Library of Entertaining Knowledge* was aimed at less serious readers who might nevertheless pick up something of value. In addition, the Society produced a *Penny Magazine* and a *Cyclopaedia* issued in sheets at 1d. each.

The foundation of the Society was the work of a remarkable figure in English public life, Henry (afterwards Lord) Brougham. He was educated in Edinburgh, at the High School and University. Of great mental and physical powers and of boundless ambition, his interests lay in every sphere. Before he was nineteen he had written two papers on scientific subjects which were printed in the *Transactions of the Royal Society*.[1] He became lord chancellor in the Whig government of 1830. Outside parliament he was a popular figure; inside he had been perhaps, the most powerful orator in the House of Commons. Education was one of his many interests, and not merely one branch of education but education in all its branches. He promoted bills in parliament, he was largely responsible for the founding of London University, and with Birkbeck he shared in the founding of the London Mechanics' Institute. 'There is not a man living', wrote Francis Place, 'who has a stronger desire to have the people instructed than Mr. Brougham, not one who has exerted himself more than he has to promote that object.'[2]

Installed in 1825 as Lord Rector of Glasgow University, he defended classical education in his Inaugural Discourse, but explained that it might well have a utilitarian aim. He assumes that the improvement of the mind is an object to be aimed at by all, that it is the indispensable duty of every man, as far as his own immediate wants leave him any portion of time unemployed. The improvement of the mind, he thinks, is best achieved through the medium of the classical languages,

[1] Aspinall: *Lord Brougham and the Whig Party*, p. 2.
[2] *Place Papers*, British Museum Additional Mss., 27823, fol. 248. Quoted in Aspinall, p. 232.

and in this way rhetorical skill and eloquence may be acquired.[1] These latter, however, have their practical uses. Even in times of peace and in lands blessed with free institutions—

> *Pacis comes, otiique socia, et jam bene constitutae reipublicae alumna eloquentia,*

for eloquence can be employed in the diffusion of information.

'To diffuse useful information—to further intellectual refinement, sure forerunner of moral improvement—to hasten the coming of the bright day when the dawn of general knowledge shall chase away the lazy, lingering mists, even from the base of the social great pyramid;—this indeed is a high calling.' When he speaks of diffusing useful information and driving away the lingering mists 'even from the base of the social great pyramid', Brougham was thinking of the future work of his society. He goes on to express his belief that the 'highest intellectual cultivation is perfectly compatible with the daily cares and toils of working men.' But he cannot close without an answer, and also a warning, to those who fear and would therefore oppose the extension of education to the People:

'To those, too, who feel alarmed as statesmen, and friends of existing establishments, I would address a few words of comfort. Real knowledge never promoted either turbulence or unbelief; but its progress is the forerunner of liberality and enlightened toleration. Whoso dreads these let him tremble; for he may be well assured that their day is at length come and must put to sudden flight the evil spirits of tyranny and persecution, which haunted the long night now gone down the sky.'[2]

---

[1] Inaugural Discourse, in *Speeches*, III, 73 *et seq.* Cf. Newman: *Idea of a University*, on 'Knowledge its own End'. Newman argues that liberal knowledge is self-sufficient and has no ulterior object, and it is doubtful if he would agree with Brougham on 'intellectual refinement, sure forerunner of moral improvement'.

[2] Inaugural Discourse, in *Speeches*, III, 96.

CHAPTER XVI

BUILDING THE NATIONAL SYSTEM OF EDUCATION IN ENGLAND

A NATIONAL system of education for England was slow in coming—so slow that few, if any, of the early pioneers of popular education lived to see it. Every effort of voluntary organization was exhausted, every individual demand in parliament defeated, before the legislators were prepared to act— and those acts were so hesitant and so widely spaced that it was not until 1902 that anything like a complete system had taken shape. The efforts of voluntary organization went back to the end of the seventeenth and the beginning of the eighteenth century with the S.P.C.K. and its charity schools. During the eighteenth century and the first part of the nineteenth, some of the children of the poor might learn to read in the dame schools, the Sunday schools, the ragged schools, or in the industrial schools for pauper children, all of which were limited efforts on the part of private money-makers, philanthropists, or the Poor Law authorities. The village dame schools were described in a verse of 1742 as kept by—

> A matron, whom we schoolmistress name,
> Who boasts unruly brats with birch to tame.

and whose pupils were—

> Awed by the power of this relentless dame.[1]

In Worcester nearly a century later about six hundred children were said to be attending 'dame schools, and the various receptacles for the children of the lower classes, at small weekly

[1] By William Shenstone in *The School-Mistress*.

sums'.[1] Idealists in parliament pressed for state intervention and the provision of a system of schools. Whitbread introduced a bill in 1807, Brougham in 1820, and Roebuck in 1832. Roebuck proposed that every child in Great Britain and Ireland should have to attend school between about the ages of six and twelve. But all these bills were defeated. Speaking in support of his bill in 1820—with the evidence behind him of a Select Committee on the Education of the Lower Orders— Brougham alleged that before the recent creation of elementary schools on the systems of Bell and Lancaster only about one twenty-first of the population was receiving education and that England was perhaps the worst-educated country in Europe.

The work of Bell and Lancaster was indeed the most considerable voluntary movement to provide elementary instruction for the masses. Yet their work was split and their energy divided by a religious difference: Bell was an Anglican clergyman, Lancaster a Quaker. The quarrel between them— between their supporters rather than between the two men themselves[2]—was nominally due to a dispute as to which was the originator of a system, which each employed, of elementary instruction by selected pupils or monitors. But in reality the quarrel represented a deeper struggle between the Church of England and the Nonconformists for the control of education, a struggle which gravely hampered the work of making a national system and of which the traces still exist. Dr. Andrew Bell was a most remarkable man—financially perhaps the most successful who ever devoted a large part of his life to elementary education. Both fortune and fame he owed to India. There his ability, his Scottish education completed at the University of St. Andrews, and his capacity for making powerful and influential friends, stood him in good stead. He gave successful courses of lectures and held many regimental chaplaincies— 'some of these offices may have been sinecures; but there is

[1] *Report on Education in Worcester* from the Letter File of the Society for the Diffusion of Useful Knowledge.

[2] Mrs. Trimmer, in her *Comparative View of the New Plan of Education promulgated by Mr. Joseph Lancaster* (1805), p. 20, described Bell as 'the original inventor of the admirable plan which Mr. Lancaster has adopted'.

good proof among his papers that none of them were sine-salaries'—and he left in 1796 after nine years with £25,000.[1] But it was as superintendent (this time without emolument) of the Military Male Orphan Asylum set up at Madras for the destitute children of English soldiers by European or native mothers that Bell hit on the plan which he was to bring home from steaming Madras and spend the rest of his life in further-ing. This plan was the use of monitors who, under the guidance of the schoolmaster, could teach what they had already learnt to the younger children, thereby making possible the great economy of running a school of large numbers by a single teacher. His new method was now introduced into some of the existing church schools in England. His work aroused con-siderable enthusiasm and won the support not only of Southey, a poet laureate whose prose was better than his poetry and who added a *Bell* to his *Nelson* and his *Wesley*, but also of Words-worth and of Coleridge.

Joseph Lancaster was not, like Bell, a man of the world. He ended his life a disappointed man in New York. His financial incompetence had led his friends and supporters to take from him the direction of his educational work. Yet he had had his day, with the personal support of George III. In his 'teens Lancaster had dreamed of going out to Jamaica 'to teach the poor blacks the word of God'. In the outcome he established what became a famous school in the Borough Road, London, and developed his monitorial system. He showed, perhaps, a deeper belief in education than Bell, and gave careful attention to the training of his better pupils in order to make them quali-fied teachers, which perhaps suggested the more systematic pupil-teacher method of training long to be used in elementary education. The fruit of Lancaster's success in the Borough Road was the formation in 1808 of the Royal Lancastrian Society, later renamed the British and Foreign School Society. The movement gained ground and influential support; schools and pupils grew in numbers. The teaching, although based on Bible-reading, was undenominational and so aroused the fear

[1] R. Southey: *Life of the Rev. Andrew Bell*, I, 110, and II, 21.

and jealousy of the Anglicans. In 1811 they founded the National Society for Promoting the Education of the Poor in the Principles of the Established Church. The new society took over many of the schools of the older S.P.C.K. Between them the societies of Bell and Lancaster made a real contribution to the work of popular instruction. The Anglican society was naturally the wealthier and larger organization and claimed that between 1815 and 1830 its schools increased in number from 564 to 2,609 and that by 1833 over a million children were under instruction.[1] Had it not been for the invincible rivalries between the Church of England and the Nonconformists something like a national system might have been founded upon the parochial schools. The monitorial system, however, was in spite of the hopes and beliefs of both Bell and Lancaster only a makeshift. The most rudimentary and mechanical education only could be given by monitors, who were children themselves and not yet sure of what they were teaching. Elementary education would demand eventually not only schools but also adult teachers.

The year after Bell was buried as a national figure in Westminster Abbey parliament quietly voted the first grant to education. The triumph of the Whig government in the passage of the great Reform Act of 1832 had awakened the hopes of the educationists, but though parliament refused Roebuk's bill it agreed in 1833 to a sum of £20,000 being given in aid of private subscriptions for the erection of school buildings. There was as yet no government machinery for dealing with education, and the money was therefore appropriated by the Treasury to local applicants, where private subscription would at least equal the amount of the grant, on the recommendation of the National Society or the British and Foreign School Society, and distribution of the money was arranged through those societies. Thus was taken the first small, but important, step in the making of a national system. In 1839 Lord Melbourne's govermnent, on the initiative of Lord John Russell, created by Order in Council a Committee of the Privy Council to superintend the expendi-

[1] R. Gregory: *Elementary Education*, p. 25.

ture of sums voted for the purpose of education, and this committee claimed that in future building grants would carry with them a right of inspection. The committee gained almost from the start the services as secretary of an able administrator, Dr. Kay, afterwards Sir James Kay-Shuttleworth. As a physician who had worked through the cholera epidemic of 1832 in Manchester, he had a first-hand knowledge of the squalid social conditions of the slum population. He believed that education could act as a civilizing force and it was due to his good sense and tact that state aid to education was firmly established in these first experimental years. For there was still, on the part of the Church of England and of other religious bodies, strong resistance to any tendency on the part of the state to control education. The creation of the new committee was opposed, the education grant of the same year was carried by two votes only, and the committee was forced to abandon its project of setting up a single training college for teachers with a general course of religious instruction. As a result training colleges came to be set up, like the elementary schools, under the auspices of the Church or the Nonconformists. The bitterness of the rival Protestant bodies—a bitterness which to-day it is hard to appreciate—continually checked educational development and made it slow and laborious. It made the creation of a national system a work of complicated compromise, the details of which are incredibly dull and almost without significance to the great majority of Englishmen of to-day.

The wrangles went on. Meanwhile, not only were many children growing up illiterate and being exploited in the factories when to-day they would have been in school, but the existing schools and the prevailing monitorial system were known, through the reports of the inspectors, to be far from satisfactory. In 1846 the committee introduced the pupil-teacher system. In certain selected schools young persons could be appointed at the age of thirteen as pupil-teachers with a small stipend during a five-year apprenticeship, and at the end of that time could compete for the Queen's Scholarships to complete their preparation in a training college. Head teachers and training colleges were assisted with grants, and successful pupil-teachers were eligible for proficiency grants and later on for pensions. In 1847 the committee's management clauses allowed a share of state aid to go to denominational school bodies other than the two existing societies, and this benefited Roman Catholics, Wesleyans, and, later, the Jews. The same year 1847 saw the state grant to education rise to £100,000. Ten years later the grant was more than five times larger than that. State participation in education was in fact growing rapidly, if quietly. Bureaucracy was showing what appears to be a natural tendency to widen its sphere of operation. In the years 1850–8 several bills for the extension of state control over education were defeated in parliament. But at the same time by Order in Council the bureaucracy was somewhat strengthened. Palmerston's government in 1856 set up a Department of Education which combined the chairmanship of the committee and that of the Department of Science and Art, a department attached since 1853 to the Board of Trade. The Lord President of the Council was chairman of each of the departments as he had been previously of the committee. But since he was a peer a new office of vice-president was instituted which gave education an official spokesman in the House of Commons, a spokesman who was virtually a minister of education.

The rapidly mounting cost of education did not go unobserved and it was often wondered whether the money was bringing a proper return. In 1858 a parliamentary commission under the Duke of Newcastle as chairman was appointed 'to enquire into the present State of Popular Education in England, and to consider and report what Measures, if any, are required for the extension of sound and cheap elementary instruction to all classes of the People'. The very wording of the terms of reference—especially the words 'sound and cheap'—recalls the practical and businesslike attitude of the Victorians. A vast amount of information was collected from England and abroad; Matthew Arnold, greatest of the Victorian poets but himself an inspector of schools, as befitted the son of the great headmaster, went to France to report on its education; and the

Newcastle *Report* when it appeared in 1861 gave great attention to a statistical picture of English education. Its conclusions were, on the whole, optimistic, if not complacent. It did not recommend compulsory education; indeed, it estimated that only about 4·5 per cent of children did not at some time attend school. But although this might be so it was pointed out that attendance was irregular, children left school too young, and the quality of the instruction they received was often poor. A common age for poor children to leave school was before eleven, and only one child in twenty, of the poorer classes, received any education after thirteen. The *Report* also drew attention to the evil conditions existing in many of the dame schools and other uninspected schools, especially in London where 'none are too old, too poor, too ignorant, too feeble, too sickly, too unqualified in one or every way, to regard themselves, and to be regarded by others, as unfit for school-keeping'.[1] The commissioners suggested that in addition to the government grants elected boards should be set up in counties and boroughs to levy rates, and to use them to assist schools on the basis of the result of an examination of the children in reading, writing, and arithmetic.

The use of local rates for elementary education had been suggested before but it was clear that any suggestion that local boards should interfere with church schools would arouse acute denominational opposition. This the government was not willing to incur. The idea of 'payment by results', however, was attractive. It appealed to the administrator and economist in Robert Lowe, then head of the Education Department, and he made it part of the revised code of 1862, the new edition of the collected and codified minutes, of both the earlier committee and the department, which had first been put together in 1860. In future the payment of grants to school managers was made dependent on attendance and on the result of an examination of each child by an inspector. There were, then and since, many criticisms of the system. To those made at the time Lowe answered by maintaining of the education he provided: 'If it

[1] Newcastle *Report*, I, 90–5.

is not cheap it shall be efficient; if it is not efficient it shall be cheap.' The new method of payment, Lowe thought, would make public money 'a spur to improvement', and 'not a mere subsidy, but a motive of action'.[1] The cost of education was certainly cut down for the time being in the following years, and the attendance of children at school rose. Indeed, there was something to be said for the system. It gave a stimulus to the inefficient schools and teachers, and probably reacted to the children's interest because it at least ensured that they did get a thorough drilling in the 'three Rs'. For there is nothing like an examination to keep up standards. But the system was applied perhaps in a too mechanical manner—'mechanical' was the word applied to it later by Matthew Arnold; it was a heavy burden to the teachers, and sowed suspicion between them and the inspectors.

The system lasted, with modifications, for about forty years, and with all its shortcomings was probably a good enough rough and ready method of achieving a degree of efficiency in elementary education. What was needed—and what was needed for many years to come—was more and better school buildings, more and better trained teachers, and above all, perhaps, an end to the denominational conflict. For the elementary-school teachers had on hand a gigantic task— nothing short of the taming and fitting for something like civilized life of the children of the new manufacturing districts. And Kay-Shuttleworth's criticism of the revised code was perhaps the justest. He argued that a test of reading, writing, and arithmetic was not in itself a fair test of the real civilizing work of the elementary schools. In the schools of northern England there had 'floated a constant supply of an immigrant semi-savage population, bred on the moors of the Pennine Chain'. Such children had 'to be taught to stand upright—to walk without a slouching gait—to sit without crouching like a sheep dog. They have to learn some decency in their skin, hair and dress.' From the thieving of the London streets and the most squalid slums 'children have of late years been netted in

[1] Hansard, vol. 165, col. 229 (13 February 1862).

shoals—got into schools, have been won, tamed, and in some degree taught'.[1]

The next great step forward was the Education Act of 1870. Demand for a national system was still growing: there had been further bills introduced in parliament, further inquiries. Population was increasing, and more children were needing instruction. English education appeared to be behind that of many Continental countries, and international events were suggesting a connexion between education and national power. In the American Civil War the more advanced North beat the South; in Europe Prussia, with its developed system of education, beat Austria. At the same time in England a wider class was finding admission to political power. The Reform Act of 1867 gave the vote to the working men of the towns which provoked from Lowe the remark that 'we must educate our masters'. When the Liberals returned to power in 1868 Lowe became Chancellor of the Exchequer in Gladstone's first cabinet and W. E. Forster was placed in charge of education. The Bradford woollen industry had made Forster a wealthy man, but he had married the daughter of Dr. Arnold, and was known as an educational reformer.

Forster, when he introduced in 1870 his bill to provide for 'public Elementary Education' in England and Wales, did not forget the nation's need of an educated electorate, the importance of educated citizens as a foundation of national power—'we must make up the smallness of our numbers by increasing the intellectual force of the individual'—nor that education might assist to clear the country of social abuses, such as crime and misery. But he stressed in particular the clamant economic need. 'We must not delay. Upon the speedy provision of elementary education depends our industrial prosperity. It is of no use trying to give technical teaching to our artisans without elementary education; uneducated labourers—and many of our labourers are utterly uneducated—are, for the most part, unskilled labourers, and if we have our work-folk any longer

[1] J. Kay-Shuttleworth: *Four Periods of Public Education as reviewed in 1832, 1839, 1846, 1862*, pp. 580–7.

unskilled, notwithstanding their strong sinews and determined energy, they will become overmatched in the competition of the world.'[1]

Around Forster surged once more the denominational conflict and the radicals, with Joseph Chamberlain to the fore, founded at Birmingham in 1869 the National Education League to press the government for an education unsectarian, free, compulsory, and universal. Those who wished to maintain a denominational system formed the National Education Union, but there were clergy and other ministers of religion on both sides and issues were confused.

The result was, not unnaturally, a compromise. The Act of 1870 did not destroy the existing denominational schools. 'Our object', said Forster in introducing the bill, 'is to complete the present voluntary system, to fill up gaps.' He aimed at providing good schools throughout England and Wales, but it must be done with 'the least possible expenditure of public money' and with 'the utmost endeavour not to injure existing and efficient schools'.[2] This meant that the existing denominational schools were left as they were in those districts where they already effectively met local needs, and in fact government grants to them were increased. Where the existing provision of education was not sufficient, increased voluntary effort was welcomed and six months were given for this to be forthcoming. There was, as events showed, a great response to this. Where deficiencies were still found, local *ad hoc* school boards were to be elected by the ratepayers in school districts (i.e., municipal boroughs and civil parishes), and these school boards had the power to levy a local rate for the purpose of building schools and employing teachers. Thus came into existence what is known as the Dual System—voluntary schools and board schools existing side by side. The school boards could also if they chose make by-laws to compel the attendance of children between five and thirteen. School fees continued, but those parents who could not afford to pay could apply for free

---

[1] Hansard, vol. 199, col. 465 (17 February 1870).
[2] *Ibid.* 443-4.

admission for their children. Under a conscience clause parents were free to withdraw their children from religious instruction in any grant-aided school, that is to say a denominational school as well as a board school. Religious instruction was to be given either at the beginning or the end of the day's time-table so as not to interfere with attendance at other lessons. By the clause suggested by Mr. Cowper-Temple, and subsequently known as the Cowper-Temple clause, religious teaching distinctive of any particular denomination was not to be given in the board schools. The Act did not provide free compulsory education as many people vaguely suppose, and many of the school boards did not, in fact, use the local powers given them to enforce school attendance, but the Act was nevertheless a most important step forward. It did at least use the authority of the state to make elementary instruction universal in the sense that eventually—for country districts were often slow about it—schools were made available to all who wished to make use of them.

Further Acts in 1876 and 1880 had the effect of making elementary education compulsory, and by 1899 the school-leaving age was raised to twelve. In 1891 parents were enabled, on demand, to obtain free education for their children, but it was not until after the First World War that fees in the elementary schools were formally abolished. During the years which followed the Education Act of 1870 expansion was rapid and with it went increasing government grants and mounting local education rates. In 1886 a Royal Commission was appointed, under Lord Cross, and reported two years later. Though the members of the Commission were not unanimous, their work led eventually to a variety of changes and improvements. The 'payment by results' system was radically modified, more subjects found their way into the curriculum, and drill, physical exercises, football, and cricket began to be a part of a pupil's life. In 1890 Day Training Colleges for intending teachers were established in universities and university colleges, and meanwhile the pupil-teacher system underwent considerable modification. Teaching methods in the schools slowly improved, becoming less mechanical and more calculated to catch the interests of the child.

The country was still, however, short of a comprehensive system of education, state provision of cheap secondary education was sadly lacking, and the complicated administration was growing more confused. 'Administrative Muddle' is the expression used by the foremost historian of modern English education.[1] The Education Department was responsible for the Dual System of elementary education. But elementary education was already producing its higher elementary or higher-grade schools which were in effect giving a more advanced, something approaching a secondary, education to older and brighter children. These more advanced schools, in so far as they provided scientific or technical instruction, might also be receiving grants from the Science and Art Department, as also might the much older endowed grammar schools which had been brought under the control of the Charity Commissioners. The great public schools remained wholly independent. The local administration of elementary education was in the hands of over 2,500 school boards and a great number of school attendance committees (set up, where there were no school boards, by the Act of 1876) and school managers, but there was as yet no direct public provision of secondary schools. Secondary education was open in the main only to the children of parents who could afford to pay the fees at public or endowed schools or at the private schools run for profit, and these latter were sometimes of poor character and educational standard.

Meanwhile also, in a haphazard, unplanned, and uncoordinated way, other forms of education, technical, adult, and university, were growing up. Perhaps it was because this country gained in the Industrial Revolution so great a start over its competitors that it was so slow to develop a system of technical education. For many years those engaged in industry and manufacturing acquired their training by means of apprenticeship, but this was not sufficient when the Continental nations

[1] J. W. Adamson: *English Education, 1789–1902* (1930): 'Administrative Muddle' is the title of chap. xvi.

began to provide for their peoples a general education and a specialized training. International exhibitions, like the Great Exhibition of 1851 and the Paris Exhibition of 1867, revealed that foreign craftsmen were rivalling those of Britain. The Royal Society of Arts and its president Prince Albert urged the claims of science, as did also in their several ways Ruskin, T. H. Huxley, and Herbert Spencer. A leading chemist, Baron Playfair, part of whose education had been in Germany, wrote a pamphlet in 1852 to reveal the superiority of German technical education. Fifteen years later Playfair was still pointing out the same danger: 'France, Prussia, Austria, Belgium, Switzerland, possess good systems of industrial education . . . and England possesses none.' At the same time (1867) A. J. Mundella, Nottingham manufacturer and later vice-president of the Committee of Council on Education, spoke from experience of his hosiery branches in Germany: 'The education of Germany is the result of a national organization which compels every peasant to send his children to school, and afterwards affords the opportunity of acquiring such technical knowledge as may be useful in the department of industry to which they are destined. . . . If we continue to fight with our present voluntary system we shall be defeated.'[1]

The Science and Art Department did something to encourage these subjects by conducting examinations and making grants to schools where the pupils were successful. Thus the upper forms of elementary schools and some of the endowed grammar schools and private schools introduced science into the curriculum, and teachers who could qualify themselves might augment their incomes by taking evening classes. Further encouragement was given by the Devonshire Commission on technical education and by the foundation in 1880 of the City and Guilds Institute. This body assisted the teaching of applied science in schools and evening classes, instituted its own examinations, and set up two technical colleges in London which served as an example to other parts of the country. At

[1] Playfair and Mundella were quoted by J. Scott Russell: *Systematic Technical Education for the English People* (1869).

the same time Quintin Hogg was developing his evening institutes, which came to be known as the Polytechnics; taken over a little later by the London County Council, they came to make an important contribution, by day and evening classes, to practical and commercial education. The rapid industrialization of Germany after the formation of the German Empire in 1871 and the increasing competition of the United States led to another Royal Commission on technical education in 1884 which brought about in 1889 the passing of the Technical Instruction Act. The newly created local authorities were empowered to levy a rate to provide technical education, and in 1890 the work of the evening institutes was expanded. In 1902, with the passing of the Education Act of that year, the local authorities took them over. But it was not until after the First World War, in 1922, that the Institution of Mechanical Engineers, in collaboration with the Board of Education, began to award a series of certificates for advanced work in the technical subjects. In 1906 several schools of advanced scientific or technical study which had come into existence since 1845, a school of science, a school of mines, and the City and Guilds Central Technical College, were brought together as the Imperial College of Science and Technology in the University of London. But what was most important for technical education, as the commission of 1884 pointed out, was a firm foundation of general, that is secondary, education, and this was not easily obtainable before 1902. Here then was another crying reason for the public provision of secondary education which was only answered by the Act of that year.

The widespread interest in popular education early in the nineteenth century was discussed in the last chapter. That interest makes the background of the later movement for adult education. In 1873 the University of Cambridge commenced its University Extension lectures at Derby, Leicester, and Nottingham; London and Oxford followed the example of Cambridge. In 1903 was formed the association soon to be known as the Workers' Educational Association; in 1906 the first tutorial class started at Rochdale under R. H. Tawney as tutor, with the financial help of New College, Oxford. The idea spread and was taken up by all the universities. After the First World War government financial support was forthcoming by way of grants to cover the payment of tutors. What such classes supply is education of a non-vocational character, that is to say, history, literature, political theory, philosophy, economics, but not accounting, typewriting, shorthand, woodwork or engineering, which latter subjects are the field of the technical schools and evening institutes. Adult education, although those who attend the classes are relatively few, has opened the field of liberal education to those who, irrespective of wealth, class or religious belief, wish to pursue some intellectual interest.

It was partly the movement for the education of adults, partly the increasing need of technical training, which led to an expansion in the number of universities. Scotland was well supplied in this respect, but England had at first only Oxford and Cambridge, and Wales had no university institution until the foundation of St. David's College, Lampeter, in 1827. London University began in 1828 with what was to be University College; it was non-sectarian, 'that godless institution in Gower Street' as its enemies called it. Anglican opposition produced, as a rival, King's College in 1829. A few years later a compromise was reached: the University of London was created to grant degrees for which students from both colleges were to be candidates. From 1858 London began to examine external candidates as well as its own internal students, that is to say, private individuals or students at other institutions could take its examinations and obtain its degrees. Since the foundation of University and King's a number of other colleges have become part of what is now the very large and complicated organization of London University. After London came Durham in 1832. Medical colleges came into existence in some places, for example, at Leeds and Birmingham. During the second half of the century university colleges were established by local effort in the larger towns of England, though most of them received their charters as full universities not until the early years of the next century. Manchester University, for example, originated with Owens College opened in 1851, and received its charter in 1903; University College, Bristol, founded in 1876, attained university status in 1909.

Financially the university colleges owed much to private benevolence. It was not until 1889 that the Treasury gave them assistance. Government grants have greatly increased since then, but the universities have retained their independence. They grew out of the local industrial life of the great cities and had therefore an early and natural bias towards science, but in time they came to provide the courses to be found elsewhere, both in arts and sciences. Meanwhile the older universities of Oxford and Cambridge had been reformed, searching written examinations had been introduced, science laboratories had been built between 1855 and 1880 at Oxford and a little later at Cambridge, and the old classical curriculum had been modified to admit all the modern subjects. Thus during the nineteenth and early twentieth centuries the old and the new universities were tending to approach each other in their curricula. Both waited, unconsciously, for the secondary schools produced by the 1902 Act to give them a vast new reservoir of students on which to draw.

Curiously enough Wales, after having been far behind England, got ahead in respect of secondary education. A wave of national feeling in the seventies and a demand for home rule led to a departmental committee of inquiry under Lord Aberdare, which reported in 1881. It led to the foundation of two university colleges, Bangor and Cardiff (Aberystwyth had been founded in 1872, and the three colleges were incorporated in the University of Wales in 1893) and also to the Welsh Intermediate Act of 1889. This Act made use of the new local government machinery of the county and county borough councils; they were to appoint education committees and provide secondary and technical education in their areas. There came into existence in Wales a system of secondary or intermediate schools, as they were called, intermediate because their education was between that of the elementary schools and that of the universities. The success of the Act for Wales led to fresh demands for similar provision in England and, in 1894, the government appointed a commission under James (afterwards Lord) Bryce 'to consider what are the best methods of establishing a well-organized system of secondary education in England'. The Bryce *Report* gave 'birth to the Board of Education; in essentials it was also the wet nurse of the Education Act of 1902'.[1]

The Bryce *Report* recommended that there should be a single comprehensive central authority for English education. This was brought into existence by the Act of 1899. The new Board of Education amalgamated the former Education Department and the Science and Art Department and took over the educational duties of the Charity Commission. The Board consisted of a number of ministers of the crown, and with characteristic English inconsistency it never met. But its chief, the President of the Board of Education, was a member of the government and virtually minister of education. It was another forty-five years before this term was brought into official use.

In addition to the creation of a strengthened central authority the Bryce Commission, although implying the retention of the School Boards for what was properly elementary education, recommended the use of the new local authorities to supply secondary education where such schools were wanting: 'We conceive experience to have conclusively shown that private enterprise cannot be entirely relied on, and that the duty of seeing that an adequate supply of secondary instruction is provided must be thrown on a public authority.'[2] Increasing awareness of the shortcomings of the existing position was making a further big reorganization of education inevitable sooner or later. A determined and persistent administrative reformer had meanwhile found his way through the Department of Education into a position of influence behind the scenes. This was Robert (afterwards Sir Robert) Morant, who as tutor to the Royal family of Siam had assisted in the organization of that state's education. By 1895 in the Department at home a special inquiries branch was working under Michael

[1] Adamson, *op. cit.*, p. 467.   [2] Bryce *Report*, I, 273.

(afterwards Sir Michael) Sadler, and Morant, in this branch, was able to contrast the chaotic administration of our own education with the carefully centralized system of certain foreign countries, especially those of France and Switzerland which he was sent to study. In fact, by appointing Morant, Sadler had found 'the man who in a few years' time was to re-model English educational machinery'.[1] Morant's position was strengthened by the situation—a situation of which he skilfully took every advantage—of the London School Board which found as a result of the decision of the courts what Morant already realized, that it was not legal to spend its money on more advanced education; it was legally restricted to elementary education in a narrow sense. Many higher-grade schools were thus shown to be acting illegally, and it was therefore urgent that the position should be cleared up officially.

The Act of 1902 was the outcome. The bill in parliament was sponsored by the prime minister, Balfour, who depended behind the scenes on the masterly guiding hand of Morant, now picked out to step into the office of permanent secretary of the Board in the following year. The full bitterness of both political and denominational conflict was aroused. It was a Conservative bill that had been introduced; it was opposed even by Bryce himself who had done so much in his *Report* to prepare the way for it; it was denounced by Lloyd George. Outside parliament the Nonconformist minister Dr. Clifford worked up feeling against the bill and urged passive resistance. The Nonconformist objection was that the rates were now to be used to maintain the Church schools—not a very plausible objection since the taxes had long been used for this purpose. Refusal by individuals to pay rates and in Wales refusal by local education authorities to operate the Act were weapons used. But in spite of the return of the Liberals in 1906 the Act remained. Indeed, as Bryce's biographer, himself a great Liberal, has written, 'so

---

[1] R. C. K. Ensor: *England 1870–1914*, p. 318. Morant, however, was extraordinarily successful in furthering his own career at Sadler's expense. Michael Sadleir speaks of Morant's 'ruthless personal ambition' in his memoir of his father, *Michael Ernest Sadler*, p. 148.

much educational progress has been accomplished under the Act of 1902 that much of the criticism then levelled against it from the Liberal benches seems now to be lacking in perspective'.[1]

The Education Act of 1902 abolished the school boards and school attendance committees and transferred their functions to the new local authorities. These latter had not existed in 1870. The Local Government Acts of 1888 and 1894 had created the county and county borough councils and the urban district, rural district, and parish councils. The councils of counties and of county boroughs were now to be local education authorities for both elementary and secondary or higher education,[2] while, in deference to local public opinion but destroying the unity of the scheme, the councils of the larger boroughs and larger urban districts were to be local education authorities for elementary education only. Every part of England and Wales fell within the area of some local education authority. The new authorities were given two important powers which had not belonged to the school boards; one was the larger part of the control and maintenance of the voluntary or denominational schools, the other was, in the case of a county and county borough council, the power to supply secondary education. The rates were to be used for the maintenance of the voluntary elementary schools as well as for the provision of secondary education. Government grants were to be paid in future directly to the L.E.A.s, and not as formerly to the school managers. Those local education authorities responsible for secondary education were 'to promote the general co-ordination of all forms of education' and to use the rates for this purpose; they were 'to have regard to any existing supply of efficient schools or colleges' and also to any steps taken under the earlier Technical Instruction Acts.[3]

[1] H. A. L. Fisher: *James Bryce*, I, 325.
[2] Part II of the Act dealt with 'Higher Education' which was described as 'education other than elementary'. Part III dealt with 'elementary education', and local education authorities for elementary education only came to be known as 'Part III Authorities'.
[3] Education Act, 1902, Part II.

The Act was, in fact, a compromise. The Dual System remained with an elaborate sharing of duties between L.E.A.s and the voluntary authorities. The L.E.A. appointed two of the six managers of a voluntary school; the managers provided the school building (the school being known as a non-provided school because not provided by the L.E.A.), but the school was maintained by the L.E.A. The L.E.A. controlled the instruction given except religious instruction; the managers appointed the teachers subject to the consent of the L.E.A. Though a compromise the Act proved in practice to be sound in its main principles. It brought comparative order—about 300 local authorities taking the place of over 2,500 school boards and nearly 800 school attendance committees—out of administrative chaos. It put secondary education on a firm foundation. The new secondary school, according to the board's *Regulations*, was to offer 'a general education, physical, mental, and moral'. How far secondary education had moved, however, beyond the old classical curriculum was evident in the subjects which were to make up a four-year course. These subjects were to include English, geography, history, a language other than English, mathematics and science, and drawing. It was still expected that Latin would be taken; as a modern language most schools did French. It was such a course of general education that became a preparation for the School Certificate (set by the universities), a leaving examination on which matriculation could be gained which gave entrance to the universities. To-day, by calling all post-primary education secondary, we tend to obscure the distinctive characteristics which must mark the education of the selected rather than the average mind.

The Act was of fundamental importance in the creation of a national system of education in England for it brought into existence what is known as the 'educational ladder'. It was now possible for the clever child to pass from the elementary school to the secondary school with a scholarship or free place—otherwise moderate fees were charged—and then on to the university. The vast expansion of the educational system since its small beginnings is indicated briefly and clearly by comparative figures; in 1833 the government made its first grant to education of £20,000; in 1914 the government grants and the local rates for education together amounted to £30,000,000. And it was still possible, before the Act of 1944, and perhaps even after it, to say that changes following the Act of 1902 'have resulted in further progress in many directions but they have not materially altered the general structure of the system so far as the provision and maintenance of educational institutions are concerned'.[1]

[1] *Outline of the Educational System in England and Wales* (H.M.S.O., 1934), p. 41.

CHAPTER XVII

NINETEENTH-CENTURY SCHOOLBOYS

T HE opportunity of a full education has, until very recently, been offered only to the few. In the past those born into the charmed circle of wealth and social influence were alone able to undergo those social, intellectual, and spiritual processes which are conveniently summed up as education, and which fitted those so moulded to take their place in society and to fill the most important positions in the land. In the two centuries between 1721 and 1922 thirty-six men have occupied the position of British prime minister. All except four were born into wealth or easy circumstances. Seventeen of them went to school at Eton, five at Harrow, and four at Westminster; seventeen went to Oxford, thirteen to Cambridge.[1] It was not until Lloyd George became prime minster in 1916 that a boy, born into really humble circumstances and educated in the elementary school and later by his own efforts only, reached the top. Men born outside the charmed circle had to pick up their education as best they might, in the poorer private institutions or, as time went on, in the crude elementary schools provided by the Church or by public funds. Only the most gifted child of exceptional stamina could hope to overcome the obstacles which barred the road to anything like a liberal education. And the difference between the education of those inside the charmed circle and those outside was not merely a difference of wealth and social class; it was also a difference of school curriculum. The boy who went to the famous public school learnt Latin and Greek, and through them as a medium

[1] Hon. C. Bigham: *Prime Ministers of Britain*, p. 346.

could enter upon the cultural heritage of the ages; the boy who did not go, might pick up a smattering of Latin as a meaningless drudgery in some private or endowed school, or might merely go through a schooling in reading, writing, and arithmetic, or with that and some newer form of secondary education might pass, with scarcely any of the traditional educational background behind him, to the coming subject of science. The kind of education provided depended upon the family position of the child; what use was made of the education received depended upon the abilities and character of the recipient. To illustrate the vastly different educations which offered in the nineteenth century, two well-known public figures can be used as examples: H. A. L. Fisher, historian and minister of education, and H. G. Wells, scientist, novelist, and utopian social reformer.

H. A. L. Fisher was born into the charmed circle. When he entered this world on 21 March 1865, at 3 Onslow Square, London, his father, trained for the Bar, was private secretary to the Prince of Wales. As children, wrote Fisher himself, 'We heard of him hunting and shooting and going to grand dinners and balls, and skating at Sandringham when we wanted him at home, and we knew how indulgent he could be to us when we were allowed down to dessert before bed-time'. But the elder Fisher was also the cultured gentleman. He had taken a First in Classics at Oxford, and could write Greek and Latin verse. 'I think', wrote his son, 'that my father was a beautiful scholar in the old Oxford sense of the term. He was not learned. He had no German . . . but the great classics, Homer, Aeschylus, Pindar, Virgil, he knew intimately and was able to communicate his love and admiration for their work to others.' This was the gift he gave to the son who came to think of it as the most valuable part of education: that a child 'should hear soon and often the great masterpieces of poetry from the lips of one who feels their beauty and can transmit it'.[1]

The young Fisher grew up in the cultivated and prosperous security of an established family plunged in the intellectual

[1] *An Unfinished Autobiography*, pp. 4–5.

and political interests of the great, and with a tradition behind it of canons and bishops, soldiers and fellows of Oxford colleges. His mother also had good and interesting family connexions, with France and with India, and to her Fisher owed much. She was the mother of eleven children, and the care of her family was her one predominant occupation. Her education was the slight one of so many ladies of good birth; she had never been to school or university, but she had learnt in France a perfect and colloquial French and 'the piano sang under her exquisite touch'. She could put a real animation into the classes she held around the nursery table and could make of education an exciting adventure. How many of our college-trained teachers can do that? 'She was', said Fisher, 'my first teacher and my best.'

From a preparatory school at Maidenhead, which he did not enjoy, Fisher passed at the age of thirteen to Winchester. He was in Du Boulay's House, and there was fag to Edward Grey, good scholar but better fisherman, foreign minister in 1914. Among his other contemporaries were two destined later to play an important part in English education, Robert Morant and L. A. Selby Bigge, later permanent secretary at the Board under Fisher. Fisher himself, who had missed through illness a scholarship at Winchester, became nevertheless one of the most distinguished boys at the school. He gained first place in the scholarship examination for New College, Oxford, and he won school prizes for Greek iambics, the Latin essay, and also for the English essay and for modern languages. He played cricket for the second eleven, he was an enthusiastic member of the rifle corps, and already in the school debating society he showed signs of his later political development by supporting the Liberal Party, then, under Gladstone, in its halcyon days.

Fisher enjoyed to the full his schooldays at the oldest of English public schools, and whatever their shortcomings may have been he was eminently fitted to benefit from their very great advantages. 'I enjoyed', he confesses, 'every moment of my life at Winchester; the work, the games, the society of my fellows and of the masters, and the compelling beauty of the old buildings, of the College Meads, and of the sweet water-meadows among which the College is set, were all delightful. The teaching was picturesquely irregular, some of it most brilliant and inspiring, some quite inefficient. I well remember my first hour in class or "up to books". The master, or don as we called him, though a fine classical scholar, was notoriously incapable of preserving discipline. Two boys were playing fives at one end of the room; one boy was sawing away the leg of the master's table; the remainder were yelling as loud as their lungs would permit. Everyone was in the best of humour. It was pandemonium.'[1]

Lest such a description should suggest that serious education was neglected, let Fisher himself describe the solid work of Greek and Latin composition. The master would 'set two long "tasks" in prose and verse; a fine piece of Shakespeare for instance, for Greek iambics or a sonnet from Wordsworth for Latin elegiacs, and these exercises were to be done in a boy's free time during the week. I took an immense pleasure in committing my English poetry or prose, as the case might be, to memory and in turning over possible renderings in Greek or Latin on country walks or in spare moments of the working day. I am sure that there could have been no finer education in literary taste. Before I left Winchester I think that I had rendered most of the finest speeches in Shakespeare into Greek or Latin.'[2] On the other hand Fisher admits that in going through the classical texts too much time was spent on minute study of grammar, and boys did not always realize that they were expected to supplement class drill in the details of grammar with general reading of the classics outside. Many boys might therefore pass through a public school without gaining the full advantage from it. The very best boys did, of course, add in their own reading to the classical curriculum of the form-room. What Gladstone had read in his spare time at Eton was phenomenal.[3]

Reflecting in later years on his own education Fisher was

[1] *An Unfinished Autobiography*, p. 37.   [2] *Ibid.*, p. 38.
[3] See the list given in Morley's *Life*, I, 33.

inclined to admit, however, that it might have been too restricted. 'Looking back I recognize that our intellectual training was too one-sided. We hardly touched the skirt of the sciences. The vast field of modern knowledge was a closed book to us; but we learned to enjoy the beauties of literature, and those of us who had any turn for history or for exact classical scholarship found every opportunity for exercising and improving those gifts.'[1]

When Fisher entered the university in 1884 he came to an Oxford which was only but recently reformed and turned into something like a real national institution. Since the commission of 1852–4 New College had been transformed from what had been a small annex of the established Church, confined to Wykehamists and with fellows who must be celibate, into a progressive institution of two hundred members, and admitting as commoners boys from any school, provided they could pass the college entrance examination and that their parents could pay the college fees. At Oxford, though not enjoying his undergraduate as much as his schooldays, Fisher settled down to the hard work necessary for Classical Moderations and 'Greats'. Success in the former depends upon a sound previous training in Latin and Greek for the examination is largely linguistic in character. Such training Fisher had acquired at Winchester and he now made the necessary additions to it. He achieved his First Class in 1886 and went on to the further two-year course in philosophy and ancient history for 'Greats'. This is the course taken by the very best 'Arts' students at Oxford; it is a real training for the finest minds and a 'First in Greats' gives a man an intellectual hallmark which nothing else can give. This Fisher gained in the summer of 1888. This qualification is indeed not a bad one for any profession in life; it is particularly appropriate to the study of medieval and modern history, and a better qualification, perhaps, than a First in the School of Modern History itself. This school Fisher did not take, but he became nevertheless one of the great Oxford historians.

[1] *An Unfinished Autobiography*, p. 40.

281

19

After he was elected a fellow of New College in the autumn of 1888 he finally decided to turn to modern history as his subject, with the purpose of college teaching in view. He need not have done this; fellowships in those days were granted on the most liberal terms; he might have worked for the Bar or some other profession, or have turned to philosophy in which subject he was regarded as having distinguished himself as an undergraduate. It was perhaps his feeling that something of more practical value than philosophy was desirable as a life's work that turned him towards modern history: 'keenly interested in public life, he felt the need for studies having a direct bearing thereon.'[1]

When the choice was made, New College allowed him to continue his historical study, first in France and then in Germany. In the Latin Quarter Fisher drank in the magic of the Middle Ages; he knew and lived among the greatest French scholars of the day; he studied palaeography at the École des Chartes; he met Taine and Renan. Among French scholars he found a standard of work and exacting labour not known in Oxford. 'Such ardour as that which prevailed among my fellow students in history was new to me. I had not known what work could be until I found my place among them.'[2] The great medievalist Ducange, he was told, worked for fourteen hours on his wedding day. The high reputation of the German universities took him in the autumn of 1890 to the university of Göttingen, and in the spring to Dresden and Weimar. The language he knew already and he turned quickly to the study of the medieval economic history of Germany and also to wide reading in German literature.

He returned to Oxford as a tutor and lecturer in modern history and threw himself into the teaching of the undergraduates at New College. He was qualified academically—if ever a man were qualified—for the study of history. His teaching, his research, his travels abroad—'in the vacations he worked in the British Museum or in the Paris Archives or the Bibliothèque Nationale, pursued the problem of the moment

[1] David Ogg: *Herbert Fisher*, p. 32.   [2] *An Unfinished Autobiography*, p. 63.

to German archives or to the libraries of Rome'[1]—were the foundations on which he built his notable books, most of all the brilliant, readable synthesis he produced towards the end of his life, the *History of Europe*. Here then was a man who had the very best that English and Continental education could give. That education prepared him both for the academic and the political life. Eventually he was drawn away—to be vice-chancellor of Sheffield, to India, to the cabinet to become Lloyd George's minister of education. 'If I may judge from my own experience', he wrote, 'there is always a haunting feeling that learning and scholarship and the lettered life can bring content only if combined with some more practical from of active service to the community . . . the ordinary Englishman craves for action . . . Administration, politics, travel, philanthropy lure him away from his books.'[2]

Very different was the early setting for the life of H. G. Wells. Born in the year after Fisher, it was on 21 September 1866 that he saw the light in the small bedroom above the little shop of 47 High Street, at Bromley, Kent. Sprung from a tradesman's family there was around him none of the accumulated tradition, culture, and *savoir faire* of the ages. Wells's father was gardener, shopkeeper (china and glassware), and professional cricketer. His mother had been a lady's maid. The young Wells was brought up among scenes of domestic drudgery, while his mother attempted to teach him the truths of the Established Church and to be respectable. 'As I knew her in my childhood', he wrote, 'she was engaged in a desperate single-handed battle with our gaunt and dismal home, to keep it clean, to keep her children clean, to get them clothed and fed and taught, to keep up appearances.'[3] Mrs. Wells's toil was unending; she was troubled with the customers as well as by domestic cares; she cleaned and cooked, darned and mended. Her husband was cheerful but not particularly successful; he read while not playing cricket, he bought books at sales, and borrowed them from the local literary institute.

[1] *Ibid.*, Mrs. Fisher's introduction.   [2] *An Unfinished Autobiography*, p. 87.
[3] *An Experiment in Autobiography*, I, 69.

She struggled most to keep up appearances. Her children had not carelessly to take off their coats lest they should expose the mends in their undergarments; the children must not mix with common children. She was anxious to give them the elements of learning. A big sheet of paper was posted up in the kitchen to teach the letters of the alphabet and the figures. She started her children on reading and writing, and then sent them on to a dame school, kept by two unqualified old ladies 'in a room in a row of cottages near the Drill Hall'.

Between the ages of seven and eight Wells broke his leg, and found himself set up on the parlour sofa and made a fuss of for some weeks. His father brought him illustrated books from the literary institute, and he read and read, books about the countries of the world, about natural history, a life of Wellington, a history of the American Civil War, and the bound volumes of *Punch*. All this reading, casual and undirected as it was, gave him a little later on a curious superiority to his Bromley schoolfellows, none of whom came from bookish homes. At this time (1874), says Wells, 'it was being realized by the ruling classes that a nation with a lower stratum of illiterates would compete at a disadvantage against the foreigner. A condition of things in which everyone would read and write and do sums, dawned on the startled imagination of mankind.'[1] Bromley had its National School, but it had also a small private school for those whose parents thought themselves a little above the former, and to it—Mr. Morley's Academy, in the High Street—Wells was sent when he was nearly eight. The prospectus of the school had indicated a curriculum of 'writing in both plain and ornamental style, Arithmetic logically, and History with special reference to Ancient Egypt'. Wells found that the history consisted largely of lists of dates and enactments, and that the schooling was mostly in copperplate writing, long addition sums, and simple book-keeping. His companions came from poor middle-class families in the town or were boarders from London public-houses whose homes were not very suitable for their up-

[1] *Ibid.*, p. 84.

bringing. Mr. Morley did almost all the teaching, Mrs. Morley giving some little assistance with the youngest pupils. Mr. Morley was a teacher of the old school, ranting at his pupils, beating them with his cane, but nevertheless pushing them through the schooling necessary to pass examinations set by the private schoolmasters association, known as the College of Preceptors, and then to jobs as clerks. His teaching, Wells thought, was 'better than that of the crudely trained mechanical grant earners of the contemporary National School which was the only local alternative', and Morley showed a certain liking for the young Wells whose interest in grammar or arithmetic was greater than that of his fellows. At the age of thirteen, then, Wells found himself in the first place for book-keeping in the examination of the College of Preceptors; he had a fair knowledge of mathematics including a start in trigonometry; and he had been taught bad French 'out of a crammer's text-book'.

Affairs in the Wells family became more difficult when the father broke his leg in 1877, which put an end for him to any serious cricket. The mother took a post as a housekeeper, and the young Wells, like his brothers before him, was apprenticed to a draper. The life of a cash-desk clerk he found almost unbearable; he lost his job, and was then for a few months a pupil teacher at Wookey in Somerset. There followed a short interval in the gentleman's house where his mother was employed. There the inquisitive youngster was allowed to take books from the library up to his room: he read something of Voltaire and Tom Paine and *Gulliver's Travels*; he discovered Plato's *Republic*. Next came a short spell working for a chemist in Midhurst. For that a smattering of Latin was desirable, and in that subject Wells now managed to obtain some lessons at the Midhurst Grammar School, an old endowed school now revived by the Endowed Schools Commissioners. Here in a few weeks, Wells found great advantage and tremendous stimulus. He took the evening classes in science, and came back to take the examinations and so earn the grant available to a school providing such instruction. But without a settled job, he was persuaded by his mother to take another opportunity in a draper's—this time in Southsea. And now he felt recalcitrant, not against his mother, 'but against a scheme of things which marched me off before I was fifteen to what was plainly a dreary and hopeless life, while other boys, no better in quality than myself, were enjoying all the advantages—I thought they were stupendous advantages in those days—of the public school and university. I conveyed my small portmanteau to Southsea with a sinking heart.'[1] This second incarceration in a draper's lasted two years, from 1881 to 1883. He was in a well-run and humane business, but he found the life one of extreme tedium. He dreamed, like Hardy's *Jude the Obscure*, of his Midhurst Latin, as something which symbolized emancipation. His desperation grew; he wrote to the headmaster at Midhurst; he broke once more with the drapery business and became a student-assistant at Midhurst Grammar School. Meanwhile he had been adding to his knowledge by reading one of the useful popular compilations of those days; it was, perhaps, Cassell's *Popular Educator*.

The move to Midhurst Grammar School in 1883 was the turning-point in Wells's career. The headmaster was determined to take full advantage of the grants payable by the Education Department for evening classes in science. Some of the classes he organized were genuine ones, but in some Wells was the only student and following the course consisted simply in reading by himself a good text-book. But in the examination Wells did very well. The Education Department was at this time trying to improve its science teaching in the country at large, and one way to do this was to produce better teachers of science. To this end it was offering a number of free student-ships, with a maintenance grant, at the Normal School of Science, South Kensington. This was a science teacher training college, part of the group of technical institutions which grew later into the Imperial College of Science and Technology, which, as Wells put it, 'has become a constituent of that still vaster, still more conspicuously acephalic monster, the University of London'.[2] Wells sent in an application and

[1] *Ibid.*, p. 146.   [2] *Ibid.*, p. 209.

was successful; he was accepted for a course as a 'teacher in training' under the great scientific figure of the day, Professor Huxley. But science had not been Wells's only occupation at Midhurst. He had been reading Plato's *Republic* and Henry George's *Progress and Poverty*; he was beginning to make for himself the image of a better world in which the selfishness of individualism should give place to the interest of the common weal.

When in 1884 he commenced his work in biology at the School of Science, Wells came for the first time into direct contact with what he had previously been only reading about. 'Here were microscopes, dissections, models, diagrams . . . specimens, museums. . . . Here was I under the shadow of Huxley, the acutest observer, the ablest generaliser, the great teacher, the most lucid and valiant of controversialists.' Wells worked hard during his first year. At the end of it he gained a first class in zoology, and he was reappointed to continue his studies, in other departments of the school, for a second, and then for a third year. He turned to physics and geology, but as time went on he lost interest and did not do as well again as he had done during his first year. He had discovered meanwhile Carlyle's *French Revolution* and the works of Blake. In these years in London—with the background of life in cheap 'digs', his poverty and his wide, discursive interests—Wells narrowly missed complete ruin. As a serious scientist he was regarded as a failure when he left South Kensington. He turned, to make a living, to teaching once more, and to journalism and writing. He took his B.Sc. of London University in 1890. His later success was due to his inherent genius as a writer—and to chance. His education had been throughout haphazard and ill-directed; he was an able man who, through circumstance, missed the steady, progressive training of the public school and the older universities which launched men like Fisher on to great careers. Of Fisher's brothers one became an admiral, another the chairman of Barclay's Bank. Fisher suggested that any one of the three could have been successful in the career of the others. Perhaps even more interesting it might be to speculate on what Fisher would have become had he been born in the Bromley High Street and what Wells might have been had he proceeded to Winchester and New College from 3 Onslow Square.

What is the true education, who can say? For the best men the classical education may still, perhaps, be best. Gladstone thought it the true education, though he realized that this could be the case only for the few. 'It can only apply in full', he said, 'to that small proportion of the youth of any country, who are to become in the fullest sense educated men.'[1] Gladstone, H. G. Wells did not consider a really educated man. 'He was educated', wrote Wells in the *Outline of History*, 'at Eton College, and at Christ Church, Oxford, and his mind never recovered from the process.'[2] But Wells's editorial advisers did not agree, and there is a battle in the footnotes between Wells himself, Professor Ernest Barker, and Professor Gilbert Murray. Gladstone, like Peel, gained the 'double first' in classics and mathematics. 'Men with such a training', said Barker, 'were genuinely and nobly trained for statesmanship.' But, objected Wells—'With no knowledge of ethnology, no vision of history as a whole, misconceiving the record of geology, ignorant of the elementary ideas of biological science, of modern political, social and economic science, and modern thought and literature!' Gilbert Murray pointed out, however, how much the good man read *outside* the old classical curriculum—'A good man was rather laughed at if he did not know Shakespeare and Milton.' Fisher's education was the classical education at its best; Wells's education though haphazard was sufficient to show him some of the deficiencies of the old and the need for an inclusion of modern science. But we are discovering to-day that it is impossible to teach everything; the school curriculum has been vastly overloaded. The best education, perhaps, is that which stretches a man's abilities to the full and gives him the feeling of rising superior to his environment. And that either classics or science may do.

[1] Morley's *Life*, II, Appendix, Letter to Lord Lyttelton.
[2] H. G. Wells: *Outline of History*, II, 663-4, with footnotes.

CHAPTER XVIII

EDUCATION: YESTERDAY AND TO-DAY

THE industrialization of western Europe with its stringent technical demands had made imperative the establishment of national systems of education to the creation of which the social and ethical needs of the new urban populations and the demand of the democratic and socialist movements for popular rights had also contributed. But the two world wars, in which governments perforce appealed to the masses for steadfast courage and self-sacrifice on an unprecedented scale, have greatly stimulated the work of completing and broadening those educational systems the main foundations of which had been laid during the nineteenth century. The Education Act of 1918 had as its object for England and Wales 'the establishment of a national system of public education available for all persons capable of profiting thereby'. The idea of a national system, open to all, was thus at length clearly expressed in this country. The Act was the result of the fruitful co-operation of two men, Lloyd George and H. A. L. Fisher. Ability, genius, and the nation's need had raised the people's representative to the premiership, but when at the end of 1916 he called upon the scholar and historian, H. A. L. Fisher, then vice-chancellor of Sheffield University, to become president of the Board of Education, Lloyd George showed a genuinely British determination to build for the future upon the foundations of the past.

In defeated Germany political revolution replaced the kaiser with the democratic republic of Weimar, which set the tone for an attempted democracy in education. The principle of the *Einheitsschule* was introduced: there were to be for all German children four years in the common primary school, or *Grundschule*, before they proceeded to different types of school.

In France the First World War stimulated a demand for greater educational equality. *La guerre égalitaire avait inspiré le vœu d'une école égalitaire*,[1] and politicians of the Left pressed for the *école unitaire* or *école unique*, under which latter name the idea became more widely known. The object was to bridge the gulf which existed in France, inside the state system, between elementary and secondary education. They were not parts of an end-on system, but parallel systems which did not meet. The new suggestion was to put a uniform single type of school for all children between six and twelve in place of both the elementary schools on the one hand and the preparatory classes for the *lycée* on the other. Such a proposal if it weakened the *lycée* was also a threat to the classical tradition in France, a tradition somewhat strengthened by the disappearance of German from French schools as a result of the war and also by the belief that it was the classical tradition which distinguished the Latin peoples from the Teutons.

But the French proposal was indicative only of a tendency and did not result in sudden fundamental change. Both in France and in Germany the classical tradition maintained an important influence over the educational system as a whole and was, of course, particularly strong in the sphere of secondary education. Elsewhere, in some cases, changes in education were greater and more far-reaching. In Russia revolution, defeat, and communist victory only after bitter civil war faced the new government with a vast task of reconstruction and a still vaster task of economic and social development. After some initial blundering and experiment, the government faced the educational problem and introduced bold measures: the greatest possible multiplication of schools and teachers, universal elementary instruction with the aim of conquering illiteracy, and the training necessary to turn out technicians of every kind in the greatest possible numbers. In Turkey, a similar problem faced Kemal after the Turkish revolution and

[1] Quoted by E. R. Curtius: *The Civilisation of France* (1932), p. 188.

the achievement of national independence. The provision of elementary education, compulsory, free, and secular—a continuation in the revolutionary Near East of the Western revolutionary liberalism of France at the end of the eighteenth century—was an essential part of the policy of a country whose determination was to be modern. Upon a foundation of common elementary instruction it was possible to base a more limited structure of secondary, higher, and technical education.

The general consolidation and expansion of national systems of education in Europe and America was but one aspect of the wave of optimism which followed 'the war to make the world safe for democracy'. In the international sphere this optimism showed itself in the foundation of the League of Nations, as a means of preventing war. A new interest in history, and especially modern history, sprang up in the schools and universities; the League's Committee of Intellectual Co-operation was at work on plans for the revision of history text-books to purge them of distorted, nationalist points of view and was also occupied with the possibility of bringing a single international language into use; 'civics', 'citizenship', conferences, vacation courses, summer schools—all these and many more phenomena of the kind represented a well-meaning faith in education. If only man could be rightly informed, it was thought, then he would choose the right path.

But by 1929 a recession set in. The world economic slump brought widespread unemployment. The problem and the tragedy of an 'educated proletariat' was revealed at its worst, perhaps, in Germany. There in the early thirties fully qualified engineers drove taxis and highly cultured men of letters walked the streets. The situation was well epitomized in the current story of an advertisement for a railway porter which stated: 'No one with a qualification lower than that of the doctorate need apply.' In England, university men and women with good degrees and a teacher's diploma in addition were forced by circumstance to take appointments in the elementary schools. In such circumstances much of the idealism associated with education was doomed to wane. The European tradition of humanism and liberalism was challenged from Left and Right. It had been rejected already in 1917 by Russia for Soviet education left little room for human freedom, and the Soviet experiment aroused a new interest when economic slump in the West suggested that the capitalist system had broken down; but liberal humanism was rejected in the heart of Europe in 1933 when desperation engendered by economic depression revived the aggressive nationalism dormant in Germany. Hitler seized his opportunity to possess himself of the state and destroy the weakly German democracy. He turned its educational machinery to the production of Nazi fanatics, soldiers, and efficient, uncritical technicians. It soon became clear that education was a term which might have very different meanings; a national system of education could be made to serve various ends, either the highest or the most devilish known to man.

At the same time even in the most advanced countries of the world education was producing its own problems. Education—at least in its highest and most cultivated forms—is something which is its own reward. It forms, or makes possible, a kind of intellectual enjoyment which is appreciated only by the few. In so far as it is a search for the secrets of knowledge it is a search for something which is not there—or, at least, is beyond human ken. The discovery of one truth opens the road to others hazily perceived on the mental horizon, the solution of one problem opens up many more. The joy of all this lies in the search itself. But this is a truth unwelcome to the multitude. Idealists and the more advanced among the working classes had conceived of education as an opportunity which must be open to all, or they thought of knowledge as power, the means to political and social ends. Popular education, therefore, now seemed to expose a sham. A gaping spiritual and intellectual void began to appear. Religious faith was destroyed or weakened by the rationalism which had spread to the masses with the advance of education. The eager youth who sought through education to find the true way of life, to find what was right and what was wrong in economics and politics, discovered that the professor of the liberal universities could not tell him and appeared to have abandoned the search for truth in favour of a pleasant game of weighing the arguments on the one hand against those on the other. At the same time in those same universities research was going on in every conceivable subject and was producing a most formidable mass of verbiage. In America, in particular, the goal of the Ph.D. degree, awarded for an approved academic thesis and all but essential for any-one who aims at a university post, encouraged the annual output of mediocre, stereotyped compilations complete with their *apparatus criticus* of footnotes and bibliography. Scholars were writing their theses in order to become professors, and pro-fessors were lecturing and writing to produce more scholars to write, in their turn, more theses. In Europe it was partly the half-discovery by the masses of the emptiness, for the masses, of the intellectual life that led to a wave of disillusion and the reaction against the liberal state—the reaction which the world knew as Fascism. To enjoy the weighing of pros and cons is an acquired taste; the strong man, the leader who will decide for them, makes a powerful appeal to the masses.

But victory in 1945 allowed liberalism a second chance; al-though victory at the same time presented the world with another totalitarian challenge almost more formidable than the one the Allies met in Hitler's Germany. To each party in the new struggle the proper training of the young appeared as of paramount importance. And in the optimism of victory the West forgot, for the time being, its disillusion of the thirties. History repeated itself, but on a grander scale: a new League— U.N.O.; a new Committee of Intellectual Co-operation— U.N.E.S.C.O.; a new wave of social and economic reconstruc-tion—a socialist government in Great Britain, a Truman administration in the United States, and everywhere new policies, plans, and projects in education. 'Nowhere', wrote two leading educationists in a broad, authoritative survey of the international education scene, 'was it considered sufficient merely to construct again what had already existed before the war. In every country there was a strong demand for a radical reform of education, a reform which would extend access to educational resources more generously than before to all alike, and which would, at the same time, serve to orientate education in a new direction, making it better adapted to serving the social needs of a new age.'[1]

Such a statement did, indeed, summarize the restless, half-formed educational demands engendered by the war; and it was, perhaps, characteristic of the modern professional educationist. In many countries reforms along these lines have taken, or are taking, place. These reforms amount, in general terms, to consolidation and expansion of the existing means of education. National systems already existed in western Europe, and the principle of equality of opportunity was already inherent in Western democracy. Something like the *école unique* existed in the United States; the educational system was so truly accessible that in the great cities, at least, a child could rise 'from the gutter to the university'. In England the 'educational ladder' made it possible for the really able child of humble parents to rise to the professional class. At the same time a child of only average ability might miss his chance of a free place, and be passed in life by a child no abler but whose parents could afford the fees to give him secondary and higher education. So long as well-to-do parents wish and are able to pay to educate their children more expensively, it will be difficult or impossible to have complete equality, but the state system should—and in western Europe, to a large extent, now does—provide a tolerably good education which opens to all the gate of opportunity. Opportunity, yes—but recent reforms go beyond this. They are made with the objects of extending education 'to all alike' and of making education serve 'the social needs of a new age'.

The most concrete examples in the West of these tendencies are the raising of the school-leaving age and the attempt to provide a secondary education for all. In making this provision for all there is something novel in the history of education; it

[1] 'The War and Education' in *The Year Book of Education* (1948), by the editors (Dr. N. Hans, of King's College, and Professor J. A. Lauwerys, of the Institute of Education, London).

means the attempt to educate children of an age at which the majority of children in the past were not in school at all. Common experience—especially the experience of popular education in the United States—has shown the difficulty of teaching an academic curriculum to an ordinary, unselected, mass of children. Attempts have therefore to be made to adapt the curriculum to the child, or alternatively different curricula have to be offered and children have to choose or be selected in some way for the different, alternative, secondary curricula. Thus between the primary and the secondary stages of education there may be an intermediate period of trial and observation, as in the recent *classes nouvelles*, the bottom classes in the French *lycée*, where the newcomers were watched with a view to finding whether or not they should take Latin and where their particular aptitudes lay. Expansion of the educational system to provide a longer period of schooling for all has meant, in England, greatly increased public expenditure, pressure for new school buildings, an urgent demand for more teachers and to meet it various emergency schemes of teacher-training, and a multiplicity of educational and training grants, maintenance grants, and scholarships for higher education. To begin the educational process below the compulsory school-age, nursery schools have been increased in number. At the other end adult education has been widened, and state-supported youth clubs and youth movements have grown up. In higher education, also, there has been vast expansion, particularly on the scientific side. The war stimulated industrial production and led to the development of new industries or branches of industry, mechanized the fighting services, and was instrumental in opening or speeding up research work in many different fields. All this had led to a sudden increased demand for scientists and technicians which has been a spur to the public provision of higher scientific and technical education.

The most significant of all the movements in Western education, the raising of the school-leaving age and the attempt to provide general secondary education, are strongly marked in France and England. In France, an official committee under M. Paul Langevin, drew up a thorough-going scheme of educational reform which, although not fully carried out, suggests the main tendencies of development. The Langevin Commission proposed compulsory education of some kind up to eighteen. First, all children would go through the primary stage until eleven; then, at the next stage, to which they would all pass, they would, by means of the *classes nouvelles*, be sorted out into those branches of study for which they appeared most suited. At fifteen a more important division would take place. Those children who had shown intellectual ability would proceed to courses of study, classical, modern, technical, or artistic, leading to one of the *baccalauréats*. This examination at eighteen would admit to higher education. The children who, at fifteen, did not show intellectual capacity would pass into classes of a practical and vocational nature as a preparation for apprenticeship. On lines comparable with those suggested by the Langevin Commission was the great educational reform carried out by the English Education Act of 1944.

The Education Act of 1944 was a measure partly the result of the demands engendered by the war and of an intelligent forecast by the government in power of the kind of demands likely to be made at its conclusion and partly the result of a gradual internal development in English education itself. The status of teaching as a profession had been considerably raised by the work of H. A. L. Fisher. Apart from his famous Act, he procured a superannuation scheme for teachers; he appointed the committees under Lord Burnham which raised and standardized in a national scale teachers' salaries (which previously had varied from area to area); and by the Board's recognition of two school examinations, School Certificate and Higher Certificate—both conducted by university examining bodies—he set objective, external standards at which the secondary schools could aim and by which they could measure the success they achieved. The Act of 1918 itself gave wider powers to local authorities, and fixed the period of compulsory school attendance at five to fourteen. Below the age of five, local authorities might establish nursery schools, and the authorities were given increased scope in the provision of physical training, recreation, and medical inspection. But most significant for the future was the direction to local education authorities that they should make provision in central schools or special classes for the older and abler children and those who remained at school after fourteen. In addition, for the majority of children who left school at fourteen, the local authorities were to provide continuation schools, attendance to be part-time from fourteen to eighteen. The provision for compulsory continued education never came into force, largely because in the post-war years a demand for economy arose, but the plan for central schools or classes to give rather more advanced instruction proved a starting-point for much which was to happen in the coming years.

Between the Acts of 1918 and 1944 a number of reports, by the Board of Education's Consultative Committee or other committees under the aegis of the Board, appeared and influenced in official and political circles the opinion which contributed to the preparation and passing of the important measure of 1944. *The Education of the Adolescent*—issued in 1926 and produced by the Consultative Committee under the chairmanship of Sir Henry Hadow, vice-chancellor of Sheffield University—considered this very problem, referred to the Committee by the Board, of provision for the children who remained at schools, 'other than secondary schools', until fifteen, that is to say, the problem of post-primary or higher elementary education. Already voices had been raised to maintain that education should be provided in two stages, primary and secondary, for all. And indeed the Hadow *Report*, roughly speaking, endorsed this view—though it took eighteen years before it was expressed in the provisions of an act of parliament.

The Hadow *Report* pointed out that the problem was not new, that it had been recognized in the Fisher Act, and that the English elementary schools of their own accord were pushing up to more advanced courses of instruction. Nor was the problem limited to England and Wales. It was present, in fact, wherever there was an organized system of elementary education; one could not draw an arbitrary line at the age of twelve, thirteen, or fourteen, and say that at that age education finished: some children would always show the capacity to go further. In Scotland, primary schools had given rise to secondary schools; in the United States the Junior High School had come into existence to satisfy the needs of those who could go further than the elementary school without necessarily completing a full course of secondary education; in Germany the *Mittelschule*, in France the *école primaire supérieure*, served the purpose of higher primary instruction.

The Committee recommended that at the age of eleven plus all children should move from the elementary or primary school to a secondary school or to a central school (or a senior and separate department of the existing elementary school); it suggested also the third possibility of a junior technical school (virtually a secondary school with a technical bias) but did not go into this. The Committee even suggested changes in terminology, which eventually came about as the result of the 1944 Act: the word 'primary' should be substituted for elementary to describe education up to eleven plus; the word 'secondary' should be widened to cover all post-primary education whether in a secondary or a central school; the existing type of secondary school should be called a secondary grammar school, and the new type, the central school, should be called a secondary modern school. There should be an examination at the end of the primary course, on the lines of the existing examination in arithmetic and English for scholarships and free places, for the purpose of selecting pupils for the different types of secondary school, and the school-leaving age should be raised to fifteen. It was thought that the new school, the modern school, could give a secondary education with a practical bias. Its aims the *Report* stated to be: 'The forming and strengthening of character—individual and national character'—through the inspiring environment of a good school; 'the training of tastes which would fill and dignify leisure' by means of music, art, literature, woodwork, and history; 'the awakening and guiding of the intelligence, especially on its practical side'. In this reference to the 'practical side', the Committee at last appeared to remember British dependence on industry and the fact that the children in the modern schools would be going out to the manual jobs of industry, agriculture, and commerce. The Hadow *Report* contained, in essentials, the principles of the Act of 1944. But to apply these principles—as the Committee recognized—would involve changes in administration. In the outcome, the school-leaving age was not raised. Nevertheless progressive local authorities did press on with schemes of reorganization in the following years, and selected children for secondary, selective central, or non-selective senior schools. The less progressive authorities did little reorganization, and such authorities, with many old, unsuitable school buildings, had not therefore made the preparations which would make easier the carrying out of the 1944 Act. In such areas the provision of secondary education for all, in any real sense, proved a slow and lengthy proceeding.

The authors of the Spens *Report* of 1938, nominally on secondary education, found themselves accepting the Hadow principle of the two stages of primary and secondary education, and therefore found it impossible to do other than consider together all forms of post-primary education. The proposal of a multilateral school, which was to include all these forms in one school building, was considered, but rejected. The *Report* adhered to the suggested Hadow plan of three separate schools of secondary status—grammar, modern, and technical. It was considered that there should be generous provision of technical schools, and many of the existing junior technical schools could be raised to full secondary status. Selection by examination must take place for the different types of secondary school, but there must be an ample number of grammar-school places available and ultimately fees should cease for the grammar schools as for modern schools. The *Report* stressed the essential requisite of 'parity of status' between the different types of secondary school. A further report in 1943, the Norwood *Report* on the *Curriculum and Examinations in Secondary Schools*, added to the verbiage now accumulating in these publicly financed inquiries, and accepted the main suggestion of the threefold division of types in secondary education. The Fleming *Report* of 1944 on *The Public Schools and the General Educational System* was more novel in its subject matter, and suggested a possible relationship in which local education authorities could send a certain number of children to the public schools, with free places or payment of fees graded in accordance with parents' incomes.

Another report in 1944 was that of the McNair Committee on *Teachers and Youth Leaders*, platitudinous as are so often the reports of committees but important because the government's intended programme of educational reconstruction would call for an increased number of qualified teachers, and because the McNair *Report* did in fact suggest the lines on which teacher-training has since been reorganized.

The outcome of this long-continued process of inquiry and discussion, stretching back to the days of the Hadow *Report*, and even earlier, was the Education Act of 1944. This was, in its planning of the system as a whole, the most comprehensive of our education acts, yet in true British tradition it was no revolutionary measure and brought to the statute book provisions which had already gained a large measure of tacit support; it was the work of the National, not the Labour, Government, and was carried through with a Conservative minister, Mr. R. A. Butler, in charge of education. The Board of Education now became a Ministry, and in future it was to be the duty of the minister of education not only to superintend education but 'to promote the education of the people of England and Wales and the progressive development of institutions devoted to that purpose, and to secure the effective execution by local authorities under his control and direction, of the national policy for providing a varied and comprehensive educational service in every area'.[1] Thus the responsibilities and the power of the central authority were increased. At the same time local administration was simplified and its

---

[1] *Education Act*, 1944, Part I, 1.

obligations enlarged. The Dual System did not entirely disappear. Denominational schools were finding the costs of building to meet the needs of reorganization very heavy, but compromise was reached over public financial help and the measure of public control. County council and county borough councils alone were now to be education authorities (the old distinction between Part II and Part III authorities disappeared), and the provision of education at three defined stages was made a duty. 'The statutory system of public education shall be organized in three progressive stages to be known as primary education, secondary education, and further education; and it shall be the duty of the local education authority for every area . . . to contribute towards the moral, mental, and physical development of the community by securing that efficient education, throughout those stages, shall be available to meet the needs of the population of their area.'[1]

The school-leaving age was raised to fifteen (this came into force in 1947), and was to be further raised to sixteen when 'it has become practicable'. Fees disappeared in all schools maintained by the local authorities. For those children who left school at fifteen there was to be free compulsory part-time education in county colleges, for the equivalent of one day a week during working hours. But this bold measure—an attempt to do what H. A. L. Fisher had tried to do in 1918—was not to come into force at once. Careful planning, new building accommodation, and an increased supply of teachers would first be necessary. The Act also provided that, subject to a conscience clause, religious instruction and school prayers at the beginning of the day should take place in all schools maintained by the local authorities. In addition, of course, local authorities could provide nursery schools for small children under the age of five, had obligations with regard to provision of special treatment and education for disabled or defective children, and could also, where thought necessary, provide boarding-schools. As for the independent schools outside the

[1] *Ibid.*, Part II, 7.

State system, the minister was given powers to inspect, to register, and to deal suitably with unsatisfactory schools.

The outstanding feature of the new organization of education under the 1944 Act was that all children, aged between eleven and twelve, were to pass to some form of secondary education. This was an important innovation—for in Great Britain to-day the effort is made to educate children to a later age than has ever before been attempted. The Act left to the local authorities a certain discretion as to the way they would carry out its provision. The most usual way was to provide three types of secondary school—with a selection examination at eleven plus—and this procedure was so general as to give rise to the expression 'the tripartite system'. Thus, the grammar school—previously, the only kind of secondary school—offers an academic curriculum suited to children who stay at school at least until sixteen, and many of whom stay on for two years more, to specialize in the sixth form and go on to a university; the secondary modern school offers a general education intended for the majority of children; the secondary-technical school gives a general education, but directed towards the practical work of industry, commerce, or agriculture. Some authorities however, including London, decided to build multilateral or comprehensive schools, including all kinds of secondary education in one school. It was hoped that, between the different kinds of secondary school, there would be parity of esteem. But this did not come about—the grammar retained its priority. There was great competition at eleven plus to get into the grammar schools, and great disappointment for those who did not—affecting parents, perhaps, more than pupils. This, no doubt, helps to explain the growth in the number of comprehensive schools. The Public Schools flourished alongside the state system of education. They and the older universities of Oxford and Cambridge retained or even increased their reputation in popular esteem.

The expansion of the educational system has, of course, involved a considerable growth of bureaucracy and expense. Governments were remarkably willing to make money available. A new Keynesian economics was in the ascendant, economic reconstruction, development, and expansion went ahead, and in the 1950's Britain entered upon a period of full-employment and prosperity which made the description 'the affluent society' a familiar one. In such conditions the country could take in its stride the vastly increased expenditure on education. Never before, in this country, was so much spent on education—and the expenditure has continued to grow rapidly—not only on the essentials such as school buildings and teachers' salaries, but also on scholarships and grants (never, anywhere, have students been so well off as in Britain), on conferences, inspection, supervision, examining, committees, courses, travelling expenses, and also on educational research often of a rather nebulous character. Any criticism of what was regarded as progress in full spate was dismissed as obscurantist and old-fashioned.

Additional schools and larger schools meant more teachers, and to provide more teachers an expansion of training facilities was necessary. To meet the immediate post-war demand, emergency training colleges were opened, accepting for one-year courses candidates with lower academic qualifications than usual. But most of their students were young men and women who had passed through the hard school of war service; what they lacked by way of paper qualifications they made up for by experience, vitality, and enthusiasm. Some of the emergency training colleges later were made permanent (with the then-prevailing two-year course) and became part of the system, for there was a general expansion of training colleges, training teachers for primary and secondary modern schools, and also of university departments of education, preparing teachers for grammar schools.

In the organization of teacher training a considerable change was made as a result of the McNair proposals, a change which was in keeping with the post-war expansive mood in the social and educational sphere. Institutes of Education were created— university bodies which link all the training colleges of an area with its university. The Institutes of Education aimed at bringing together all those being trained as teachers, whether primary or secondary, at encouraging research, and at raising the standard of the training colleges by contact with the university spirit. Such aims were wide and are difficult of realisation, but Institutes have come to be generally accepted. It would be agreed that there has been a considerable improvement in the training colleges—they had suffered previously from poverty, from being too small for effective staffing and economical management, and from poor buildings and equipment—but, of course, it is possible that improvement might have come about by other means. The McNair committee was not unanimous in its findings; half its members, indeed, advocated instead of the Institutes an improvement of the existing Joint-Board system for teacher training, and their view was that it would be better 'to see the training colleges acquiring a higher status by reason of their own work and merits than that they should attempt to derive it from their connection with the universities'.[1] In any case, the pattern of teaching training may not yet be firmly fixed: already there is a move towards a merging inside the university of the Institute and university department of education in a Faculty or School of Education, and voices have also been heard advocating taking teacher training outside universities altogether, as in Scotland.

Added to all this—the reconstructive and expansionist tendencies following the Second World War—were two vitally important and largely unforeseen factors, a large population increase with its growing pressure, stage after stage, on the educational system and a shortage of scientists and technicians relative to the increasing demand from a more and more mechanized and complex industrial system and from more and more mechanized and scientific military services. These new factors led to a great expansion of the educational system and to a special emphasis on science and technology: the expansion has been great, and it is still going on, though some people think that the scale and pace of the expansion are not even yet great enough. More than ever before, the importance of education is

[1] *Teachers and Youth Leaders* (McNair *Report*), p. 59.

realised: the State knows it as essential in a technological age, for it makes possible both successful competition in the economic sphere and also the scientific research necessary for nuclear defence; the individual senses that economic prosperity has opened gateways of opportunity, and sees that education leads to professional success and social status.

The increase in population has been popularly termed 'the bulge in the birth-rate'. An exceptionally large number of children were born in the years immediately after the war—British casualties were relatively light—when the service men were demobilised and returned home to marry and start families. The number of children in the publicly-maintained primary and secondary schools increased from about 5,000,000 in 1945 to nearly 7,000,000 in 1960. The pressure on the schools was considerable—teachers were scarce, and still are in spite of expanded universities and training colleges, classes were too large, school buildings were overcrowded and too few. Apart from the bulge, British education is being influenced also by the 'trend' and the 'swing'. The trend is seen in the large numbers of children staying on in school after the age of fifteen, now that secondary education is free. As a result the sixth forms in grammar schools have increased greatly in size. The swing is the movement, in keeping with the demands of industry, away from the Arts subjects to science and technology. The trend has brought heavy pressure on the universities. Most of the boys in the sixth forms would, by pre-war standards, have been qualified for entry; but now universities ask for two or three subjects studied in the sixth form and carried to successful Advanced Level in the General Certificate of Education. Even among these pupils the universities still select, and thus competition to get in has become very severe. The swing, at the same time, has led to especial pressure on the scientific departments of the universities and on technical colleges outside.

To meet the pressure on the schools by the bulge, big building programmes were undertaken. Several thousand new schools have been built, and existing schools have been enlarged and improved. In secondary education the most controversial question has been—what kind of secondary education? Should there be selection of pupils for grammar and secondary modern schools or should there be a common school—the comprehensive school? Local Education Authorities are free to choose, and the comprehensive school has grown in popularity. Some authorities have made interesting experiments in compromise. In general there has been reluctance to drive the claims of either side in the controversy to extremes, and the typically English love of compromise has been at work. Secondary modern schools have often found themselves able to put some children in for the G.C.E.—an examination really intended for grammar schools. Comprehensive schools have been on their guard against lowering of standards and have given careful attention to their grammar sides. The *Crowther Report*, published in 1959, advocated the putting into effect of the two unfulfilled provisions of the Act of 1944—raising the school-leaving age to sixteen and providing county colleges for compulsory part-time education to the age of eighteen. But—with the existing shortage of teachers —the realisation of these proposals must be difficult.

In higher education, too, expansion has been considerable. Training colleges have been expanded, and the two-year course extended to three years. University departments of education have also been increased in size. The universities themselves have been much enlarged. The number of students, now about 110,000, has doubled since before the war, and is expected to go up to 170,000 by 1970. New universities have been created, at Brighton and York, for example, and others are on the way. Technical education has also been enlarged—both outside and inside universities—and a number of senior institutions have been designated as Colleges of Advanced Technology, granting a diploma in Technology which is held to be on a par with a university degree. The *Robbins Report* on Higher Education published in 1963 led to a still greater expansion, in which the C.A.T.s were to become universities.

With the vast expansion of education and with it of educational administration there is always the danger that the lasting human values in education may be forgotten. The increasing use of mechanical aids and devices, the growing interest in teaching machines, take the emphasis away from the personal relationship between teacher and taught. Yet up to now the dynamic of education has been the teacher's interest in individual boy or girl. It would be regrettable, too, if the tutorial method— perhaps the greatest educational asset of Oxford and Cambridge—should be endangered by the great and sudden expansion of universities. Committees, administration, the sheer growth in numbers are already taking up too much of the time of professors and lecturers, time which should be given to teaching and research.

If we look at the educational picture as a whole, however, by far the most outstanding feature is the extension of education, to the whole population, which never before in history has been carried so far. This is apparent in England, it is apparent in Europe; it is a common feature of capitalist America and of communist Russia. However different schools may be in aim and spirit, in each case the mass of children are passed through them. Education for all—today that is the practice, whether in the West or in the communist East. That practice is based on the needs of modern society which, whether capitalist or communist, is fundamentally dependent upon industrial production and upon mechanized and scientific agriculture.

The long story of European education reveals that each and every period and territory has had very much the kind of education which its own way of life has made necessary and possible —whether it was the specialized training of the medieval knight or clerk, some form of apprenticeship which reproduced the manual skills of peasant or craftsman, or the primary and secondary education of recent times. But to-day, more than ever, education is essential; the highly complex industrial system depends upon it. But that system itself, with its vast output of material wealth, provides also a liberal education for the many, only dreamed of by the educationalists of the past. Life itself, in our complex and crowded communities, depends upon education, but at the same time education makes possible the good life.

BIBLIOGRAPHY

The chapter-bibliographies are intended to indicate the more important printed sources from which our information on the history of education is drawn, and also the principal secondary works in each case. Useful general surveys are:

J. W. Adamson: *Short History of Education.*
W. Boyd: *History of Western Education* (with useful bibliographies of the great educationists).
P. R. Cole: *History of Educational Thought.*
E. P. Cubberley: *History of Education.*

Valuable bibliographical material is to be found in the standard histories, particularly the *Cambridge Medieval History*, the *Cambridge History of English Literature*, and the *Oxford History of England*.

CHAPTER I

Xenophon: *Constitution of the Lacedaemonians*; *Cyropaedia*; *Memorabilia*; *Economics*; Plutarch: *Lycurgus* (in the *Lives*); Plato: *Republic*; *Protagoras*; Aristotle: *Politics*; Aristophanes: *Clouds*; Isocrates: *Against the Sophists*; *Antidosis*; *Panathenaicus*. (Translations in the Loeb Classics.)

K. J. Freeman: *Schools of Hellas* (1907); P. Girard: *L'Éducation Athénienne au Ve et au IVe Siècle avant J.-C.* (1889); R. L. Nettleship: *Theory of Education in Plato's Republic* (1935); R. C. Lodge: *Plato's Theory of Education* (1947); M. J. Mather: *Histoire de l'École d'Alexandrie* (3 vols., 1840–8); H. I. Marrou: *Histoire de l'Éducation dans l'Antiquité* (1950)

CHAPTER II

Plutarch: *Marcus Cato* (in the *Lives*); Cicero: *De Republica*; *De Oratore*; *Orator*; *Brutus*; Tacitus: *De Oratoribus*; Quintilian: *Institutio Oratoria*; Marcus Aurelius: *Meditations* (edition of A. S. L. Farquharson with translation and commentary); St. Augustine: *Confessions*. (Translations in the Loeb Classics.)

A. Wilkins: *Roman Education* (1905); A. Gwynn: *Roman Education from Cicero to Quintilian* (1926); W. Warde Fowler: *Social Life at Rome in the Age of Cicero* (1909).

CHAPTER III

Epistle to the Romans; for the Fathers, see Migne's *Patrologia Cursus Completus*, Latin Series and Greek Series, especially St. Augustine: *De Doctrina Christiana* and *De Ordine*; Augustine's works in English translation, 15 vols., edited M. Dods, vol. IX *On Christian Doctrine*; Martianus Capella: *De Nuptiis Philologiae et Mercurii* (ed. A. Dick, Leipzig, 1925); Aelius Donatus: *Ars Grammatica* (ed. Keil in *Grammatici Latini* (Leipzig, 1880), which also contains Priscian).

C. J. Cadoux: *The Early Church and the World* (1925); F. A. Wright and T. A. Sinclair: *History of Later Latin Literature* (1931); P. R. Cole: *Later Roman Education in Ausonius, Capella and the Theodosian Code* (1909); J. A. Lalanne: *L'Influence des Pères de l'Église sur l'Éducation Publique pendant les cinq premiers Siècles de l'Ère Chrétienne* (1850); P. Alfaric: *L'Évolution Intellectuelle de Saint Augustin* (1918); T. J. Haarhoff: *Schools of Gaul—A Study of Pagan and Christian Education in the Last Century of the Western Empire* (1920).

CHAPTER IV

See the detailed bibliographies in the *Cambridge Medieval History*, vol. VI, chaps. xxiv and xxv. For chivalry and knightly training especially *L'Histoire de Guillaume le Maréchal* (ed. Paul Meyer, 3 vols., 1891–1901); Joinville's *Histoire de Saint Louis*; Froissart's *Chroniques*; Chaucer's *Canterbury Tales* (Prologue); Malory's *Morte d'Arthur*. For education of a bookish kind, *Educational Charters and Documents* (ed. A. F. Leach); Capella, Donatus, and Priscian, see above; Bede's *Ecclesiastical History*; Einhard's (or Eginhard's) *Vita Caroli Magni Imperatoris* (ed. L. Halphen in the *Classiques de l'Histoire de France au Moyen Age*); FitzStephen: *Vita Sancti Thomae* (*Materials for History of Thomas Becket*, III, Rolls Series); Alexander Neckham: *De Naturis Rerum* and *De Laudibus Divinae Sapientiae* (Rolls Series); Vincent of Beauvais: *De Eruditione Filiorum Nobilium*.

E. Prestage (ed.): *Chivalry* (1928); L. Gautier: *La Chevalerie* (1891); T. L. Jarman: *William Marshal* (1930); G. G. Coulton: *Medieval Panorama* (1938), and *Europe's Apprenticeship* (1940) (a survey of medieval Latin with examples); A. Clerval: *Les Écoles de Chartres* (1896); P. Abelson: *The Seven Liberal Arts* (1906).

CHAPTER V

See also bibliography for Chapter IV.

Alcuin: *De Pontificibus et Sanctis Ecclesiae Eboracensis Carmen* (*History of the Church of York,* I, Rolls Series); William of Malmesbury: *De Gestis Regum Anglorum,* V (Rolls Series); Higden: *Polychronicon,* with English translation of John Trevisa, I and II (Rolls Series).

A. F. Leach: *Schools of Medieval England* (1915); *English Schools at the Reformation* (1896); article on 'Schools' in *Encyclopedia Britannica* (11th edition). For a bibliography of the educational works of Leach see *Schools of Medieval England.* For a critical review of this work by another medieval scholar, see A. G. Little in the *English Historical Review,* XXX. Kathleen Edwards: *English Secular Cathedrals in the Middle Ages* (1949).

CHAPTER VI

John of Salisbury: *Metalogicon* (ed. C. C. J. Webb); *Chartularium Universitatis Parisiensis* (ed. H. Denifle and E. Chatelain, 4 vols.); *Statuta Antiqua Universitatis Oxoniensis* (ed., with introduction, Strickland Gibson).

Hastings Rashdall: *Universities of Europe in the Middle Ages* (3 vols., ed. Powicke and Emden, 1936); and 'The Medieval Universities' in the *Cambridge Medieval History,* VI, chap. xvii, revised by G. R. Potter; H. Denifle: *Universitäten des Mittelalters bis 1400* (I, *Entstehung der Universitäten,* 1885); S. d'Irsay: *Histoire des Universités* (I, *Moyen Age et Renaissance,* 1933); C. E. Mallet: *History of the University of Oxford* (3 vols., 1924–7); J. B. Mullinger: *University of Cambridge from the Earliest Times* (3 vols., 1873–1911); N. Schachner: *Medieval Universities* (1938).

CHAPTER VII

A. F. Leach: *History of Winchester College* (1899); J. D'E. Firth: *Winchester College* (1949); H. Maxwell Lyte: *History of Eton College* (1911); F. Paulsen: *Geschichte des gelehrten Unterrichts,* I (1919); W. Rein (ed.): *Encyclopädisches Handbuch der Pädagogik,* II (1904), article by C. Nohle, with bibliography, on *Deutsches Knabenschulwesen, seine Geschichte;* K. Kehrbach (ed.): *Monumenta Germaniae Paedagogica,* I (1886); A. F. Leach: *Early Yorkshire Schools,* I (1889), and II (1903), in the Yorkshire Archaeological Society *Record Series),* and his *Educational Charters and Documents;* D. Gardiner: *English Girlhood at School* (1929); Eileen Power: *Medieval English Nunneries* (1922).

310

CHAPTER VIII

Erasmus: *Opera Omnia* (Leiden Edition, 1703–6); *Epistolae* (ed. P. S. Allen, 11 vols.); Vives: *De Anima et Vita*, and see below under Foster Watson.

W. H. Woodward: *Studies in Education during the Age of the Renaissance, 1400–1600* (1906); *Erasmus concerning Education* (1904); P. S. Allen: *Age of Erasmus* (1914); Foster Watson: *Vives on Education* (1913, with English translation of the *De Tradendis Disciplinis*); *Vives and the Renascence Education of Women* (including Hyrde's English translation of Vives's *De Institutione Feminae Christianae* and Foster Watson's translation of Vives's *De Officio Mariti* (1912)); T. Corcoran: *Renovatio Litterarum* (1925); *Studies in the History of Classical Teaching* (1911).

CHAPTER IX

See also bibliographies for Chapters III, VII, and VIII.

Luther: *An die Ratsherren aller Städte deutsches Lands, dass sie Christliche Schulen aufrichten und halten sollen*, and *Eine Predigt dass man Kinder zur Schule halten solle*; translated in F. V. N. Painter: *Luther on Education* (1889); *Monumenta Germaniae Paedagogica* contains collections of *Schulordnungen* and K. Hartfelder's *Philip Melanchthon als Praeceptor Germaniae*; *Melanchthoniana Paedagogica* (ed. Hartfelder); Melanchthon's *Visitation Books* (*Unterricht der Visitatorn an die Pfarhern ym Kurfurstenthum zu Sachssen* (1528)), German and Latin versions in *Corpus Reformatorum* (ed. C. G. Bretschneider), XXVI; *Ratio Studiorum et Institutiones Scholasticae Societatis Jesu* (ed. G. M. Pachtler, S. J., in the *Monumenta Germaniae Paedagogica*; English translation by A. R. Ball).

F. Paulsen: *German Education, Past and Present* (1908); *Geschichte des gelehrten Unterrichts*, I (1919); F. de Dainville: *La Naissance de l'Humanisme Moderne* (1940); T. Hughes: *Loyola and the Educational System of the Jesuits* (1892); A. P. Farrell: *The Jesuit Code of Liberal Education* (1938); T. Corcoran: *Renatæ Litteræ* (1927); A. Schimberg: *L'Éducation morale dans les Collèges de la Compagnie de Jésus en France sous l'Ancien Régime* (1913); C. de Rochemonteix: *Un Collège de Jésuites au XVIIᵉ et XVIIIᵉ Siècles—Le Collège Henri IV de la Flèche* (1889, 4 vols.); G. Dupont-Ferrier: *Du Collège de Clermont au Lycée Louis-le-Grand, 1563–1920* (*La vie quotidienne d'un collège parisien pendant plus de trois cents cinquante ans*) (1921, 3 vols.).

CHAPTER X

Roger Ascham: *The Scholemaster, or plaine and perfite way of teaching children to understand, write and speak in Latin tong* (1570); J. Brinsley: *Ludus Literarius: or, the grammar school* (1612. Ed. E. T. Campagnac, 1917); *Letters and Exercises of the Elizabethan Schoolmaster* (John Conybeare. Ed. F. C. Conybeare, 1905); C. Hoole: *A New Discovery of the Old Art of Keeping School* (1660, but written twenty years earlier. Ed. Campagnac, 1913); R. Mulcaster: *Positions wherein those circumstances be examined necessarie for the training up of children* (1581); *The first part of the elementarie which entreateth of right writing of our English tong* (1582); *Lily's Rules Construed* (with the *Carmen de Moribus*), translation by W. Haine (1638); W. Kempe: *The Education of Children in Learning* (1588); *Milton—Private Correspondence and Academic Exercises* (translated from the Latin by Phyllis B. Tillyard, 1932).

A. F. Leach: *English Schools at the Reformation*; A. M. Stowe: *English Grammar Schools in the Reign of Queen Elizabeth* (1908); Foster Watson: *The English Grammar Schools to 1660* (1908); J. H. Brown: *Elizabethan Schooldays* (1935); T. W. Baldwin: *William Shakspere's Petty School* (1943), and *William Shakspere's Small Latine and Lesse Greeke* (1944, 2 vols.); G. A. Plimpton: *Education of Shakespeare* (1933); R. W. Chambers: *Thomas More* (1935); C. H. Firth: *Oliver Cromwell* (1890); Hilaire Belloc: *Cromwell* (1934); D. L. Clark: *John Milton at St. Paul's School* (1948); E. M. W. Tillyard: *Milton* (1930).

CHAPTER XI

Baldassare Castiglione: *Il Cortegiano* (1528, Translated into English as *The Courtier* by Sir Thomas Hoby, 1561); Sir Thomas Elyot: *The Boke named The Governour* (1531. Ed. with introduction by Foster Watson in Everyman Series); H. Gilbert: *Queen Elizabeth's Academy* (ed. F. J. Furnivall, 1869); Francis Bacon: *Advancement of Learning* (1605); J. A. Comenius: *The Great Didactic* (1657, translated by M. W. Keatinge, 1910); Montaigne: *Du Pédantisme* (*édition critique* with introduction by G. Michaut, 1936).

F. P. Graves: *Peter Ramus and the Educational Reformation of the Sixteenth Century* (1912); I. Parker: *Dissenting Academies in England* (1914).

CHAPTER XII

See also bibliographies for Chapters VI, VII, and XIV.
Jean-Jacques Rousseau: *Émile* (1762, vols. V and VI in the *Œuvres*,

Bry edition. English translations by W. H. Payne, and B. Foxley in Everyman series); *Minor Educational Writings of Rousseau* (translated by W. Boyd, 1911); *Educational Writings of John Locke* (ed. J. W. Adamson, 1922); *Pestalozzi's Educational Writings* (translated by J. A. Green, 1912); Froebel: *Education of Man* (1826, translated by W. N. Hailmann, 1894).

John Morley: *Rousseau* (1873); W. Boyd: *The Educational Theory of Jean-Jacques Rousseau* (1912); John Adams: *Evolution of Educational Theory* (1912); M. G. Jones: *The Charity School Movement* (1938); C. Wordsworth: *Social Life at the English Universities in the Eighteenth Century* (1874); D. Winstanley: *University of Cambridge in the Eighteenth Century* (1922).

CHAPTER XIII

See also bibliographies for Chapters XVI and XVIII.

Marquis de Condorcet: *Rapport et Projet de Décret surl' organisation générale de l'instruction publique présentés a l'Assemblée Nationale, au nom du comité d'instruction publique* (1792); Joseph Priestley: *Miscellaneous Observations relating to Education* (1778); Herbert Spencer: *Education* (1861); Matthew Arnold: *A French Eton* (1864); *Reports of Commissioners* (Henry Barnard, etc., U.S.A. Bureau of Education, created 1867); the vols. of Henry Barnard's *American Journal of Education* (1856–80); Henry Barnard: *National Education—Systems, Institutions and Statistics of Public Instruction*, I (German states), II (Switzerland, France, Belgium, Denmark, Russia, Turkey, etc.) (1872); *Systems, Institutions and Statistics of Scientific Instruction applied to National Industries in Different Countries* (Austria, German states, France, Belgium, etc.) (1872); Newcastle Commision *Report* on popular education (1861), IV, Reports of the Assistant Commissioners, Matthew Arnold, *Systems of Education in use in France, Holland, and the French Cantons of Switzerland*, and Mark Pattison, *State of Elementary Education in Germany*; Samuelson Commission *Report* on technical instructions (1882–4), 'to inquire into the instruction of the industrial classes of certain foreign countries in technical and other subjects, for the purpose of comparison with that of the corresponding classes in this country' (considered France, Switzerland, Germany, Austria, Belgium, Holland, Italy); *Special Reports on Educational Subjects* (Education Department, England and Wales, 1896 onwards), especially vol. I, R. L. Morant: *French Systems of Higher Primary Schools*, M. E. Sadler: *Realschulen in Berlin, and their bearing on modern Secondary and Commercial Education*, and vol. III, Morant: *National Organisation of Education in Switzerland*; Sadler, *Problems in*

Prussian Secondary Education for Boys, with special reference to similar questions in England.

E. H. Reisner: *Nationalism and Education since 1789* (1922); F. E. Farrington: *French Secondary Schools* (1910); G. Weill: *Histoire de l'Enseignement secondaire en France, 1802–1920* (1921); F. Paulsen: *German Education, Past and Present,* and *Geschichte des gelehrten Unterrichts* II (1921); W. Lexis and G. J. Tamson: *General View of the History and Organisation of Public Education in the German Empire* (1904); P. Barth: *Geschichte der Erziehung in soziologischer und geistesgeschichtlicher Beleuchtung* (1911).

CHAPTER XIV

See also bibliography for Chapter VII, and biographies of eighteenth- and nineteenth-century figures.

Clarendon *Report* (1864) on the great public schools; Taunton *Report* (1868) on the other endowed schools; A. P. Stanley: *Life and Correspondence of Thomas Arnold, D.D.* (1844); S. Butler: *Life and Letters of Dr. Samuel Butler* (1896); *Autobiography of Leigh Hunt* (1850. Ed. J. E. Morpurgo, 1949).

R. L. Archer: *Secondary Education in the Nineteenth Century* (1921); E. C. Mack: *Public Schools and British Opinion* (1938–41. I, 1780–1860; II, since 1860); T. C. Worsley: *Barbarians and Philistines* (1940); Fleming *Report* (1944); Spencer Leeson: *The Public Schools Question* (1948).

CHAPTER XV

The publications of the Society for the Diffusion of Useful Knowledge (1826–46. *Library of Useful Knowledge, Library of Entertaining Knowledge, Penny Magazine,* etc.); Charles Knight: *Passages of a Working Life* (1864–5, 3 vols.); James Hole: *History and Management of Literary, Scientific and Mechanics' Institutes* (1853); Thomas Cooper: *Life of Thomas Cooper* (1872); Henry (Lord) Brougham: *Speeches* (1838, 4 vols.); Thomas Pole: *History of the Origins and Progress of Adult Schools* (1816).

A. E. Dobbs: *Education and Social Movements, 1700–1850* (1919); *Final Report,* Adult Education Committee (Ministry of Reconstruction, 1919); E. Halévy: *Growth of Philosophic Radicalism* (1928); G. Wallas: *Francis Place*; G. D. H. Cole: *Robert Owen* (1930); *Journal of Adult Education* (Oct. 1931, R. Peers, 'Thomas Cooper—The Leicester Chartist'; April 1933, T. L. Jarman, 'Charles Knight: an Educational Pioneer').

CHAPTER XVI

See also bibliography for Chapter XIII.

R. Southey: *Life of the Rev. Andrew Bell* (1844); J. Kay-Shuttleworth: *Four Periods of Public Education* (1862); Education Acts of 1870 and 1902; parliamentary debates in Hansard; *Reports* of Royal Commissions (Newcastle on popular education, 1861; Bryce on secondary, 1895; Samuelson on technical, 1882, 1884).

R. Gregory: *Elementary Education* (1895) (the history of the National Society); H. B. Binns: *A Century of Education* (1908) (the centenary history of the British and Foreign School Society, 1808–1908); F. Smith: *Life and Work of Sir James Kay-Shuttleworth* (1923); J. W. Adamson: *English Education 1789–1902* (1930); H. C. Barnard: *Short History of English Education from 1760–1944* (1947); S. J. Curtis: *History of Education in Great Britain* (1948); A. N. Lowndes: *The Silent Social Revolution* (1937); C. Birchenough: *History of Elementary Education in England and Wales* (1938); F. Smith: *History of English Elementary Education* (1931); R. L. Archer: *Secondary Education in the Nineteenth Century* (1921); H. A. L. Fisher: *James Bryce* (1927); B. M. Allen: *Sir Robert Morant* (1934); Michael Sadleir: *Michael Ernest Sadler* (1949); A. Abbott: *Education for Industry and Commerce in England* (1933); F. Schneider: *Geltung und Einfluss der Deutschen Pädagogik im Ausland* (1943).

CHAPTER XVII

H. A. L. Fisher: *An Unfinished Autobiography* (1940); David Ogg: *Herbert Fisher* (1947); H. G. Wells: *An Experiment in Autobiography* (1934, 2 vols.); Geoffrey West: *H. G. Wells* (1930).

CHAPTER XVIII

See also bibliographies for Chapters XIII–XVII.

Education Acts of 1918 and 1944; *Reports* of the Board of Education's Consultative Committee (especially the Hadow report on the *Education of the Adolescent* and the Spens report on secondary education); *Reports* of the Norwood, Fleming, and McNair committees; *15 to 18: The Report of the Central Advisory Council for Education* (Crowther Report 1959); *Reports of the Ministry of Education* (annual).

Year Books of Education (since 1932), especially the vol. for 1948 containing 'The War and Education' by the editors, and 'England and Wales' by A. C. F. Beales; S. J. Curtis: *Education in Britain since 1900* (1952); I. L. Kandel: *Comparative Education* (1937); N. Hans: *Comparative Education* (1949); R. Peers (ed): *Adult Education in Practice* (1934); A. Flexner: *Universities: American, English, German* (1930); H. C. Dent: *Education Act, 1944* (1944).

Guides to the education system today are—*Education in Britain* (H.M.S.O. 1960); and short books by H. C. Dent, G. A. N.

Lowndes, W. O. Lester Smith, and A. P. Alexander. Dealing with
contemporary educational problems are— G. H. Bantock: *Freedom
and Authority in Education* (1952); O. Banks: *Parity and Prestige in
English Secondary Education* (1955); R. Pedley: *Comprehensive Education* (1957); A. Yates and D. A. Pidgeon: *Admission to Grammar Schools*
(1957); F. Stevens: *The Living Tradition* (1960); H. C. Dent: *Universities in Transition* (1961); C. P. Snow: *The Two Cultures* (1959);
J. Vaizey: *Education for Tomorrow* (1962); and a good survey article
by Ben Morris, 'Educational Change in the United Kingdom since
World War II', in *Phi Delta Kappan*, Nov. 1961.

APPENDIX TO BIBLIOGRAPHY

Among the new books, appearing since the original compilation
of the bibliography in 1950, may be noted:

GENERAL SURVEYS

S. J. Curtis and M. E. A. Boultwood: *A Short History of Educational
Ideas* (1953); R. R. Rusk: *The Doctrines of the Great Educators* (revised
edition 1957); A. D. C. Peterson: *A Hundred Years of Education* (1952);
H. M. Knox: *Two Hundred and Fifty Years of Scottish Education 1696–
1946* (1953); W. H. G. Armytage: *Civic Universities* (1955); M. L.
Clarke: *Classical Education in Britain 1500–1900* (1959). G. Baron:
Bibliographical Guide to the English Educational System (1960) is a useful
guide to books.

CHAPTERS I AND II

E. B. Castle: *Ancient Education and Today* (1961); W. Barclay:
Educational Ideals in the Ancient World (1959).

CHAPTER III

'The Christian Fathers and the Moral Training of the Young',
by E. B. Castle, in *Brit. Journal of Educational Studies 1954–5* (vol. 3).

CHAPTERS VI AND VII

A. H. Smith: *New College and its Buildings* (1952)

CHAPTER IX

A. C. F. Beales: *Education under Penalty* (English Catholic education 1547–1689 (1963)).

BIBLIOGRAPHY

CHAPTER XI

John Dury: *The Reformed School* (1650. Edited H. M. Knox); W. A. L. Vincent: *The State and School Education 1640–60* (1950); G. C. Brauer: *The Education of a Gentleman* (1955); J. W. A. Smith: *The Birth of Modern Education . . . the Dissenting Academies* (1954); N. Hans: *New Trends in Education in the Eighteenth Century* (1951); D. C. Douglas: *English Scholars 1660–1730* (2nd ed. 1951).

CHAPTER XII

Evelyn Lawrence (ed.); *Friedrich Froebel and English Education* (1952); H. M. Pollard: *Pioneers of Popular Education* (1956); Kate Silber: *Pestalozzi* (1960); E. M. Standing: *Maria Montessori* (1957).

CHAPTER XIV

T. W. Bamford: *Thomas Arnold* (1960); F. J. Woodward: *The Doctor's Disciples* (1954); D. Newsome: *Godliness and Good Learning* (1961); Josephine Kamm: *How different from us . . . Miss Buss and Miss Beale* (1958)

CHAPTERS XV AND XVI

B. Simon: *Studies in the History of Education 1780–1870* (1960); T. Kelly: *George Birkbeck* (1957)

CHAPTER XVI

S. J. Curtis and M. I. A. Boultwood: *An Introductory History of English Education since 1800* (1960); J. Murphy: *The Religious Problem in English Education* (1959); W. H. G. Armytage: *A. J. Mundella* (1951); A. V. Judges (ed.): *Pioneers of English Education* (1952); J. Leese: *Personalities and Power in English Education* (1950); W. F. Connell: *Educational Thought and Influence of Matthew Arnold* (1950); E. Eaglesham: *From School Board to Local Authority* (1956); D. S. L. Cardwell: *The Organisation of Science in England* (1957); B. Simon: *Education and the Labour Movement 1870–1920* (1965).

INDEX

Abelard, Peter, 93, 94, 95, 107
Academy, the, 17
Acts of Parliament (*see also* Education Acts)
  Act of Supremacy (1534), 163
  Act of Uniformity (1662), 163
  Chantries Acts (1545, 1547), 161
  Five Mile Act (1665), 192
  Reform Act (1832), 259
  Reform Act (1867), 264
  Schism Act (1714), 191
Adult Education, 269
Aelfric, 70, 77
Alberic, 94, 95
Albert, Prince, 268
Alberti, Leon Battista, 131
Alcibiades, 17
Alcuin, 67, 73–6
Aldhelm, 73, 74, 75
Alexander the Great, 19–20, 35
Alexandria, 20–1, 35, 41, 50
Alfred, King, 59, 67, 76–7
Allen, William, 247
Anabaptists, 146
Andrews, C. F., 15n.
Antioch, 41
Antoninus, 35–6
Antony, Mark, 34
Apuleius, 29
Aquinas, Thomas, 104, 159
Aristarchus, 139
Aristophanes, 11, 16, 17
Aristotle, 10, 14, 19, 38, 74, 91, 93, 104, 105, 159, 179, 198
Arnold, Dr., 64, 228, 235–6
Arnold, Matthew, 261, 263
Artaxerxes, 7
Ascham, Roger, 183, 187
Asser, 77
Athens, 7, 10, 11, 12, 13–19, 50
Aubrey, John, 172
Augustine, St., 71, 72
Augustine, St., bishop of Hippo, 35, 44, 46–50, 51, 52
Aurelius, Marcus, 33, 34–5, 36
Austria, 199, 305
Averroes, 104

Bacon, Francis, 139, 160, 179, 180–2

Bacon, Roger, 79, 139
Barker, Ernest, 288
Barnes, Thomas, 232
Basedow, 209
Basil, St., 42–3
Bates case, the, 191
Bayle, 134
Beard, Dr. Thomas, 169
Beaufort, Cardinal, 116
Beaufort, Lady Margaret, 122
Becket, Thomas, 79–80, 92, 93, 99
Bede, 66, 72, 73, 74
Bell, Dr. Andrew, 257–8, 259
Bentham, Jeremy, 253
Bernard of Chartres, 95, 96
Bible, the: and private judgement, 145, 147, 151; the Authorized Version, 169
Bigge, L. A. Selby, 279
Biondo, 131
Birkbeck, Dr. George, 249–50
Bismarck, 216
Board of Education, inception of, 272
Boccaccio, 140
Boëthius, 70, 74, 104, 105, 115
Boswell, James, 202
Botticelli, 129
Boyer, Rev. James, 232, 234
Braithwait, Richard, 187
Brethren of the Common Life, at Deventer in the Netherlands, 141–2
Brinsley, John, 187
British and Foreign School Society, 247, 258, 259
Brothers of the Christian Schools, 196, 222
Brougham, Lord, 244, 254, 257
Browning, Oscar, 11
Bryce, Lord, 272, 273
Bryce Commission, 272
Burke, Edmund, 240
Burnet, Bishop, 170
Burnham, Lord, 296
Butler, R. A., 229, 300
Butler, Samuel, 235

Caesar, 65
Calvin, 152, 153, 154

318

INDEX